WIGS AND GUNS

Wigs and Guns

IRISH BARRISTERS IN THE GREAT WAR

ANTHONY P. QUINN

with a Foreword by
JOHN BOWMAN

FOUR COURTS PRESS
in association with
THE IRISH LEGAL HISTORY SOCIETY

Typeset in 10.5pt on 13pt EhrhardtMt by
Carrigboy Typesetting Services, County Cork for
FOUR COURTS PRESS LTD
7 Malpas Street, Dublin 8, Ireland
e-mail: info@four-courts-press.ie
and in North America for
FOUR COURTS PRESS
c/o ISBS, 920 N.E. 58th Avenue, Suite 300, Portland, OR 97213.

A catalogue record for this title is available
from the British Library.

ISBN (10 digit) 1–85182–935–0
ISBN (13 digit) 978–1–85182–935–4

Printed in England
by MPG Books, Bodmin, Cornwall.

For Ann, and also:

Here's to you, men I never met,
Yet hope to meet behind the veil,
Thronged on some starry parapet,
That looks down upon Innisfail,
And sees the confluence of dreams …
One river born from many streams.

Æ

Foreword

By John Bowman

In schools, hospitals and sports pavilions throughout Ireland – and in the Four Courts in Dublin – there are memorials to those who died in the Great War: a listing of those who were students, workers, sportsmen or lawyers and who did not return from the war. I can never read through these names without hearing in my head the claim in Tom Kettle's poem:

> Died not for flag, nor king, nor emperor,
> But for a dream, born in a herdsman's shed,
> And for the secret scripture of the poor.

I hear these words not because of any presumption that they necessarily apply to those listed on an Irish memorial, but rather as a reminder that one should not make assumptions about motivation when it comes to the tens of thousands of Irish who died in that war.

One of those who returned, Bryan Cooper, described Ireland as 'a land of long and bitter memories' which made it difficult for Irishmen to unite for any common purpose. And yet Cooper's own Tenth Irish Division had been composed of men of every class, creed and political opinion:

> The old quarrels, the inherited animosities were forgotten, and men who would have scowled at one another without speaking became comrades and friends. Only those who know Ireland can realize how difficult this was.[1]

Cooper was writing in 1918. Matters were presently to become even more difficult. Civil war is not always an agreed term for any conflict. But to those returning from the Great War it must have seemed as if there were three confusing civil wars being fought out in Ireland between 1919 and 1923.[2]

Known collectively as The Troubles, the bitter memories from this period were to skew perceptions of what had happened between 1914 and

---

1. Bryan Cooper, *The Tenth (Irish) Division in Gallipoli* (Dublin, 1993), p. 137.
2. Given personnel involved it could be argued that the 1919–21 War of Independence and the Troubles in the North East from 1920 to 1922 can be joined with the Civil War of 1922–23 as three variants of civil war on the island.

1918. And some simply managed to air-brush the Great War out of their family history. This despite the fact that for every Irish Volunteer in the Easter Rising there were an estimated sixteen nationalist volunteers at the front fighting for 'the freedom of small nations'. Writing in the context of the fiftieth anniversary of 1916, F.X. Martin suggested that outside of Northern Ireland it was

> difficult to find men and women who will acknowledge that they are children of the men who were serving during 1916 in the British Army, the R.I.C., the D.M.P., and Redmond's Irish National Volunteers. This is the 'Great Oblivion', an example of national amnesia.[3]

Some simply forgot. Others – with no memory nurtured – did not seem to even know of their family connections. Some remained silent from a misplaced sense of embarrassment. Yet others may have been intimidated by those adopting a superior sneer. The war memorial at the entrance to St Stephen's Green at the top of Grafton Street in Dublin was once colloquially spoken of as 'Traitor's Gate'. And it is probably still true that only a fraction of those who pass through its portals are aware of its history or purpose.

As a schoolboy I got my first inkling of the depth of bigotry about the war from the scribbled 'corrections' in public library books. Later, on a youth-hostelling tour of Wicklow, I encountered it more directly when a sing-song was interrupted by one hosteller objecting to the singing of 'It's a long way to Tipperary'. He announced that 'no genuine Irishman would ever sing that shoneen song'. This created general embarrassment – with many baffled English and continental visitors asking what he meant. I don't think any of us at breakfast the next morning succeeded in explaining where the protester was coming from.

Latterly, of course, these issues have been treated in a more mature fashion. Many date this from a speech by Sean Lemass, then taoiseach, at the King's Inns in 1966.[4] But there were some earlier signs of a thaw.[5] And in recent years a considerable amount of scholarly work on Ireland's role in the war has been published. Anthony Quinn's contribution to this scholarship is now welcomed. No longer is the memorial in Dublin's Four Courts simply another list of names of the fallen: in these pages their all too short lives can be recalled.

3. F.X. Martin, '1916 – myth, fact and mystery', *Studia Hibernica*, no. 7 (1967), p. 68.
4. See Keith Jeffery, *Ireland and the Great War* (Cambridge, 2000), p. 135.
5. See, for instance, Eamon de Valera's tribute to John Redmond a decade before, in Maurice Moynihan (ed.), *Speeches and statements of Eamon de Valera* (Dublin, 1980), pp. 576–78.

Contents

Illustrations

Plate section appears between pages 72 and 73.

MAPS

FIGURES

xi

Illustrations from A.P. Quinn collection, unless otherwise indicated.

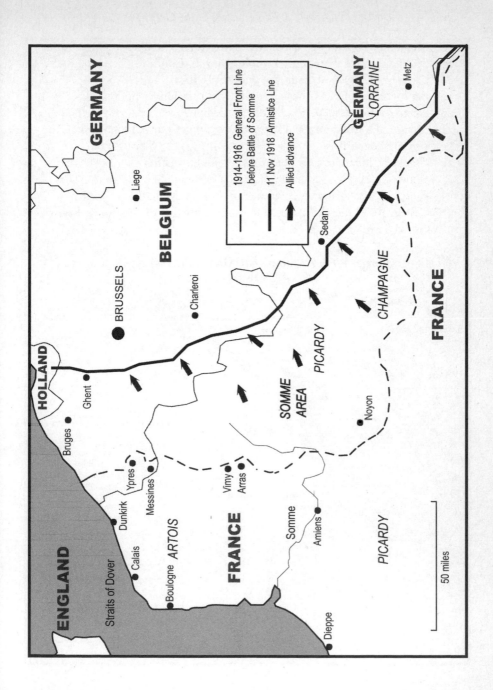

Map of Western Front

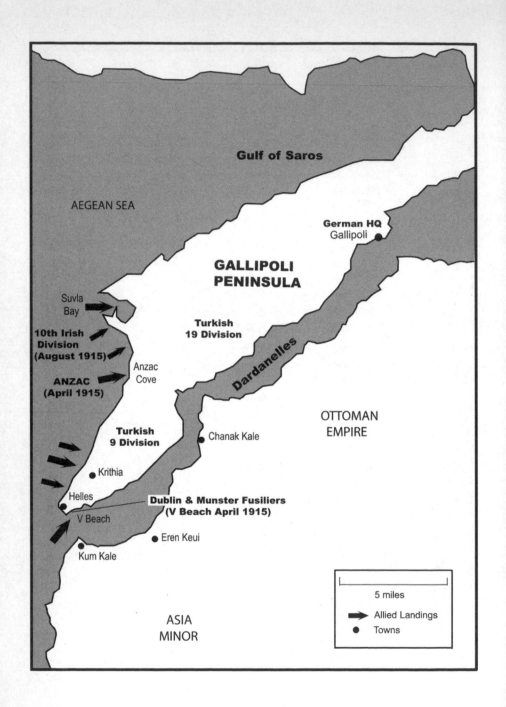

Map of Gallipoli

Abbreviations

ASC	Army Service Corps
Bn.	Battalion
CR	Connaught Rangers
CWGC	Commonwealth Graves Commission
DMP	Dublin Metropolitan Police
DU	Dublin University
GAA	Gaelic Athletic Association
ILT&SJ	*Irish Law Times and Solicitors' Journal*
IMR	*Irish Memorial Records, 1914–1918*
IOC OTC	Inns of Court Officers Training Corps
IRA	Irish Republican Army
IWM	Imperial War Museum, London
MC	Military Cross
NUI	National University of Ireland
OTC	Officers Training Corps
PRO	Public Record Office [National Archives]
RAC	Royal Air Corps
RAMC	Royal Army Medical Corps
RDF	Royal Dublin Fusiliers
RDFA	Royal Dublin Fusiliers Association
RIC	Royal Irish Constabulary
RIF	Royal Irish Fusiliers
RIR	Royal Irish Rifles, renamed Royal Ulster Rifles following the partition of Ireland
RIReg	Royal Irish Regiment
RMF	Royal Munster Fusiliers
RND	Royal Naval Division
RUI	Royal University of Ireland
TCD	Trinity College Dublin
TNA	The National Archives, London (PRO)
UCD	University College Dublin
UVF	Ulster Volunteer Force
WDL	War Dead List
WFA	Western Front Association
WO	War Office (its papers are housed at the PRO)

Acknowledgments

THANKS TO THE MANY people and organisations who encouraged my efforts and provided advice, information and support during my research and writing. My gratitude is due to my friends and colleagues over the years: in the civil service, the legal profession, writing groups, the Irish Writers' Union and Irish PEN; and many historical, literary and other voluntary societies, and especially those listed below. For any omissions, I plead forgiveness because all assistance was appreciated.

Ann, m'anam chara, buíochas, especially for compiling the bibliography and much more. Our family: Anthony M. Quinn for his computer, photographic and journalistic skills; Bláithín and Paul for their artistic skill; Jeannette for her business acumen and for conveniently living near the Public Record Office, National Archives, Kew; my brother John, for garnering press cuttings and making other practical inputs; hill-walking and rambler friends in Na Coisithe who savoured stories and slide-shows of my travels on the killing fields of Flanders and Gallipoli.

The Irish Legal History Society, especially the Hon. Mr Justice Geoghegan, Judge John Martin, QC, Professors W.N. Osborough, N.M. Dawson, and D.S. Greer, the Hon. Mr Justice A. Hart, Robert D. Marshall, Daire Hogan, Dr Colum Kenny, and Felix Larkin. The academic referees provided useful insights.

The members and staff of the Bar Council and Law Library, Four Courts, Dublin, especially Jerry Carroll, director, and Jennefer Aston, consultant librarian, John McCoy and Dan Boland, organisers of remembrance services; Hugh Mohan, SC, chairman, Bar Council, Conor J. Maguire, SC, former chairman of the Bar Council, Jim Bridgeman, Frank Callanan, SC, Keara Donnelly, Dr Kenneth Ferguson, Brendan Gogarty, Gerard Humphries, Brendan Kilty, SC, John McGuigan, John O'Donnell, SC, James O'Reilly, SC, Seamus Ó Tuathail, AS, and various editors of the *Bar Review*. Benchers of the Honorable Society of the King's Inns, Camilla McAleese, under-treasurer, Jonathan Armstrong, librarian, and the assistant librarian, Isabel Duggan, for her enthusiastic research beyond the call of duty. In accessing King's Inns archives, the index to barristers' admission papers compiled by Julitta Clancy and Margaret Connolly was very helpful.

The Royal Dublin Fusiliers Association (RDFA), especially my intrepid climbing companions in the Turkish heat of August 2001 on the Kiretch Tepe (Kirectepe) mountain ridge, Gallipoli, when we followed the footsteps of the 10th (Irish) Division: RDFA chairman, Tom Burke, MBE; Dr Timothy Bowman, David Buckley, Joe Gallagher, Philip Lecane, Dr David Murphy and Nick Broughal. RDFA members on the journeys of remembrance to Flanders and the Somme, especially Des Byrne, Sean Connolly, Brian Moroney, the late Pat Hogarty, A.P. (Tony) Behan, Nial Leinster, John Moore, Ken Doyle, Leo Collins, Marjorie Quarton, Leo Enright, Philip Lecane, the Kavanaghs and the honorary lay chaplain, Pat Cummins (formerly a Fianna Fáil TD) who resolved any residual doubts about the significant nationalist credentials of Irish participants in the Great War.

For detailed data about regiments, battles and individuals: the Western Front Association, and specifically Willie Lennon, Kilcoole; Hal Giblin, Liverpool; Gwen Prescott, Cardiff; Nigel Wood, Nottingham; Alan W. Gregson, Chester; and D. Holroyd, Liversedge, West Yorks. (re the King's Shropshire Light Infantry); Jack Kavanagh, Co. Durham; Frank Liston, Wirral; Alex Shooter (re Royal Irish Rifles); James Brazier, editor, WFA bulletin; and Ann Clayton, editor of *Stand To*. The Gallipoli Association, especially D.R. Saunders, editor of *The Gallipolian*, Claire and Michael Bogan, Malachi Doyle, Canterbury, Kent, and Sinead O'Hanlon.

The late Myfanwy Thomas, president, Edward C. Thomas, chairman, and Colin Thornton, Richard Emeny, Larry Skillman and Anne Harvey of the Edward Thomas Fellowship. Rory and Deirdre McCormack, Wokingham, Berks., for data on Dr Patrick S. Walsh, KC. Bill Simpson, former TCD librarian and Robin Adams, now librarian, and the staff, especially Aisling Lochhart and Felicity O'Mahony, manuscripts department, and also Jean O'Hara, records office. The Friends of the Library, TCD, especially Aidan Heavey, BL, Anne Marie Diffley, Monica Henchy, Henry Murdoch, BL, and Hugh Fitzpatrick; Dr Eilis Ní Dhuibhne, National Library of Ireland and TCD; Dr R. Refaussé, archivist, Representative Church Body, Dublin; Brigid Clesham, archivist, the Neale, Co. Mayo. Patricia Byrne and Marian Keyes, librarians, and the staff of Dalkey and Dun Laoghaire public libraries. Staff at Donegal County Library, Letterkenny. Caroline Carr, Donegal County Museum, Letterkenny; Paddy Harte and Tommie Francis, Co. Donegal Book of Honour committee, for alerting me to the family connection between Tony Blair, MP, British prime minister, honorary bencher of King's Inns, and William Alfred Lipsett, an Irish barrister killed in the Great War.

Staff at the Commonwealth Graves Commission; the National Archives, Kew; the Imperial War Museum, London, especially Alan Martin; R.W. O'Hara, and the late Mick Dalzell, freelance records searchers; National War Museum, Ottawa; and Declan P. Hughes, Irish Veterans Memorial Project.

Members of Foxrock Local History Club, notably Liam Clare, Padraic and Moira Laffan; Dun Laoghaire Borough Historical Society's members Mona O'Donnell, Seamus O'Connor, Anna and Colin Scudds, the late

Robert Brennan, Dermot Dwyer, Anthony Walsh and Michael McGovern. Michael Simons, Ian Cox and the staff, Exchange Bookshop, Dalkey, Co. Dublin. Conor Kostick and Lorcan Collins, organisers of the 1916 rebellion walking tours, Dublin.

Many individuals generously responded with information following my queries and letters in the *Irish Times, Irish Examiner*, and my other articles and reports especially: Henry Tierney, for data on his late uncle, Herbert Tierney, and for speaking at the Bar remembrance services; Dr Gerald Morgan, TCD; Eddie Sullivan, Waterford; Paul McCandless, Banbridge, re Smyth family; Manus Nunan, QC, Colchester; the late A.W.R. (Brian) Fitzmaurice; Jerry Langton, Dublin; Jack O'Connell, Schull Books, Ballydehob, Co. Cork; Tom Crozier, Colchester, and also Brian O'Brien, Rathkeale (re William Magee Crozier); Dr Michael Solomons, Dublin for information on Robert B. Burgess; Seoirse Plunkett, Dublin, Lady Barraclough, Peter Plunkett, London and Dr C.J. McCormack, Portlaoise, for information on the Plunketts; Jerry Holland, Bandon, for information on Cornelius MacCarthy and Gerald O'Brien, also from Co. Cork, for his encouraging postcards; Dr Joseph C. McKenna, Sligo (grand-nephew), Prof. J.B. Lyons (biographer), and Jack Kavanagh, former president of the Institution of Engineers in Ireland for data on Tom Kettle; Oliver Fallon, Connaught Rangers Association and Patrick Lewin, London, for background on Frederick H. Lewin; Michael Lee, RTE, for information on his great uncle, Joseph Bagnall Lee; John Lillis for data on Martin M. Lillis; C. Chomley Farran, Dublin (re Edmund C. Farran); Robert Wood (re J. Rowan Shaw); John W. de Courcy; Joe Moran, Celbridge (re Royal Flying Corps); Tadhg Moloney, Royal Munster Fusiliers Association; Danny Tiernan, Connaught Rangers Association; Major (retd) Jack M. Dunlop, curator, Royal Inniskilling Fusiliers Museum, Enniskillen; James Scannell, local historian; Patrick Casey, medals collector; Dr Jim Stacey, Dungarvan and Dr John Nolan, as Registrar, NUI; John Roche, baritone, for alerting me to Percy French's friendship with Sir John Ross, last lord chancellor of Ireland; Jeff Kildea, Sydney, barrister and historian; M. O'Connell, Cahirciveen, Co. Kerry, James Taylor, Wexford, and the late Leslie Mallon, solicitor, Dublin re Poole Hickman; Billy Patton, Old Court House, Lifford; Gerry Gallick, St Columb's cathedral, Derry; Kirsten Noone, TCD; and Wendy Spearing, London re Capt. R.H. Cullinan.

The Irish Courts Service, especially P.J. Fitzpatrick, director and Helen Priestly, newsletter editor. Brian Lowry and Shirley Mallon, Court Service of Northern Ireland, and John Creaney, QC, facilitated me in tracing relevant memorials in Belfast. The O'Morchoe, chairman, members and staff, the Royal British Legion, Republic of Ireland.

Archivists and record keepers of schools and other educational institutions especially: Dr Clare Rider, Inner Temple; Lesley Whitelaw,

Middle Temple, and also Brig. Charles Wright, under-treasurer, London; Prof. John Turpin, National College of Art and Design, Dublin; John Looby, SJ, Clongowes; the late Dr Patrick O'Donoghue, CM, Castleknock, Co. Dublin; Oliver Murphy, museum curator, and Gerald Conlon, annual editor, Belvedere College, Dublin; Jerome O'Donovan, Christian Brothers College (CBC), past pupils' union, Cork; Ninian Falkiner, St Columba's College, Rathfarnham, Dublin; Georgina Fitzpatrick, St Andrew's, Dublin; Keith Haines, Campbell College, Belfast; R.L. Bennett, headmaster and Lt.-Col. Mark Scott, MBE, estates manager, Portora Royal School, Enniskillen; Sue Cole, Charterhouse, Surrey; Tim Pearce and Christine Leighton, Cheltenham; A.J. Linnell, headmaster, Reading School and Kerr Kirkwood, Old Redingensian Society; Russell Muir, Old Reptonian Society, Derby; Alice Blackford, assistant keeper of archives, Oxford University; Caroline Dalton, archivist, New College, Oxford; Micheal Stansfield, archivist, Merton College, Oxford. Liam O'Meara and Michael O'Flanagan, Inchicore Ledwidge Society, Dublin, and the enthusiasts at the Ledwidge Museum, Slane, Co. Meath and all those, including Ulick O'Connor, who celebrate Ledwidge. Tim Carey, GAA museum, Croke Park, Dublin and later Dun Laoghaire-Rathdown County Council's heritage officer; the Revd David Pierpoint, archdeacon of Dublin; and Martin Joyce.

My various writing mentors and editors, especially Bryan McMahon, RIP, Bill Long, Sean McCann, Joe O'Donnell, Mary Russell and John McKenna; David Rice and Sean Egan, memoirs facilitators; Kieron Wood and Fiona Ness, *Sunday Business Post*; Terri McDonnell, Round Hall Press; Liam McAuley, letters editor, and Kevin Myers, columnist, *Irish Times*; Vincent Browne, S. Burke and N. Reddy, *Village Magazine*; Martha McCarron, Peter Mooney, Kevin Haugh and Cliodhna Ní Anluain producers, *Sunday Miscellany*, and Tom McSweeney, *Seascapes*, RTE Radio 1; Paul Clarke, UTV; Phil Murphy, *Ireland's Own*; and Ken Finlay, *Southside People*.

Authors and historians, especially Dr John Bowman, Philip Orr, Charles Lysaght, BL, Ian Passingham, Middlesex, who generously shared their sources and knowledge. Dalkey Writers' Workshop, and to Maeve Binchy and Joseph O'Connor who encouraged my efforts. The co-operation of Penny and Emma Bailey-Hayden at Dalkey Business Centre, and of Michael Adams and the staff of Four Courts Press was much appreciated.

Thanks to copyright holders for permission to include quotations, especially John Murray, publishers, for permission to reproduce the extract from John Betjeman's poem, 'Ireland on Sunday' and also Colin Smythe Ltd on behalf of the estate of Diarmuid Russell for the extracts from the poem 'Salutations' by George Russell (Æ). If, through inability to locate the present copyright owners, any copyright material is included for which permission has not specifically been sought, apologies are tendered in advance to proprietors and publishers concerned.

   Gratitude to the kind and friendly people of Church Hill and Gartan, Co. Donegal, including the Revd Brian Smeaton, David and Claire Slattery, Gerald and Alice Doherty, Niall McGinley, Vicki and Kelvin and especially Nellie Gallagher, who welcomed Ann and our family to the local community and provided serenity for quiet writing and reflection. During the Great War, injured Belgian soldiers found constructive repose making a path near Gartan in the Glenveagh Castle gardens. There, I reflect about war and peace along the Belgian walk, a tranquil legacy from wartime.

   Finally, special thanks are due to Dr John Bowman, RTE, for writing the foreword, and to Julitta Clancy, for making the index.

ANTHONY P. QUINN

Roll of Honour

Prologue

FOR MANY CENTURIES, there have been connections between law and various types of combat. Lawyers are familiar with fighting during their professional duties in the cut and thrust of adversarial litigation as advocates in court cases. Also, the legal profession has been a source of recruits for armies in various conflicts during many eras. For example, around the time of the Norman invasion of Ireland in the twelfth century, the scholar and prelate, John of Salisbury, wrote:

> They do not alone fight for the State who, panoplied in helmets and breastplates, wield the sword and dart against the enemy; for the pleaders of causes, who redress wrongs, who raise up the oppressed, do protect and provide for the human race as much as if they were to defend with the sword the lives, fortunes and families of citizens.

At the start of the Great War in 1914, the *Irish Law Times and Solicitors' Journal*, quoting the English *Law Journal*, traced the legal profession's involvement in the British army during armed conflicts.[1] Barristers were never content to limit their fighting instincts to professional duties. Lawyers' sense of public service and inclination towards sharp encounters encouraged them into the arenas of politics and war. In England, armed members of the Inns of Court and Chancery under Lord Lyttelton defended Oxford in the reign of Charles I. During the English Civil War, lawyers on the parliamentarian side included Ireton who became lord president of Munster under Oliver Cromwell. Lawyers, commanded by Chief Justice Willes, defended the English monarchy against the Jacobites in 1745.

As explained by Dr Patrick M. Geoghegan, the 1798 rebellion against British rule was conceived and executed by lawyers and a high proportion of protagonists on opposing sides were barristers.[2] The most notable among the revolutionary United Irishmen were: Theobald Wolfe Tone, Henry Sheares (who resigned his commission in the British army), his brother John Sheares, and also Beauchamp Bagenal Harvey who was executed in

1. *ILT&SJ*, xlviii (1914), at p. 281.
2. *1798 and the Irish Bar* (Dublin, 1998).

Wexford. Robert Emmet's brother, Thomas Addis Emmet, expelled from the Irish Bar for 'seditious and traitorous conspiracy', became a distinguished member of the New York Bar. On the loyalist side, the Lawyers' Corps of yeomanry included Catholics and Protestants. During that era when a French invasion was threatened, English barristers formed a body of volunteers, the Inns of Court Rifle Corps. It became known as the Devil's Own and later evolved into the Inns of Court Officer Training Corps. Volunteers from the lawyers corps participated in the Boer War.

Following the tradition outlined above, it is not surprising that many Irish lawyers volunteered for service in the British forces during the Great War, known also as the First World War. Some had previously trained with the Ulster Volunteers, raised following the initiatives of Sir Edward Carson, KC. In contrast, some Irish lawyers such as Patrick Pearse, a qualified barrister, were strongly nationalist.

The main purpose of this book is to record and commemorate twenty-five Irish barristers who died in the Great War and are listed on the Bar Memorial in the Four Courts, Dublin. Their lives are described in narrative form in the wider Irish and European contexts in the respective chapters and are also outlined in appendix 1. In appendix 1, the headings, such as rank, unit, dates of birth and death, and memorial records follow the general format of *Irish winners of the Victoria Cross*.[3] That publication includes over 200 VC winners compared with much fewer barristers killed in the Great War. In this book more detail is included in the profiles in appendix 1 especially for the notable and interesting names: Tom Kettle, Frederick Lewin, Gerald Plunkett, Willie Redmond, and Arthur P.I. Samuels.

Chapter 1 sets the scene by outlining in narrative form some unusual aspects of the lives of the twenty-five listed barristers, and also traces the evolution of remembering the Irish participation in the war. Complexities and connections between conflicting strands of Irish history are woven into the text. Chapter 2 traces the educational and other backgrounds which influenced enlistment. Chapter 3 deals with remembrance in various modes, direct and indirect, formal and informal. The epilogue provides conclusions, linked to current trends in a pluralist Ireland as part of a European Union in which former enemy nations now co-operate peacefully.

It is beyond this book's scope to deal in detail with the Irish solicitors and solicitors' apprentices who died in the First World War. Nevertheless, they are listed in appendix 2 and aspects of some of their careers, deaths and remembrance are included in the text where relevant. Non-lawyers, paralegal personnel such as clerks and officials employed by the legal

---

3. Richard Doherty and David Truesdale, *Irish winners of the Victoria Cross* (Dublin, 2000).

profession and in the courts system, also volunteered to serve in the war. As a topic for further research, it would be worthwhile emulating the example of Dr Gerald Morgan, who campaigned to have names of non-academic staff recorded on the war memorial in Trinity College, Dublin.

Although there has recently been increased Irish awareness of the Great War, much basic information is not known generally outside specialist circles such as military historians and regimental enthusiasts. Therefore, some relevant background information is included to assist readers and to reduce reliance on other books. The select chronology in appendix 3 outlines significant political milestones in Ireland, relevant to this book. The chronology also includes military events on the war fronts so that individual lives and deaths can be placed in context as part of wider history without repeated recourse to other texts. Appendix 5 provides keys to abbreviations and military and other terms to help the general reader. This book was based on detailed research in many diverse areas and sources but it is not intended as a dry academic exercise. Personal references enliven the book and add to the history of evolving attitudes towards remembrance. Conscious of the debates among professional historians about revisionism both in Ireland and Britain, various sides of the arguments are outlined. Recognition of traditional nationalist views did not blind visions of a pluralist Ireland which enshrines diverse strands including those favouring involvement with the Allied cause and closer Anglo-Irish relations.

Sources and bibliography are listed in detail. At this stage, however, a general overview of basic literature and sources will assist readers. Roy Foster, in *The Irish story: telling tales and making it up in Ireland*,[4] analysed many conventional attitudes and fallacies inherent in Irish folk memories. Despite analysis by historians of Roy Foster's calibre, however, inherent human needs will continue to inspire people to commemorate their martyrs and heroes.

Basic facts are available in Henry Boylan's *A dictionary of Irish biography* (3rd ed., Dublin, 1998) and also in standard texts on the Great War. Many are in paperback editions, especially those by Lyn Macdonald, *1915*, *Somme*, *They called it Passchendaele: the story of the third battle of Ypres*, and Robert Rhodes James, *Gallipoli* (London, 1965 and 1999). John Laffin's *Panorama of the Western Front*, including an annotated version of a panoramic plan sketched by Georges Malfroy during the Great War (London, 1994), put battle-lines in context.

Books by Myles Dungan, broadcaster and author, helped to make Irish aspects of the Great War accessible to a wide readership. *An atlas of Irish*

4. London, 2001.

history, ed. Sean Duffy (Dublin, 1997), contains a chronology and facts enlivened by excellent maps. Daire Hogan's *The legal profession in Ireland, 1789–1922* (Dublin, 1986) provides basic information on the legal system's history. Also useful is E. Hall and D. Hogan (eds) *The Law Society of Ireland, 1852–2002: portrait of a profession* (Dublin, 2002).

Current information on military records, rolls of honour, regiments and museums was provided by two excellent reference guides: Norman Holding, revised by Iain Swinnerton, *The location of British army records, 1914–1918* (4th ed., Federation of Family History Societies, Bury, Lancs., 1999) and Terence and Shirley Wise, *A guide to military museums and other places of military interest* (10th revised ed., Knighton, Powys).

Taken into account were more recent publications and research on war and remembrance by eminent historians, especially John Bowman, Terence Denman, Keith Jeffery, Tim Bowman, Jane Leonard, John Horne, Alan Kramer and Niall Ferguson. Critical attitudes are balanced by Gary Sheffield's *Forgotten victory, the First World War: myths and realities* (London, 2001), which refutes assumptions about the futility of the conflict.

There is a substantial body of poetry inspired by the Great War, and relevant verses by Irish and English poets, including Francis Ledwidge, Tom Kettle and Edward Thomas, are quoted throughout the text. For literary references, some books are especially useful: Jon Silkin (ed.), *The Penguin book of First World War poetry* (2nd edition, London, 1996), Anne Powell, *A deep cry: First World War soldier-poets killed in France and Flanders* (Stroud, Glos., 1998) and more recently, *Anthem for doomed youth*, Jon Stallworthy's book for the war poets exhibition in the Imperial War Museum, London, 2002/3.

A more recent book is also relevant: J. Haughey, *The First World War in Irish poetry* (Associated University Presses, London; Cranbury, NJ; and Mississauga, Ontario, 2002); Kettle, Æ and Ledwidge and the literary connections between various streams of Irish identity are examined by Professor Haughey. His approach and analysis echo and expand on the approach in this book. Literature, and especially poetry brings vital insights to understanding the Great War. Paul Fussell, an American professor of English, however, placed excessive emphasis on the literary aspects.

The Irish involvement in the Great War must be viewed against a background of Irish nationalism and unionism during the twentieth century. Therefore, the lives, deaths and remembrance of the listed barristers are placed in the wider historical context of Anglo-Irish relations and the struggle for Irish political freedom. The story of the interaction between Ireland and the British army extends beyond the limited parameters of the Great War. Recent indicators of reconciliation and the peace process are relevant. Thence, this book refers to modern commemorative events and remembrances, including those at the Irish Peace Park in Mesen, Flanders, Belgium.

Mesen, in Flemish, like many other places renowned in the military history, previously had a different name. In that case Messines, in French, was used and still appears in many military history books and maps. To assist readers, a list of the main place names in appendix 4 shows old and modern forms.

Although no bias is intended, most of the people dealt with in this book were men. The reasons are simple because women were not admitted to the Bar or to the combat units during the Great War. Also with a few exceptions, notably Tom Kettle and Willie Redmond, most of the listed barristers were not married. Included, however, is information about mothers and wives, notably the strong women in the Sheehy and Plunkett families. Women suffered pain and grief for the unredeemed loss of their loved ones.

Hilaire Belloc, in *The cruise of the 'Nona'*, hoped that the Irish would give a due position in their annals to the memory of Willie Redmond. The time is now opportune for him and his lawyer colleagues killed in the Great War to be granted that honour. As is evident from the acknowledgments, reference notes, sources and bibliography, a wide variety of sources were used when writing this book. The interpretation of the material, however, is personal to the author, and does not purport to represent the views of the Irish Legal History Society, the Bar of Ireland, or of any other organisation or individual.

This book is not intended to glorify war nor to encourage divisive bitterness. The purpose is to redress past neglect and to remedy remaining imbalances.

CHAPTER ONE

Setting the scene

There is no case of petty right or wrong
That politicians or philosophers
Can judge. I hate not Germans, nor grow hot
With love of Englishmen to please newspapers ...
Little I know or care if, being dull,
I shall miss something that historians
Can rake out of the ashes when perchance
The phoenix broods serene above their ken ...

Edward Thomas [1]

THE ABOVE LINES, WRITTEN in critical reaction to the prevalent jingoistic mood at the start of the Great War in 1914, are still relevant when describing and analysing aspects of the conflict. The soldier-poet's sceptical sentiments aptly summarise the experience and attitudes of many Irish people, especially those of the nationalist tradition.

'British soldiers' cottages': that was the term used derisively to describe the brick houses in suburban Drumcondra, on Dublin's Northside, in the 1940s and 1950s.[2] While most of the soldiers' houses were well kept, veterans' estates were not accepted as equal to those of the lower middle

1. James Bentley (ed.), *Some corner of a foreign field: poetry of the Great War* (London, Boston, Toronto, 1992), p. 92, extract from 'There is no case of petty right or wrong,' by Philip Edward Thomas (1878–1917), a Londoner of Welsh extraction educated at Oxford. Like Francis Ledwidge, another soldier-poet, Edward Thomas also wrote in the Georgian style. Despite his earlier scepticism, he enlisted as a private, but was a 2nd lieutenant with the Royal Garrison Artillery in France, when killed at the battle of Arras, Easter 1917. The Edward Thomas Fellowship commemorates the poet with walks and readings; A.P. (Tony) Quinn, 'In the poet's footsteps', *Walking World Ireland*, no. 51, Sept./Oct. 2002, p. 52.
2. Keith Jeffery, *Ireland and the Great War* (Cambridge, 2000), p. 117 refers to the Irish Soldiers' and Sailors' Land Trust as having developed small estates of houses for ex-servicemen and their families throughout Ireland. Nearly 4,000 dwellings, of a high standard, were built. Those veterans' colonies never posed a loyalist threat to the Irish Free State. Tony Dixon, in conversation with the author, recalled from his own childhood that the housing trust imposed strict rules. For example, if soldiers' widows remarried, they could lose tenancy rights. The trust was wound up in 1987. Tony Gray, *The lost years: the Emergency in Ireland, 1939–45* (London, 1998), p. 25

class. During the frugal 'forties, some tough boys were taunted as the offspring of foreign troops. British symbols were rare, even on remembrance occasions. Some veterans, however, wore poppies and collected money for the British Legion.

Enclaves of veterans' houses contrasted with the dwellings of the lower middle class: minor Irish public servants including army captains, gardaí, clerks and teachers. Some had fought in the Easter Rising 1916, the War of Independence and the Civil War. There was a communal feeling of threat due to the proximity of a colony of former British soldiers. Memories of atrocities by the Black and Tans against the Irish sometimes provoked arguments about the British legacy. Children were in awe of the men who, having fought for Irish freedom, were accorded heroic status.

Appreciating the Irish role in the Great War is a recent phenomenon, contrasting with such attitudes during earlier decades. Then, schoolteachers emphasised the Irish armed rebellions against British rule in 1798, the nineteenth century and 1916 but neglected other significant events. History lessons at school taught little or nothing about the Irish involvement in the Great War and its aftermath. It is remarkable how educators considered that the blood sacrifices of the Easter Rising could be explained or understood without reference to the wider European context. Education, later criticised as indoctrination, reinforced narrow nationalist attitudes. Residual memories of the Irish role on the Allied side were generally suppressed or ignored in nationalist Ireland. As Roy Foster wrote in *The Irish story*, 'not talking about the war was elevated to a fine art in public rhetoric'.[3]

Narrow attitudes were dominant especially in all-Irish schools such as St Patrick's, Drumcondra, and the Christian Brothers' Coláiste Mhuire, Dublin. The school building on Parnell Square was marked by a bilingual plaque stating that the Irish Republican Brotherhood (IRB), planned the 1916 Rising there. In the nearby Belvedere College, a Jesuit secondary school with a more liberal ethos, narrow attitudes and prejudices against British and Allied policies were also evident.[4]

During the Emergency, the Irish euphemism for the Second World War, many Dublin children had a sneaking regard for German spies whom they imagined as lurking in laundry-vans with Swastika brand-signs.[5] In the

describes life in the soldiers' cottages in Dublin. See, generally, Ruth McManus, *Dublin 1910–1940: shaping the city and suburbs* (Dublin, 2002), especially pp. 253–65.

3. R.F. Foster, *The Irish story* (London, 2001), p. 58.
4. Dr Garret FitzGerald, former taoiseach, speaking at the unveiling of an inclusive plaque to past pupils and staff killed in twentieth century conflicts, Belvedere College, Dublin, 15 November 2003.
5. Anthony P. Quinn, book review of Richard Doherty, *Irish volunteers in the Second World War* (Dublin, 2002) in *Sunday Business Post*, Agenda, 25 November 2001.

1950s and 1960s, the Irish-German Society promoted German culture in a fashionable non-political way. Some of the older members, however, had allegedly been involved in intelligence activities during the Second World War. In the Irish-German Society, there was a residual empathy with militaristic nationalist traditions of Germany, and its marching songs, such as Erika, were sung on the society's hikes in the Wicklow mountains.[6]

In the period after the Second World War, poppy wearing in Dublin was confined to veterans on remembrance occasions. Later, more sophisticated attitudes evolved. An IRA bomb killed eleven people and maimed many others at the war memorial in Enniskillen, Co. Fermanagh, on Remembrance Sunday 1987. In reaction to that horrific event, many Dubliners consciously decided to wear a poppy on commemorative occasions to assert the right to remembrance.[7] Red flowers were traditional in pastoral elegy and there is a natural and symbolic connection between Flanders fields and poppies.

Barristers renewed their interest in remembrance ceremonies at the Four Courts memorial, Dublin. It recalls twenty-five members of the Irish Bar who died in the First World War: Robert B. Burgess; William M. Crozier; Robert H. Cullinan; John H. Edgar; Edmond C. Farren (Farran); Poole H. Hickman; Ernest L. Julian; Cecil S. Kenny; Thomas M. Kettle; Joseph B. Lee; John H.F. Leland; Frederick H. Lewin; Martin A. Lillis; William A. Lipsett; Cornelius A. MacCarthy; Edmund Meredith; Arthur R. Moore; Hubert M. O'Connor; Gerald Plunkett; James C.B. Proctor; William Redmond; Arthur P.I. Samuels; Rowan Shaw; George B. Smyth; Herbert Tierney. Information about their family background, education, legal and military careers are included in the biographical profiles in appendix 1. Some aspects are also placed in wider contexts in narrative form throughout the book.

The lives of two of those listed, Willie Redmond and Tom Kettle were reasonably well recorded in their own writings and biographies. The names and stories of the other and mainly younger men were relatively unknown

6. Cathy Molohan, *Germany and Ireland, 1945–1955: two nations' friendship* (Dublin and Portland, OR, 1999) traces the German interest in Irish affairs during the two world wars; A.P. (Tony) Quinn, 'Happy Wanderers', recalling winter walking and youth hostelling with the Die Wandergruppe of the Irish-German Society, *Walking World Ireland*, annual, 1997; James Scannell, 'German World War Two espionage in County Dublin', lecture to Foxrock Local History Club, 13 November 2001; TG4, television documentary, 'An seamróg agus an Swastika,' reviewed by E. Kehoe, Agenda, *Sunday Business Post*, 3 February 2002; Mark M. Hull, *Irish secrets: German espionage in wartime Ireland, 1939–45* (Dublin and Portland, OR, 2003).

7. Denzil McDaniel, *Enniskillen: the Remembrance Sunday bombing* (Denver, CO and Dublin, 1997). The author James Plunkett (1920–2003), in a radio interview repeated on RTE, *Bowman's Saturday*, 8.30 (16 August 2003), spoke of Dublin's poppy tradition in Dublin and the clashes with the republican Easter lily tradition.

and therefore challenge curiosity and stimulate research. Although many of the barristers listed had distinguished academic records, few were well established in legal practice and none had taken silk as King's Counsel.

Those who served the British forces and survived the war included some KCs: Richard Manders, Registrar of Deeds and Titles, Ireland, who was commissioned as Lt., Royal Naval Volunteer Reserve. Edward S. Walsh, North West Circuit and Kenneth Dockrell, North East Circuit, joined the OTC in 1918. Charles F. Casey, SC, became Irish attorney general and later a judge of the High Court in 1951. Frank Fitzgibbon, who served in the war with the Munster Fusiliers, was father of the senior Irish Bar in the 1950s.

The most prominent KC involved in the war effort was Dr Patrick S. Walsh of the Donegal recruiting staff. Walsh had been with Padraic Pearse in his rare appearance as a barrister in a court case defending Niall McBride, a Donegal man who asserted his right to use the Irish language for official purposes. Many such links between diverse strands of Irish identity and history emerged from research.

The Journey of Reconciliation Trust influenced public opinion through its initiatives in 1998. In the presence of the British and Belgian monarchs, President Mary McAleese formally opened the Peace Park at Mesen, Flanders, Belgium. Wreaths laid at the Irish round tower included one to honour the Irish barristers killed in the Great War.

Most of those named on the Four Courts memorial, Dublin, had studied at Trinity College, Dublin, where through ignorance and apathy their memory was often neglected. Research revealed twenty-five human stories. Letters from the wider public were also very encouraging. For example, a Cork correspondent hoped that recording the barristers' stories would ' help dispel the myth that all who fought and died in the Great War came from the ranks of the unemployed, uneducated and deprived'.[8] On a family headstone in St Patrick's cemetery, Bandon, Co. Cork, the name of one of the listed barristers was hidden: Cornelius McCarthy (MacCarthy). He was drowned at sea near Malta on 19 July 1917, while serving as a 2nd Lieutenant with the 9th Bn., Royal Dublin Fusiliers. The McCarthy tombstone at Bandon graveyard was recently restored so that the name of Cornelius MacCarthy 'liveth for evermore'.

War literature revealed relevant data. For example, Philip Orr's book about the Somme includes frequent references to, and many quotations from, the diaries of Capt. Arthur Samuels.[9] Details of his career are in

8. Jerry Holland, Bandon, Co. Cork, member of local remembrance committee, in response to author's letters to *Irish Times*, 3 and 23 February 1999 and *Examiner*, Cork, 19 February 1999.
9. Philip Orr, *The road to the Somme: men of the Ulster Division tell their story* (Belfast, 1987), quoting extensively from A.P.I. and D.G.S. (Samuels), *With the Ulster*

appendix 1. In summary, he was from Howth, Co. Dublin, served in the C Coy., 11th Bn., Royal Irish Rifles, 36th (Ulster) Division, and died of wounds on the Western Front on 24 September 1916.

False trails were checked to ensure that the list of twenty-five names on the Four Courts memorial was complete in respect of Irish practising barristers who had been Law Library members. For example, Capt. James Patrick Roche (de Roiste) was a legal clerk in Manchester. That legal connection became confused and Roche was referred to as a barrister in war letters by Col. R. Feilding published as battle memoirs.[10] Capt. James P. Roche, of course, is worthy of remembrance but details would be outside the scope of this book. In summary, Roche, a talented field officer, was killed in June 1917 during the Allied victory at Messines, which also claimed Major Willie Redmond as a victim. Messines was the prelude to the third battle of Ypres, often called the battle of Passchendaele.

Raymond P.D. Nolan, shown in the *ILT&SJ*, 14 November 1914, as a barrister was killed in action at Ypres, on 5 November 1915 while serving with the Black Watch (Royal Highlanders). Capt. Nolan, who married the daughter of the Master of the Rolls, Charles Andrew O'Connor and Mrs O'Connor, could not be traced in King's Inns records, but he is listed and remembered at the Inner Temple, London.

Data from family, educational, military and legal archives, and from entrance and admission papers at the King's Inns library, and legal journals crystallised into micro images. Those jigsaw pieces fitted into place to form a larger picture composed of twenty-five distinct biographical profiles in appendix 1. Each individual profile was different but some were unique because of unusual circumstances.

Frederick H. Lewin was the only one of the twenty-five on the list who died and was buried in Ireland. He followed the military tradition of the Lewin family which can be traced back to the Bayeux Tapestry depicting the battle of Hastings in 1066 when King Harold's brother, Earl Leofwin (Lewin) was killed. Frederick H. Lewin, commissioned as a captain in the 3rd Bn., Connaught Rangers in 1914, died from injuries sustained while

    Division in France: a story of the 11th Battalion, Royal Irish Rifles (South Antrim Rifles) from Borden to Thiepval, including war diaries of Arthur Samuels (Belfast, n.d. *c.*1920, reprinted Naval and Military Press, Uckfield, 2003).

10. Rowland Feilding, *War letters to a wife: France and Flanders, 1915–1918* (London, 1930; Gliddon Books, Great War Classics, Norfolk, 1989), p. 191; Terence Denman, *Ireland's unknown soldiers* (Dublin, 1992), pp. 107, 112, 114; Anthony P. Quinn, letter, *Irish Times*, 24 March 2001, in response to Kevin Myers, 'An Irishman's Diary', 14 March 2001; see also that columnist, 13 November 2001; Michael O'Connell, Cahirciveen, to author. The RDFA tour during September 2000 visited J.P. Roche's grave at Kemmel Château cemetery in Flanders where the Irish inscription recalls the generous and manly nature of an Roisteach (Roche).

engaged on bomb practice at Charles Fort, Kinsale, Co. Cork on 8 December 1915. He is named at the Grangegorman military ceremony, Blackhorse Avenue, Dublin, but was buried in the Lewin family vault at Kilmaine (Holy Trinity) Church of Ireland churchyard, Co. Mayo, near the Galway border.

The Lewin family vault is shadowed by remnants of a 'lichen-crusted' ruined church and belfry, where to quote John Betjeman:

> ... There in pinnacled protection
> One extinguished family waits
> A Church of Ireland resurrection.[11]

Unlike the Burren mausoleum which Betjeman described as covered by 'sheepswool, straw and droppings', the Lewin family plot was recently restored and reclaimed from overgrown vegetation on the initiative of family members from England.

Frederick H. Lewin, unlike most of the other listed barristers who died in the war, came from a landlord family of the Protestant Anglo-Irish upper class listed in Burke's *Landed gentry of Ireland*.[12] The Lewins, called lords by the local people, had extensive property in the area north of Tuam, where Galway ends and Mayo begins. There the family had two mansions, Cloghans and also Castlegrove, now in ruins, destroyed by fire in the early 1920s during a vicious campaign by the IRA against the Anglo-Irish of the big houses. Trees now grow erratically between the solid stones of the ruined mansion. In the late Victorian era, when Frederick H. Lewin was a student at Cheltenham public school, before going up to Merton College, Oxford, Castlegrove was the scene for considerable social activity as noted in a contemporary account:

> [Visitors enjoyed] the hospitality of Frederick T. Lewin, Esq., JP, DL, the very lordliest of Irish west country squires. The mansion at Castlegrove is a fine, solid, square-built structure, battlemented and porticoed and having a front of hewn stone-clean as a freshly-shaven face, while the sides are covered from roof to basement in a type of variegated ivy ... On the right is the dining-room, the scene of unremitting hospitality and general merriment over meals ... In the library, there was a vast army of fiction from ... Scott down to Haggard, Lyall and Kipling.[13]

11. John Betjeman, 'Sunday in Ireland', quoted in Frank O'Connor (ed.), *A book of Ireland* (London and Glasgow, 1959), pp. 27–28. Reproduced by permission of John Murray, Publishers.
12. Burke's *Landed gentry of Ireland* (London, 1958), p. 439.
13. Mrs Power O'Donoghue, 'Castlegrove House' (1894), originally published in *Lady's*

Such literature, replete with images of British imperial glory, was available to Frederick H. Lewin in his formative years in the privileged ambience of Castlegrove. The expansive 'arboreous ornamentation of the estate', described in that contemporary account, gave way to an untidy growth of untamed woodland. Tall trees now submerge the past glory of a landlord class which enthusiastically supported the British empire and provided officers for its armies and navy.[14] Frederick H. Lewin inevitably followed the family tradition of service in the local Connaught Rangers, which Col. John T. de Burgh of the Norman Clanricarde dynasty originally raised in the late eighteenth century.

The activities and journeys of regimental associations, especially the Royal Dublin Fusiliers and the Connaught Rangers are very informative about specific areas of research. Aspects of the listed barristers' stories are enshrined in Flanders fields and on the Gallipoli peninsula. A journey of remembrance organised by the RDFA to Flanders and the Somme in September, 2000, was remarkable for many poignant incidents and serendipitous discoveries. At a welcoming dinner, Flemish officials expressed formal thanks for the Irish role in liberating Belgium from German invaders during the First World War.

A book about the second battle of Ypres, obtained on the RDFA tour, included an extract from the Canadian Roll of Honour featuring a hero of the 2nd Ypres.[15] He was one of the listed barristers: William Alfred Lipsett from Ballyshannon, Co. Donegal, who studied at St Andrew's and Trinity Colleges, Dublin. An emigrant to Calgary, Alberta, he volunteered two days after the war started and returned to Europe with the 1st Canadian Division, 2nd brigade, 10th Bn. Canadian Infantry (Alberta Regiment). Unusual for a barrister and university graduate, he refused a commission and served as a private and grenadier. Many of such basic facts were already available through systematic research in archives, and from military, educational and other records. During the RDFA tour, however, details of the human dimension came available. The Canadian Roll of Honour described William Alfred Lipsett's behaviour on the night of 22–23 April 1915 during the

Pictorial, reprinted in John A. Claffey (ed.), *Glimpses of Tuam since the Famine*, Old Tuam Society (Tuam, 1997), pp. 139–45; Patrick Lewin, London, to author, information about Lewin family and their houses; Anthony P. Quinn, 'Capt. F. Lewin', in *New Ranger*, journal of the Connaught Rangers Assoc., vol. 1, no. 1 (Boyle, Co. Roscommon, 2003).

14.   Terence Dooley, *The decline of the big house in Ireland* (Dublin, 2001), examines the considerable contribution of the landed gentry to the British armed forces in the context of the socio-economic effects of the Great War.

15.   Norm Christie, *For king and empire; 1: the Canadians at Ypres, 22nd–26th April 1915* (Ottawa, 1999), p. 70.

attack on St Julian wood as 'very cool, apparently without fear … a gallant soldier … killed within 10 or 15 yards from the German redoubt, he was deeply regretted by all ranks'. The name of Lipsett, a fearless and gallant soldier, is engraved in Ieper on the Canadian panels at the Menin Gate memorial to those buried without known graves in Flanders fields.[16]

The Ulster Tower, Thiepval, Somme, described in chapter 3, recalls the 36th (Ulster) Division in which four of the listed twenty-five Irish barristers served: Lt. William Magee Crozier, Capt. Arthur P.I. Samuels, Capt. George B.J. Smyth and Capt. James C.B. Proctor. The only Methodist among the twenty-five barristers, James C.B. Proctor, is of special interest. A unionist, he organised the Derry Volunteers, a political militia group which formed the 10th Bn., Royal Inniskilling Fusiliers and became part of the Ulster Division.[17]

On the RDFA tour of the Western Front, an appropriate mood was evoked during spontaneous poppy-picking in the roadside field near the Ulster Tower, Thiepval.[18] Poppies and other symbols are significant, as illustrated by the souvenir badges which refer to 'Somme, Ireland 1916'. Even well-informed visitors are challenged by that enigma because a symbol of Ulster's sons displaces traditional Irish nationalist perceptions of 1916 as a significant year solely because of the Easter Rising.[19]

Myth and sentiment were, however, moderated by the reality of the tensions and conflicting loyalties as Philip Orr explained regarding the 36th (Ulster) Division:

> [It was] designed primarily to include the men of the Ulster Volunteer Force (UVF). Carson and Craig, the Unionist leaders, ensured that

16. A.P. (Tony) Quinn, 'The Irish in Flanders', featuring William A. Lipsett, talk on *Sunday Miscellany* (producer Martha McCarron), RTE Radio 1, Remembrance Sunday, November 2000; Pol Ó Muiri, 'Tuarascail', *Irish Times*, 3 October 2001, referring to an exhibition, 'Before I joined the army, I lived in Donegal', County Museum, Letterkenny, Co. Donegal, October 2001, stated that over 1,000 Donegalmen, including native Irish speakers, died in the war; Anthony P. Quinn, letter re that war exhibition in Letterkenny, *Irish Times*, 14 November 2001, re William A. Lipsett; *Donegal book of honour: the Great War 1914–1918* (Dublin and Donegal, 2002).

17. As Dr Timothy Bowman pointed out in his foreword to Patrick Hogarty's *The Old Toughs: history of the 2nd Bn., Royal Dublin Fusiliers* (Dublin, 2001), the 10th Bn., Royal Inniskilling Fusiliers originated in a political militia, which was called the Derry, not Londonderry, Volunteers.

18. *Flanders Fields, 75th anniversary tape of the battle of the Somme*, also evokes a poignant mood, Noel McMaster producer for Somme Association (Belfast, 1991).

19. A.P. (Tony) Quinn, 'Remembering the Irish in World War One is relevant to reconciliation and peace' in *The Blue Cap*, journal of the Royal Dublin Fusiliers Association (RDFA), vol. 8, June 2001, pp. 15–17.

Home Rule would not be passed during the war years and that the exemption of Ulster from Home Rule would be a real option. In return, many of the men in the Volunteers would be available for service in the 36th Division.[20]

Many links between diverse traditions, Orange and Green, conflicting but complementary, emerged during my research. For example, as outlined by a controversial commanding officer, Brig.-Gen. F. Percy Crozier in his account of the 36th Division at Thiepval and the Somme slaughter: 'On St Patrick's Day, we receive shamrock from Mr John Redmond, and in replying (we) express a hope that he (Redmond) will wear Orange lilies from us on the 12th July, for luck.'[21] Ruth Dudley Edwards, a controversial historian and commentator with insights into the Orange and unionist traditions, elaborated:

> As the men of the Ulster Division emerged from their trenches on 1 July (1916), some wore orange lilies and a sergeant wore his sash. By any standards, they acted with both efficiency and bravery, but they never stood a chance. During two days, 5,500 were killed or wounded. Some companies were virtually wiped out.[22]

Two of the listed barristers, Lt. William Magee Crozier and Capt. James C.B. Proctor were killed at that fateful start to the Somme battle. Green and orange images, however, belied the horror of war on the Western Front and its brutalising effects on officers and men. General Crozier later commanded the auxiliary division of the Royal Irish Constabulary (RIC) for a brief period in 1921. He explained controversially:

> The last detailed man has sacrificed himself on the German wire to the God of War. Thiepval village is masked with a wall of corpses. The net result of the barren, glorious bloody battle of Thiepval (the 1st July, 1916 at the start of the Somme offensive) is that over seven hundred men of the West Belfast battalion of the Royal Irish Rifles prove their ability to subordinate matter to mind … A battalion is

20. Philip Orr, introduction to F.P. Crozier, *A brass hat in no man's land* (London, 1930, and Gliddon Books, Norfolk, Great War Classics, 1989), p. 19; Dr Timothy Bowman, 'Carson's army or Kitchener's men: the Ulster Volunteer Force and the formation of the 36th (Ulster Division)', lecture to RDFA, Dublin Civic Museum, 13 October 2001, also examined the relevant tensions and conflicting loyalties.
21. Crozier, *A brass hat in no man's land*, p. 102
22. Ruth Dudley Edwards, *The faithful tribe: an intimate portrait of the loyal institutions* (London, 2000), p. 312.

never really a first-class machine in a great war until it has passed the acid test of big battle with success ... Units were regarded as 'not up to much', merely because they had not picked up laurels on the field of gore, or killed as many opponents as was considered necessary. The acid test of killing and being killed had been passed by us with credit.[23]

It is interesting to speculate on the extent to which the listed barristers passed that acid test of killing, directly or perhaps indirectly as officers ordering the German enemy to be shot, before they themselves were killed. Lines from Wilfred Owen, fatally killed by German machine guns a week before the armistice in 1918, are pertinent:

> I am the enemy you killed, my friend.
> I knew you in this dark: for you so frowned
> Yesterday through me as you jabbed and killed.
> I parried; but my hands were loath and cold.
> Let us sleep now ...

To place the conflict in a wider perspective, it is salutary to visit German cemeteries such as that at Langemarck, near Ieper, which commemorates over 44,000 young soldiers, including almost 25,000 buried in mass graves.

The RDFA visits to Flanders recalled the memory of one of those listed on the main memorial at Thiepval: Thomas M. Kettle, barrister, poet, essayist and patriot. An Irish Parliamentary Party MP for East Tyrone at Westminster (1906–10), he underestimated the depth of unionist opposition to Home Rule. Although critical of the Easter Rising, 1916 which had spoilt his dream of a free, united Ireland in a free Europe, he called for an amnesty for Sinn Féin prisoners.[24] Lt. Tom Kettle, 9th Bn., Royal Dublin Fusiliers, 16th (Irish) Division, was killed near Ginchy during the battle of the Somme, on 9 September 1916. That was only a few months after the Easter Rising. During that period, Kettle's brother-in-law, Francis Sheehy Skeffington, a socialist pacifist who opposed recruitment to the army, was shot by British military in Portobello (Cathal Brugha) Barracks, Dublin, then occupied by 3rd (Reserve) Bn., Royal Irish Rifles.[25] Skeffington was sympathetic to the

23. Crozier, *A brass hat in no man's land*, pp. 128–29.
24. J.B. Lyons, *The enigma of Tom Kettle, Irish patriot, essayist, poet, British soldier, 1880–1916* (Dublin, 1983).
25. *Sinn Féin (1916) rebellion handbook* (Dublin 1916, and 1998, revised ed. with introduction by Declan Kiberd), containing at pp. 213–31, report of Royal Commission of Enquiry (Simon Commission), September 1916, which found that Francis Sheehy Skeffington and two others had not been connected with the rebellion; Leah Levenson, *With wooden sword: a portrait of Francis Sheehy*

republican socialist leader, James Connolly, who was executed after the Easter Rising. Tom Kettle's death in British army uniform could be attributed to a broken heart due to conflicting loyalties and complex attitudes, evident in the tragic course of events in Ireland and in Europe.[26]

Tom Kettle's colleague at the Bar, Edmond Chomley L. Farran, had enlisted in September 1914 in the 3rd Bn., Royal Irish Rifles. An officer in that same unit, Capt. J.C. Bowen-Colthurst, was in September 1916 found guilty but insane on a charge of murdering Francis Sheehy Skeffington while in military custody. Like Tom Kettle, Edmond Chomley L. Farran has no known grave but his name is listed on the Menin Gate memorial in Ieper. The RDFA also visited the lonely grave of John Redmond's brother, Major Willie Redmond, MP, at Loker, Flanders. There his memory has become a local icon and the Irish pub is named Redmonds. Shortly before being killed aged 56 in the battle of Messines Ridge on 7 June 1917, Willie Redmond pleaded for the consummation of peace between North and South. Stretcher bearers of the 36th (Ulster) Division brought him back to base. He became a symbol of the concept of blood sacrifice as a unifying process between the Orange and Green traditions. The credentials of Willie Redmond as a patriotic Irishman in the traditional sense were enhanced by his record, not only as a nationalist MP, but also as a prisoner in Kilmainham gaol with Parnell during the land agitation.[27]

In the Clare by-election caused by the death of Willie Redmond in 1917, Eamon de Valera of Sinn Féin defeated the Irish Parliamentary Party candidate, Patrick Lynch, KC, who later became attorney general in a Fianna Fáil government under de Valera.[28]

Herbert (Bertie) Tierney wrote letters home to Dublin from the Middle East (extracts in appendix 6). His correspondence shows that while serving in the 8th Bn., Cheshire Regiment in Gallipoli during the terrible battles of

Skeffington, militant pacifist (Dublin, 1983), generally and chap. 14, 'Murder most foul', pp. 222–37; A.P. Quinn, news feature comparing different attitudes of Kettle and Sheehy Skeffington to war and peace, *Sunday Business Post*, 23 February 2003.

26. Ulick O'Connor, speaking at the annual commemoration of Francis Ledwidge, organised by the Inchicore Ledwidge Society at the National Memorial Gardens, Islandbridge, Dublin, 29 July 2001, asserted that Tom Kettle died of a broken heart (in the political rather than in the romantic sense).

27. Terence Denman, '"A voice from the lonely grave": the death in action of Major William Redmond, MP, 7 June 1917', *Irish Sword*, journal of the Military History Society of Ireland, vol. xviii, summer 1992, no. 73, pp. 286–97; Anthony P. Quinn, speaking as winner of Ledwidge poetry award, at Ledwidge commemoration, Islandbridge, Dublin, 29 July 2001.

28. Oliver Snoddy, 'Three by-elections of 1917', *Capuchin Annual* (Dublin, 1967), pp. 341–47 and Geraldine Plunkett Dillon (daughter of Count Plunkett), 'The North Roscommon election', ibid., pp. 338–40.

August 1915, he received a letter 'giving legal news'. The writer was Patrick Lynch, KC, from Co. Clare, the home county of Herbert Tierney's mother. Tierney survived Gallipoli but was reported missing believed dead on 9 April 1916, aged 27, in Mesopotamia during the unsuccessful attempt to rescue the troops of the arrogant Major-General Townshend at Kut-el-Amara. Also serving in that event was Tom Barry, later a famous guerilla fighter in the Irish War of Independence who took the republican side in the Civil War.

Questions of national identity, related to ambiguities and apparent conflicting loyalties, challenge generalisations. War memorials at home in Ireland and abroad on the Western Front and in Gallipoli reflect a wider British and Allied culture which should not be equated simplistically with unionism or loyalism. As explained in detail in chapter 3 on remembrance, the biographer of the sculptor, Oliver Sheppard, RHA, John Turpin asserted that:

> Both memorials [to the lawyers in Dublin] were modelled at the height of the war of independence and are an assertion of the loyalist community to which most of the barristers and solicitors belonged.[29]

The position is much more complex because lawyers came from different traditions. Even within the unionist and loyalist community, there were nuances and complexities. For example, in January 1922, at the unveiling of the war memorial at Queen's University, Belfast, Field Marshal Sir Henry Wilson said:

> Scattered hither and thither over this dear country of theirs, of Ulster, and that dear land of theirs, England, were memorials of those … who were not professional soldiers, the names of men who thought it was their duty to come forward to help when their country was in danger.[30]

Wilson was later assassinated in London by two British ex-servicemen acting in the Irish republican cause.

The memorial at the Queen's University, Belfast, includes the name of John H. Edgar, of the Durham Light Infantry. A barrister from Belfast, he practised in both the Irish and English jurisdictions and thus exemplified the complexities of loyalties and nationalities. Such complexities were also

29. John Turpin, *Oliver Sheppard: symbolist sculptor of the Irish cultural revival* (Dublin, 2000), p. 127.
30. *Belfast News-letter*, 20 January 1922, quoted in Keith Jeffery, 'The Irish military tradition and the British Empire' in Jeffery (ed.), *An Irish empire? Aspects of Ireland and the British Empire* (Manchester, 1996), chap. 4, p. 107.

evident in the life and death of Capt. Arthur P.I. Samuels, whose father
Arthur Warren Samuels, had written about the likely financial effects of
Home Rule. He was a unionist MP for Dublin University and one of the few
southern unionists elected in 1918. He later served as a judge of the King's
Bench Division until 1924. The Samuels family had an unusual link with the
Easter Rising, 1916. From the smouldering ruin of the General Post Office,
Dublin, Arthur Warren Samuels, then solicitor general for Ireland,
preserved a signed copy of the Proclamation of the Republic together with
army recruiting posters upon which it was pasted.[31] Those artefacts and
other historic material, including many pamphlets relating to the nationalist
movement during the Great War, the struggle for independence and the
Civil War, are part of the Samuels Collection in Trinity College Library,
Dublin. Gathering information for political intelligence purposes may have
motivated Arthur Samuels, senior, to accumulate the artefacts. The remarkable Samuels collection reveals insights into the history of Irish nationalism
and links between diverse traditions. Included in the collection are copies of
Æ's inclusive poem, 'Salutations', and the accompanying letter to the *Irish
Times* in December, 1918, pleading for reconciliation between diverse
Irish traditions and especially those of the Easter Rising and the Great War.
That poem and its wider significance are dealt with in the context of
remembrance in chapter 3.

Arthur P.I. Samuels, a distinguished Trinity graduate, had family
connections in Ulster and his wife, Dorothy Gage Young, came from
Culdaff, Inishowen, Co. Donegal, but her family also had a residence in Co.
Antrim. He was commissioned in the Royal Irish Rifles, C Company, 11th
Bn., formed from the South Antrim Volunteers, part of the Ulster
Volunteer Force (UVF), raised by Sir Edward Carson, KC, to resist Home
Rule, if necessary by armed force against the British government. Soon after
the Easter Rising, Arthur P.I. Samuels died of wounds in Belgium, in
September 1916 during action at Messines (Mesen) with the 36th (Ulster)
Division. In a book, published in 1923, based on research on Edmund Burke
by Arthur P.I. Samuels, his father mourned the loss of his only son, a young
man of great potential who served his country.[32]

31. John S. Ellis,' The degenerate and the martyr: nationalist propaganda and the
    contestation of Irishness, 1914–1918,' in *Eire-Ireland*, vol. xxxv: 3–4, fall/winter
    2000/1, Morristown, NJ, pp. 7–33; Samuels Collection, Trinity College Library,
    Dublin; Ben Novick, *Conceiving revolution: Irish nationalist propaganda during the
    First World War* (Dublin, 2001), at p. 27 suggests that Samuels's personal collection
    reflects a double bias because it only drew on seized material and contains material
    of interest to Samuels himself.
32. Arthur P.I. Samuels, *Early life, correspondence and writings of the Rt. Hon. Edmund
    Burke, LL.D. with a transcript of the minute book of the debating 'club' founded by him
    in Trinity College, Dublin*, with extra material by A.W. Samuels (Cambridge, 1923).

From their social and family background, it is apparent that individuals among the twenty-five Irish barristers had different visions of what constituted their country and native land. Arthur Samuels, senior, was very active in Irish public affairs and lobbied politically on behalf of the Bar. Constructive in outlook and sensitive to nationalist opinion including the arguments for Home Rule, he opposed partition, but was a convinced unionist who believed that North-East Ulster could not be coerced.[33]

Therefore, the family background of Capt. Arthur P.I. Samuels conditioned him towards a vision of an Ireland linked to Britain and the empire, probably with a reluctant acceptance of a limited degree of devolved government. Such a status would, however, fall short of the Ireland envisaged by constitutional nationalists such as Tom Kettle and Major Willie Redmond: 'a semi-autonomous Irish nation existing in harmony within a multi-national British State.'[34] There are many strands of nationalism including the parliamentary tradition in which lawyers, including Tom Kettle and Willie Redmond, played a significant role.

What emerged was an Irish nation State, independent of Britain, nationalist and Roman Catholic in ethos and separated from the six counties of Northern Ireland. Irrespective of their political complexions, however, the young lawyers killed in the war would have had much to contribute to post-war Ireland, in whatever form it developed.

In Gallipoli, Turkey, during August 2001, the RDFA held a remembrance ceremony where many Irish, killed in 1915, were buried at V beach cemetery. In that beautiful place haunted with poignant Irish memories, the RDFA chairman, Tom Burke, in the presence of the local Turkish governor, presided at a ceremony. Francis Ledwidge's poem, 'The Irish in Gallipoli', with allusions to Grecian heroes, focuses on Irishmen fighting and dying in British uniforms and refers significantly to 'Our (Ireland's) cross with England's mingle ... Let Ireland weep but not for sorrow, weep.'[35] In Gallipoli, at V beach, Compton Mackenzie in 1915 searched for a rare orchid and contrasted the scent of flowers with the stench of dead horses.[36]

33. Arthur Warren Samuels, 'Election address to the electorate of the University of Dublin', November 1918, TCD Lib., Bernard Papers, 2388/95, 163.
34. Ellis in *Eire-Ireland*, vol. xxxv. p. 7.
35. Bryan Cooper, *The Tenth (Irish) Division in Gallipoli* (London, 1918), revised ed. with foreword by Dr John Bowman (Dublin 1993 and 2003), includes Francis Ledwidge's poem, 'The Irish in Gallipoli', but other versions were included in later Ledwidge anthologies: *Complete poems*, ed. Alice Curtayne (London, 1974 and 1986) and *Poems complete*, ed. Liam O'Meara (Newbridge, Co. Kildare, 1997). A.P. Quinn quoted that poem at the RDFA ceremony in Gallipoli, August 2001.
36. T. and M. Holt, *Major and Mrs Holt's battlefield guide to Gallipoli* (Barnsley, 2001), pp. 105–07; see, generally, re Irish involvement in Turkish campaign, Anthony P.

At V beach, the seaside cemetery is now planted with Japanese laurels, tamarisk bushes and rosemary, a relevant remembrance symbol in the Gallipoli context. At the nearby Helles memorial, six Irish barristers killed in summer, 1915, are named: Robert H. Cullinan, Poole Hickman, Ernest Julian, Joseph B. Lee, John H.F. Leland, Gerald Plunkett.

Research revealed the hidden story of Gerald Plunkett. His family background, like that of the Lewins, can be traced back to the battle of Hastings and the Norman invasions. There were conflicting and overlapping loyalties in the Plunkett family. Gerald's life, including education and career are detailed in appendix 1. In summary, a scion of a wealthy Irish Catholic family, Gerald Plunkett was educated by the Jesuits at Belvedere College, and graduated from Oxford. He studied at the Inner Temple, London, and the King's Inns, but was called to the Irish Bar only. A talented musician and singer, he was a keen yachtsman who joined the Royal Naval Volunteer Reserve and was commissioned as a sub-lieutenant in the Collingwood Bn., Royal Naval Division. He was killed by a Turkish bullet on 4 June 1915, while, laughing and joking, he led his men during the third battle of Krithia, inland from Helles.

Reflections on the flora at Helles and the talented men who were cut off in the flower of their youth, like Francis Ledwidge, leaving 'songs unsung', recall another Plunkett: Joseph Mary, poet and signatory to the declaration of the Republic. Shortly after marrying Grace Gifford, he was executed by the British because of his role in the Easter Rising, 1916. Those heroic events ensured that Joseph Mary Plunkett became a nationalist icon in Irish political and educational spheres. His image and reputation, combining blood sacrifice and religious symbolism, were enhanced by his mystical poem:

> I see his blood upon the rose
> And in the stars the glory of his eyes
> His body gleams amid eternal snows
> His tears fall from the skies.[37]

Irish schoolchildren who memorised that poem became well informed about Joseph Mary Plunkett, but remained unaware of Gerald Plunkett. Both were born in the same year, 1887, and attended Belvedere College, Dublin, but Joseph transferred to another Jesuit school at Stonyhurst. The close family connection between the two men became apparent from research.

Quinn, 'Gallipoli, where 4,000 Irish were slaughtered', *Sunday Business Post*, 11 November 2001.

37. Poem quoted with critical comment in Ulick O'Connor, *The Ulick O'Connor diaries, 1970–1981: a cavalier Irishman* (London, 2001), p. 313.

Gerald's father, Patrick Plunkett, married twice and his second family were about the same age as the children of his son, George Noble Plunkett, from Patrick's first marriage. A papal count and later a Sinn Féin MP and anti-Treaty republican, George Noble Plunkett was the father of Joseph Mary who was therefore Gerald's half-nephew. Patrick Plunkett was Gerald's father and also Joseph Mary's grandfather. While family sensitivities and divided loyalties were relevant, it is difficult to excuse or explain the neglect of Gerald Plunkett in Irish consciousness. That imbalance can now be redressed by remembering them both.

One of the listed barristers, Robert (Bobbie) Burgess, was on an unbeaten rugby team at Portora Royal School, Enniskillen, and later played rugby for the Dublin University team at Trinity College, Dublin.[38] He was killed in France, aged 24, on 10 December 1915 and, like many other young lawyers, his sporting and career potential ended prematurely.

In the wider context, the barristers' war memorial at the Four Courts, Dublin, should not be categorised as an Anglo-centric imperialist monument. In the era when the memorial was conceived, during the Anglo-Irish War, the Bar of Ireland on 26 March 1921, asserted its political and professional independence by passing a motion objecting to Crown forces infringing privilege by seizing counsels' briefs at the office of Michael Noyk, defence solicitor for IRA prisoners.[39]

The sentiments of Tom Kettle, who diced with death to protect civilisation against barbarism, were echoed nearly a century later by President Bush's exhortations against terrorism during the first war of the new millennium. Lord Kitchener's recruiting poster inscribed 'Your country needs you', was mirrored in reverse by pictures of Bin Laden, 'Wanted dead or alive'. The

38. Correspondence to author from Dr Michael Solomons, whose late father, Dr Bethel Solomons, played rugby with Robert (Bobbie) Burgess, as described in his autobiography, *One doctor and his time* (London, 1956), pp. 96, 172. See also Ray Rivlin, *Shalom Ireland: a social history of Jews in modern Ireland* (Dublin, 2003), pp. 34, 145, 214, 224.

(On a personal note, the author's Catholic mother, Kitty Quinn, said that the Jewish gynaecologist Dr Bethel Solomons delivered him in the Protestant Rotunda hospital, on St Anthony's feast day during the Roman Catholic Eucharistic Congress. Those pluralist origins spurred the author's efforts at Great War remembrance which entwines diverse traditions.)

39. *ILT&SJ*, lv (1921), 83. See Tim Carey, *Hanged for Ireland: the forgotten ten, executed 1920–21, a documentary history* (Dublin, 2001), chap. 2, quoting Michael Noyk (a republican solicitor of the Jewish tradition), 'Thomas Whelan,' *An tOglach* (Dublin, winter, 1967); Tim Carey in conversation with author indicated that many lawyers were reluctant to become involved in defending republican prisoners in 1920–21; TG4 Munla television documentary, 'An deichniúr dearmadta' (The forgotten ten), 2002; Richard Bennett, *The Black and Tans* (Staplehurst, Kent, 1959, 2001), p. 124 refers to Capt. Bagally (Baggally) as a barrister and prosecutor under Restoration of Order in Ireland Regulations.

second Gulf War in Iraq during 2003 was more controversial, but the coalition forces were inspired to a large extent by the conviction that they were fighting for freedom.

War propaganda and recruiting images, like conflict and militarism, are blunt instruments which result in the deaths of many people. To quote the eminent Irish historian, Joseph Lee, such people 'were innocent of the calculations of their masters'.[40]

Despite the human and institutional frailties, it is relevant to recall a French tribute to Kettle: 'He died, a hero in the uniform of a British officer, because he knew that the faults of a period or of a man should not prevail against the cause of right or liberty.'[41]

Positive aspects of the lives and achievements of lawyers killed in the war are outlined in this book and especially in the biographical details in appendix 1. The tragic enormity of death as a dominant theme was moderated by the participants' heroism inspired by their sense of history and honour. A verse of Patrick Shaw-Stewart is apt:[42]

> Achilles came to Troyland
> And I to Chersonese:
> He turned from wrath to battle,
> And I from three days' peace.
> Was it so hard, Achilles,
> So very hard to die?
> I will go back this morning,
> From Imbros over the sea;
> Stand in the trench, Achilles,
> Flame-capped, and shout for me.

40. Joe Lee, NUI Cork, 'A modest proposal for commemorating the dead', *Sunday Tribune*, 11 November 2001.
41. Tom Kettle, *The day's burden and other essays with memoir by his wife, Mary Sheehy Kettle* (Dublin, 1968), p. 37.
42. Quoted in Holt, *Battlefield guide to Gallipoli*, p. 244 and Ronald Knox, *Patrick Shaw-Stewart* (London, 1920), p. 159. Shaw-Stewart served in the Hood Bn., Royal Naval Division. Emulating his colleague Rupert Brooke, he was inspired by Grecian classical heroes. Shaw-Stewart, like Ledwidge, survived Gallipoli but both lives of great literary potential were lost on the Western Front in 1917. Patrick Shaw-Stewart is remembered on the roll of honour at Inner Temple where he was a student but not a barrister.

CHAPTER TWO

Education, training and enlistment

> Then lift the flag of the Last Crusade!
> And fill the ranks of the Last Brigade!
> March on to the fields where the world's re-made,
> And the Ancient Dreams come true!
>
> T.M. Kettle, 'A song of the Irish armies'

TOM KETTLE'S VERSE (from *Poems and parodies*, 1916) illustrates his idealistic conviction in exhorting his contemporaries to enlist in the British army and defend Belgium against German aggression which violated the rule of law and international treaties. In 1914, a recruiting poster referred to the London Treaty of 1839 as 'Britain's bond to protect Belgian's independence and neutrality against Prussia's perfidy'. There were varied motives for individual enlistment. Kettle, an Irish nationalist of the parliamentary tradition, was a trained barrister, convinced Christian, prolific author and university professor. He believed that Irish people should 'dice with death' and support the Allied armies, mainly British and French, to protect Europe and 'civilisation against barbarians' and to uphold the rule of law.[1] The word 'crusade' seems politically incorrect, currently in an Islamic context and retrospectively in the historical background of the Allied campaign in Gallipoli against the Turks during 1915. Kettle's inclusion of 'crusade' in his recruitment song was a conscious call to war in defence of Christian values. 'He was using the only means available to Irishmen at the time to resist German aggression against the ancient Christian civilization of Europe.'[2]

Just before the Great War started, there was an idealistic initiative to assert the reign of law among nations. The Scots-American benefactor Andrew Carnegie endowed the Palace of Peace in The Hague. When it was

---

1. Thomas M. Kettle, *The day's burden* (Dublin, 1968), especially essays at pp. 135–61: 'Why Ireland fought', 'The long endurance', 'Under the heel of the Hun', and 'Treating Belgium decently'; A.P. (Tony) Quinn, 'But for a dream', a quest for Tom Kettle, in *The Cross* (Dublin, 1976); Denis Gwynn, 'Thomas M. Kettle', *Studies*, lv, no. 220, winter 1966, 384; Dr Joseph C. McKenna, Sligo, letter to author; J.B. Lyons, *The enigma of Tom Kettle*.
2. Beda Herbert, 'Tom Kettle, 1880–1916', *Capuchin Annual*, 1967, pp. 420–27.

opened in 1913 as a centre to preserve peace and extend international law, a senior German official wrote to Carnegie hoping that the Peace Palace initiatives would save lives.[3] It was ironic that the Peace Palace was completed at the time when war clouds were spreading in Europe. The Kaiser was reported as having shown his contempt for the rule of law by asserting to the American ambassador in Berlin that many lawyers were among the Allied leaders opposed to Germany, including Lloyd George, Asquith and Poincaré, the French president.[4]

A peace conference was planned at The Hague for 1915 but by then Europe was gripped in terrible conflict in which the Allies, principally the United Kingdom of Great Britain and Ireland, France and Russia, joined in April 1917 by the United States of America, opposed the Central Powers: the German and Austro-Hungarian empires supported by Turkey (as part of the crumbling Ottoman Empire), and later by Bulgaria.[5]

My aim is to focus on the personal stories of the twenty-five listed Irish barristers who died in the war and to examine the circumstances and reasons why they volunteered to serve in the armed forces of the then United Kingdom, which at the time included the whole island of Ireland. Except in that context, it is not the purpose of this book to deal extensively with the wider aspects of the Great War, the First World War. It is necessary, however, to explain the context and trace the background, including the influence of education, legal training and politics on their motivations for enlisting in Irish, Welsh, English and other regiments.

A distinguished author, Anthony Cronin, writing in 1976, sixty years after the Somme slaughter in which Tom Kettle was killed, summed up the diverse motivations for enlisting:

> What sent them to their deaths were the degraded vestiges of European romantic chivalry, the glorifications of honour and gallantry which were in everything they heard or read … There were those who went for the pay and there were those who went for bread; but the spirit of the Somme was the spirit of adventure.[6]

3. *ILT&SJ*, xlvii (1913), 247; and Phyllis Hamilton, official of the Permanent Court of Arbitration, the Hague, to author at seminar organised by Brendan Kilty, barrister, in Dublin, April 2001; Simon Goodenough, *The greatest good fortune: Andrew Carnegie's gift for to-day* (Edinburgh, 1985), p. 248; Andrew Carnegie, *Autobiography* (London, 1920).
4. *ILT&SJ*, li (1917), 308.
5. For general accounts of the war: John Keegan, *The First World War* (London, 1999); Martin Gilbert, *First World War* (London, 1994, 1995); Alan Axelrod, *The complete idiots' guide to World War 1* (Indianapolis, 2000).
6. Anthony Cronin, author and alumnus of King's Inns, 'Till the boys come home', *Irish Times*, 9 July 1976, quoted in Anthony Quinn, 'Flanders fields and Irish recollections', *Capuchin Annual*, final issue (Dublin, 1977), pp. 342–50; see also Henry Harris, *The Irish regiments in the First World War* (Cork, 1968).

Aspiring young barristers, such as Robert B. (Bobbie) Burgess and Martin Lillis, had middle-class family backgrounds. Starting on precarious legal careers, they may have been attracted by the status of regimental commissions and the financial inducements of officers' pay. Young professional people were also enticed to military service by other reasons such as chivalry, honour, gallantry and adventure. Those characteristics were often evident in militarism as expressed in the spirit of professional soldiers and officers, and also reflected in public opinion. Before and during the First World War and the Irish struggle for independence (the Troubles), militarism was a common rhetoric among the various strands of Irish political life, nationalist and unionist.[7] As David Andrews, SC, former Minister for Foreign Affairs, commented in the context of the current peace process in Northern Ireland:

> The Irish (nationalist) volunteers mimicked Carson's Ulster volunteers. Both Pearse and Carson were moved by that same militarism which had swept all Europe and which would bring blood sacrifice to the GPO and the Somme in 1916. Such symmetry runs through the last century.[8]

Militarism influenced the educational systems throughout Europe, especially Germany and Britain, and to a lesser extent in Ireland. Many Anglo-Irish families, both Protestant and Catholic, sent their sons to English public schools to confirm their social status, acquire the right accent and enhance career opportunities in the army where they could indulge interests such as field sports.[9] Military education was provided by schools such as Mottingham House, Kent, advertised in Ireland 'as a Catholic establishment in a very salubrious neighbourhood for the preparation of candidates for admission to the military academies at Woolwich and Sandhurst'.[10]

Discipline and training conducive to military service was instilled through British public schools, such as Cheltenham, Charterhouse and Stonyhurst; and by Irish rugby-playing colleges, such as Belvedere, Clongowes, Castleknock and, to some extent, Christian Brothers College, Cork (in the Roman Catholic tradition); St Andrew's and St Columba's, in

---

7. David Fitzpatrick, 'Militarism in Ireland, 1900–1922', in Thomas Bartlett and Keith Jeffery (eds), *A military history of Ireland* (Cambridge, 1996), p. 379.
8. David Andrews, SC, 'Andrews on Saturday', *Irish Times*, 4 August 2001. Both Edward Carson, KC, the unionist leader and also Patrick H. Pearse, leader of the Easter Rising, 1916, were barristers. Pearse was called to the Bar in 1901 and did not persevere with a legal career, but see below, p. 50, footnote 94.
9. E.M. Spiers, 'Army organisation and society', in Bartlett and Jeffery (eds), *A military history of Ireland*, p.342.
10. *Irish Catholic directory* (Dublin, 1896), p. 44 of advertisements.

Dublin, Campbell College, Belfast and Portora Royal School, Enniskillen (in the Protestant tradition). There were rifle clubs, shooting tests and competitions, and also from 1908 officer training corps at many intermediate, grammar, and secondary schools and university colleges. The OTCs were organised by the War Office following the Haldane committee's recommendations, as part of army reforms, to ensure that there would be sufficient young officers in a new Territorial Force, replacing the Yeomanry and Volunteer Force.[11] The concept of OTCs for training cadets fell on fertile ground in upper and middle class schools to provide a framework to facilitate army service. The ethos of militarism pervaded English public schools.

The above trends can be illustrated by reference to specific individuals among the twenty-five barristers who served and died in the war. For example, Frederick H. Lewin came from the Galway/Mayo border area near Tuam, where the Lewin family of the landlord class were noted for sporting activities and service in the army, especially the Connaught Rangers. From 1891 to 1895, F.H. Lewin attended Cheltenham College, Gloucestershire, England, where many pupils took the entrance examinations to the Royal Military Academy, Woolwich, and to Sandhurst.[12] There is no evidence of F.H. Lewin taking those entrance examinations. Nevertheless, the sporting and military ethos of his education at Cheltenham, where he played on the rugby team, combined with his family military tradition, presumably influenced Lewin to enlist in the 3rd Bn., Connaught Rangers, which as part of the regular British army in Ireland had depots in Galway and Boyle. William Magee Crozier, who later served with the Royal Inniskilling Fusiliers, attended boarding public school at Repton, Derby, from 1886 to 1892. As a founder member of the Irish branch of the Old Reptonian Society, he displayed loyalty to his alma mater's ethos and traditions, which included military service.[13] Others attended typical upper class English public schools, now called independent schools. Ernest Lawrence Julian imbued Victorian values as a scholar at Charterhouse, near London, where later the poet Robert Graves (of the Royal Welsh Fusiliers) learnt the potential of modern weapons in that school's OTC. At the turn of the twentieth century, James C.B. Proctor was educated in the ethos of Reading Public School, Berkshire.[14]

11. John Creaney, QC, Belfast, to author; Col. Johnston, *Queen's University of Belfast OTC: history of the corps, 1908–1998* (updated version, Belfast,1999).
12. Tim Pearce, the Cheltonian Society, and Christine Leighton, college archivist, to author, and extracts from *The Cheltonian*, college annual, various years, and class records; Patrick Lewin, London, and Brigid Clesham, archivist, The Neale, Co. Mayo, to author, information about the Lewin family.
13. Russell Muir, Old Reptonian Society, Repton, Derby, to author; *The Reptonian*, school magazine, November 1916, and school register.
14. Thomas Hughes, barrister and MP, *Tom Brown's schooldays* (for insights into the

John Hammond Edgar was educated from 1895 to 1897 at Campbell College, Belfast, where military training was subsequently formalised. Early in 1909, Campbell College was the first school in Ireland to form a junior division of the OTC, and flag-raising ceremonies extolled imperial glory. Most pupils took the training course for certificate 'A', entitling entrance to the army at officer level. By the end of the Great War, 600 Campbellians had enlisted and 126 were killed.[15]

William Alfred Lipsett, following a family pattern, attended St Andrew's College, then in St Stephen's Green, Dublin. The school had Presbyterian connections but many students, including the Lipsetts of Ballyshannon, Co. Donegal, came from Church of Ireland backgrounds. After further education at Trinity College, Dublin and the King's Inns, Alfred left the North West circuit to practise in Calgary, Canada. Following the Lipsett family tradition, he joined the army and returned with the Alberta Regiment of the 1st Canadian Infantry Division to serve and die as a grenadier in the second battle of Ypres/Ieper in 1915.[16]

Georgina Fitzpatrick, historian of St Andrew's College, Dublin, analysed the reasons why a high proportion of its past pupils rallied to the colours. She explained how classical education conditioned youths to emulate Greek and Roman battle bravery, and how heroic English literature encouraged colonial attitudes among public schoolboys.[17] Greek mythology was evoked in the Gallipoli campaign by poets such as Francis Ledwidge and Patrick Shaw-Stewart, following the classical heroes' footsteps, and also by Rupert Brooke who died prematurely before reaching Turkey. The militaristic ethos of literature and wider culture in schools strongly influenced the young men described by Vera Brittain in her *Testament of youth* and exemplified in *Letters from a lost generation*:[18]

> The OTC provided the institutional mechanism for public school militarism. But a more complex web of cultural ideas and assumptions, some taken from the classics, some from popular fiction, some even

English public school system and specifically Rugby School) (London, 1857 and many subsequent editions).
15. Keith Haines, archivist, Campbell College, Belfast, to author.
16. Georgina Fitzpatrick to author with reference to St Andrew's College records; A.P. (Tony) Quinn, 'The Irish in Flanders', talk on *Sunday Miscellany* (producer, Martha McCarron), RTE Radio 1, Remembrance Sunday, November 2001; Christie, *For king and empire*, 1: *the Canadians at Ypres, 1915* (Ottawa, 1999).
17. Georgina Fitzpatrick, *St Andrew's College, 1894–1994: Ardens sed virens* (Dublin, 1994), p. 55.
18. Alan Bishop and Mark Bostridge (eds), *Letters from a lost generation* (London, 1999), p. 4; Vera Brittain, *Testament of youth: an autobiographical study of the years 1900–1925* (London, 1933 and 1979).

developed through competitive sports on the playing fields, was instilled by schoolmasters in their pupils, and contributed to the generation of 1914's overwhelming willingness to march off in search of glory.

In Ireland, St Andrew's College, like many other schools, facilitated army recruitment by preparing students for civil and military service examinations, in a era when there was a strong possibility of war. Almost 700 past pupils from St Andrew's enlisted for military service, and the death rate among them was 13 per cent. Schools reinforced the virtues of loyalty, honour and glory through competitive sport, especially rugby. William Lipsett played on the rugby team at St Andrew's College. Many of its *alumni* became members of Wanderers club which at the time could boast of two Victoria Cross (VC) winners among its international rugby players. Clubs such as Wanderers provided recruits in 1914 for the 'Pals' D Company (the football company) of the 7th Bn., Royal Dublin Fusiliers, following the call by its commander, Lt.-Col. Geoffrey Downing, and a circular from F.H. (Chicken) Browning, president of the Irish Rugby Football Union.[19] Glory on the sporting field was echoed and emulated on the battlefield. Despite some differences, recruitment through the Irish rugby network followed trends in other parts of the United Kingdom where Pals battalions were expressions of Edwardian civic pride.[20] Lawyers and other professionals supported such initiatives.

Two barristers, Poole H. Hickman and Ernest L. Julian, were killed in August 1915 while serving with the Dublin Pals, part of the 10th (Irish) Division in Gallipoli in 1915. F.H. Browning, who had been prominent in recruiting the Dublin Pals, died from wounds received at Haddington Road, Dublin, when returning from a route march with the Volunteer Training Corps on Easter Monday, 1916.

Before the war, rugby football also had an influential role during the formative years of Robert (Bobbie) Burgess and George B.J. Smyth, at Portora Royal School, Enniskillen, Co. Fermanagh.[21] Bobbie Burgess, who

19. Henry Hanna, *The pals at Suvla Bay, being the record of the 'D' Company of the 7th Royal Dublin Fusiliers*, with a foreword by Lieut-Gen. Sir Bryan Mahon (Dublin, 1917), pp. 13–15 (reprinted, Naval and Military Press, Uckfield, East Sussex, 2002). Cooper, *The Tenth (Irish) Division in Gallipoli*, pp. 25–26 generally, and specifically Francis Ledwidge's poem 'The Irish in Gallipoli.'
20. Dr Gerald Morgan, TCD, to author, information on the Dublin Pals; E.D.H. Sewell, *The rugby international's roll of honour* (London and Edinburgh, 1919), pp. 1–2, and 118–19; Gavin Mortimer, *Fields of glory, the extraordinary lives of 16 warrior sportsmen* (London, 2001), copy courtesy of Aengus Fanning, editor, *Sunday Independent*, illustrates the parallels between sporting and military achievements.
21. R.L. Bennett, headmaster, Portora Royal School, Enniskillen, Co. Fermanagh, to author; and author's visit to the school through the courtesy of Lt.-Col. (retd.)

played rugby on the unbeaten Portora team, 1908/09, is remembered with pride in photographs and plaques at his alma mater. A young man of splendid physique, he also learned shooting skills and was regarded as a 'good shot'. He was one of 130 international rugby players, including ten Irishmen, who died in the Great War.[22] Bobbie Burgess of the Royal Engineers was killed aged 24 when a shell hit him while he was cycling at Armentiers, France in December 1915. He was an example of Ireland's lost generation, which had great but unrealised potential to contribute much to public life.

It would be superficial and misleading to generalise about Protestant schools and colleges, and their sporting connections, as furnishing the only source of officer material for the army. Leading Roman Catholic schools catering for upward mobile business and professional classes emulated, to varying degrees, the sporting and imperial ethos of elite English schools and Irish Protestant educational institutions. The Jesuit college at Clongowes Wood, Co. Kildare, was favourable to Irish participation in the Allied war effort. As Senia Paseta points out in her analysis of the Irish Catholic elite, pro-Allied attitudes

> should not be read to signify an anti-Irish political stand. Nationalist Ireland's enthusiasm for the war effort by far surpassed the level of support for the Rising in 1916, if the number of recruits for the two causes is any measure. As in the case of games, the college merely reflected the social ambition and political conviction of its students.[23]

Prominent Clongowes alumni, mainly of the parliamentary nationalist Catholic tradition, played an active role in the Irish contribution to the Allied cause. Tom Kettle, whose father Andrew was a major supporter of Charles Stewart Parnell, transferred from O'Connell's Christian Brothers School, Dublin, to Clongowes.[24] There he played rugby, soccer and cricket and won many academic awards including a gold medal for English. Tom Kettle's study of German and French developed his European outlook, later expressed in his advice 'that Ireland to become deeply Irish must become

Mark R.H. Scott, Portora estate manager and trustee of the Inniskillings Museum, Enniskillen.

22. Gwen Prescott, Cardiff, to author.
23. Senia Paseta, *Before the revolution: nationalism, social change and Ireland's Catholic elite* (Cork, 1999), p. 42.
24. Lyons, *The enigma of Tom Kettle*, pp. 21–28; Andrew J. Kettle and L.J. Kettle (eds), *Material for victory* (Dublin, 1958); Conor Cruise O'Brien (son of Kathleen Sheehy), *Memoir: my life and themes* (Dublin, 1999), pp. 8, 12, 14, 19, 32, 62, 82, 83, on Tom Kettle (husband of Mary Sheehy, Kathleen's sister) and generally on Sheehy family, their politics and complex loyalties; the Sheehys were featured in the writings of James Joyce, *Ulysses* and *Dubliners*.

European'.[25] At a school debate on the topic of war versus arbitration, he spoke in his strong north County Dublin accent in favour of war and proclaimed the virtues of death on the battlefield.[26] Tom Kettle evolved from a radical nationalist to become a reasoned and articulate democrat. After Tom Kettle was fatally wounded by a Prussian Guards' bullet at Ginchy, Somme, on 9 September 1916, leading his beloved 9th Bn., Dublins, his old school hoped that 'his life would be an inspiration to present generations of Clongownians'.[27] Subsequent aspects of Kettle's notable career are given later in this chapter when the influence of university education is considered, and in the biographical outlines in appendix 1.

Another barrister and pastman of Clongowes, who served and died in the Great War, was Hubert (Hugh) Michael O'Connor. His father, Dr Charles Joseph O'Connor, was medical adviser to Clongowes, where Hugh was on the rugby and cricket teams. 'Well behaved and always good at games and lessons', he imbued the school ethos that the 'highest duty of a gentleman was in every circumstance of life to play the game'.[28] H.M. O'Connor developed leadership qualities which were subsequently expressed as a member of the Leinster Bar and in political activity as an independent nationalist candidate for East Limerick in 1910.[29] His military service as captain in the King's Shropshire Light Infantry and winner of the Military Cross (MC), ended in his premature demise, aged 30, at Langemarck, from wounds during the third battle of Ypres in 1917.

The close connections of the Redmond family with Clongowes was illustrated by a picture taken at the college centenary in 1914, showing three distinguished alumni, whose physical appearances were remarkably similar: William (Willie) Hoey Kearney Redmond, his older brother John Edward Redmond, leader of the Irish Parliamentary Party, and John's son, William Archer Redmond.[30] All three patriotic 'look alikes' qualified as barristers and were elected as nationalist MPs for Westminster. Each in his own way contributed to the Allied war effort: the two Williams as officers, and John as an influential advocate of Irish enlistment in the British army.

25. Thomas M. Kettle, memoir by Mary (Sheehy) Kettle, in *The day's burden*, p. 17, quoted by Ulick O'Connor at the Inchicore Ledwidge Society commemoration, National War Memorial Gardens, Islandbridge, Dublin, 29 July 2001.
26. *The Clongownian* (school annual), *1918*, pp. 148–50, obituary of Tom Kettle, including a memoir from his school-fellow and barrister, and later professor of law at UCD, Arthur E. Clery; extracts from *The Clongownian*, courtesy of Fr John Looby, SJ, archivist, Clongowes Wood College.
27. *The Clongownian*, *1917*, pp. 24–25; *1918*, p. 150.
28. *The Clongownian*, *1918*, p. 141; letter from Fr Nicholas J. Tomkin, SJ, headmaster, Clongowes Wood College: TNA/PRO, WO 339/5485.
29. *The Clongownian*, *1918*, p. 199.
30. Ibid., p. 141: see plate 1.

From 1873 to 1876, Willie Redmond attended Clongowes, where 'he was a light-hearted, good-natured, popular boy, not specially distinguished intellectually, being somewhat overshadowed by his more brilliant brother (John)'.[31] The Redmond brothers often 'expressed their intense affection in later years for their *alma mater*, ... then the principal school for the Irish Catholic middle class; it did not have a nationalist reputation'.[32] Willie Redmond was 'very loyal to Clongowes and to his old masters (the Jesuits) ... a true lover of Ireland; he was also a model Catholic ... deserving the admiration of every man who is capable of appreciating sanctity in a Catholic, and valour in a soldier'.[33]

John Redmond, trusting the British promise of Home Rule, despite its postponement because of the war, called in 1914 at Woodenbridge, Co. Wicklow, for Irishmen to join the British army and to fight 'wherever the firing-line extends, in defence of right, of freedom and of religion in this war'.[34] Willie Redmond actively supported his brother's recruitment drive, which was aimed specifically at the nationalist volunteers, but he found it a moral effort to wear a British uniform at that time. As a young man, however, he had been commissioned in December 1879, as a 2nd lieutenant in the Wexford infantry militia and 3rd (Militia) battalion, Royal Irish Regiment. He followed the 'landed gentry' family tradition which regarded the militia as an indigenous Irish body, different from the main British army. He resigned from the militia to participate in the Land League agitation and later was active in anti-recruitment campaigns during the Boer War.

A nationalist motivated by a wider patriotism in an imperial context, Willie Redmond re-enlisted in his old regiment, the Royal Irish, during his mid-fifties saying: 'If not too old to fight, at least I will not sit comfortably in an armchair and read what other men are doing and suffering.'[35] An active man, he enjoyed shooting expeditions from Aughavannagh, Co. Wicklow, Parnell's former shooting lodge, later owned by John Redmond (now an An Oige youth hostel). On 22 February 1915, Willie Redmond was gazetted as temporary captain in the 6th (Service) Bn., Royal Irish, part of the 47th

31. Ibid., p. 145.
32. Paul Bew, *John Redmond* (Dublin, 1996), p. 7.
33. *The Clongownian, 1918*, p. 146.
34. Bew, *John Redmond*, p. 38.
35. William Redmond, *Trench pictures from France*, articles mainly contributed to the *Daily Chronicle* under a pseudonym (London, 1917), p. 17, quoted in 'A wreath for Willie Redmond', by Tony Quinn, radio talk, *Sunday Miscellany*, RTE Radio 1, 1994; see also Thomas P. Dooley, *Irishmen or English soldiers? The times and world of a southern Catholic Irish man (1876–1916) enlisting in the British army during the First World War* (Liverpool, 1995), pp. 143 and 157, for references to Willie Redmond's role in the recruitment drive led by his brother John; Denman, 'A voice from the lonely grave'.

'Irish Volunteer' Brigade, 16th (Irish) Division, which was based in Mallow, Co. Cork. During training in Fermoy, as senior Catholic officer he marched his men to mass. After his death at Messines/Mesen, Flanders, in June 1917, Major Willie Redmond was buried in the convent garden at Locre (Loker). Requiem mass at the church of St Francis Xavier, Upper Gardiner Street, Dublin indicated Jesuit solidarity and loyalty expressed through the Clongowes Union.[36]

The union of Clongowes pastmen was founded in 1897 and the first president was Chief Baron Palles. He had often discussed legal topics as an equal with a neighbour in Dundrum, Dublin, a young Clongownian, Ambrose Davoren.[37] A brilliant law student at University College, Dublin and at the King's Inns, Davoren was not called to the Bar as he preferred to fight in the battlefield rather than in the courts. Ambrose Davoren was killed aged 27 on 18 July 1917, near Poperinge, Flanders, while serving with the Royal Field Artillery. Maurice Healy, in his memoirs about the Munster Circuit, recalled Ambrose Davoren reading John Buchan's *A history of the war*, and wishing to translate into Greek the historical references to heroes and loyalty to king and country.[38] Another aspirant lawyer, Vincent Connell Byrne, a solicitor's apprentice educated at Clongowes and Belvedere, was killed in action as a 2nd lieutenant with the 1st Bn., Royal Irish Rifles near Ypres on 31 July 1917.

Ideals of heroic loyalty, expressed through competitive sport and peer pressure, combined with effective recruitment techniques, rather than any inherent militarism, may have influenced many past pupils of Clongowes and similar schools to enlist in the army. Niall Ferguson, an innovative Oxford historian, while acknowledging the influence of the public school ethos, challenged generalised assumptions about the motives for enlistment.[39] According to Ferguson, the diverse and complex motives included: successful recruitment techniques, pressure from women and peer groups, and also

36. Thomas J. Morrisey, SJ, *William J. Walsh, archbishop of Dublin, 1841–1921* (Dublin, 2000), p. 302; Terence Denman, *A lonely grave: the life and death of William Redmond* (Dublin, 1995), p. 128; Kevin Myers, 'An Irishman's diary', *Irish Times*, various dates and specifically 14 March 2001.

37. Eithne Clarke, Dundrum, Dublin to author; V.T.H. Delany, *Christopher Palles* (Dublin, 1960), p. 154; A.P. Quinn, 'A briefed encounter with Chief Baron Palles', *ILT (n.s.)*, xiii, no. 12 (1995), 294.

38. Maurice Healy, *The old Munster circuit* (London and Dublin, 1939), pp. 261–62; new edition with biographical introduction by Charles Lysaght (London, 2001), reviewed by E. Hall, *Law Society Gazette*, vol. 95, no. 6, July 2001, p. 27.

39. Niall Ferguson, *The pity of war* (London, 1998, Penguin edition, 1999), pp. 201–02, 205–07; David Fitzpatrick made a similar point in 'The logic of collective sacrifice: Ireland and the British army, 1914–18' in *Historical Journal*, xxxviii (1995), 1017–30.

economic factors. Belvedere College, Dublin, was another Jesuit educational institution catering for Catholic boys from the middle and upper middle classes, including two of the barristers who died in the war. Herbert (Bertie) Tierney attended Belvedere and also an English college which was advertised in Ireland: SS. Peter and Paul, Prior Park, run by the Christian Brothers at Bath.[40] Gerald Plunkett from a leading Catholic family, connected with the earls of Fingall, had a brilliant career at Belvedere. He achieved honours each year and maintained similar standards at New College, Oxford and the King's Inns. He later trained with the OTC at Trinity College, Dublin. Gerald Plunkett was killed in Gallipoli in high summer, June 1915, while serving with the Volunteer Reserve in the Royal Naval Division.[41]

Born the same year (1887) as Gerald Plunkett, Joseph Mary Plunkett was son of George Plunkett, a papal count and non-practising barrister with Clongowes connections. Gerald also attended Belvedere College. His half-nephew, Joseph Plunkett, transferred to Stonyhurst, a Jesuit establishment in Lancashire catering for the 'top of the social heap'.[42] At Stonyhurst, Joseph Mary Plunkett joined the OTC and went on manoeuvres to Salisbury Plain.[43] Ironically, Joseph Plunkett utilised the skills and strategies learned from his British military training to try and establish an Irish republic during the Easter Rising, 1916. A member of the military council of the secret revolutionary IRB, and signatory of the proclamation, Joseph Mary Plunkett was executed by the British after the Rising.

Tom Kettle's brother-in-law, Eugene Sheehy, a pupil at Belvedere from 1892 to 1899, described the college atmosphere in his autobiography.[44] There is no clear indication from the description of Sheehy's schooldays of the reasons why he volunteered to serve as an officer in the Dublins. Sons of David Sheehy, Irish nationalist MP, Eugene and his brother Richard,

40. Henry Tierney, Dublin to author; *The Belvederian* (school annual), *1917*, extracts courtesy of G. Conran, current editor; *Irish Catholic directory* (Dublin, 1896), p. 44 of advertisements.

41. *The Belvederian*, *1916*, pp. 56–57; Dr C.J. McCormack, Portlaoise, to author, information on Plunkett family; G. Plunkett is on list of Belvederians killed in conflict during twentieth century, many during World War I, compiled by Oliver Murphy, curator of school museum, and launched in book form as *The cruel clouds of war*, at an inclusive remembrance ceremony in November 2003.

42. C.S. Andrews, *Dublin made me* (Dublin and Cork, 1979 and 2001), p. 10.

43. Moira Laffan, 'Count Plunkett and his times', paper read at Foxrock Local History Club, Co. Dublin, 14 October 1992, lecture publication no. 29, p. 12. Moira Laffan and Sr Meabh Uí Chléirigh, 'The story of Muckross Park', in *Dominican College Muckross Park, a centenary of memories, 1900–2000* (Dublin, 2000), pp. 6–8.

44. Eugene Sheehy, *May it please the court* (Dublin,1951), and especially chapter 1: 'The happiest days of my life – perhaps' (pp. 1–11) and chapters 9–11 (pp. 86–122), about army service.

followed John Redmond's call to enlist. In his memoirs, Eugene Sheehy narrated the mischievous reaction of himself and his fellow officer and barrister, Maurice Healy, during their 'futile training for a futile war'. They encountered the products of the playing fields of Harrow and Eton and 'the lofty disdain that emanates from the English public school'. Sheehy as an officer in the Royal Dublin Fusiliers commanded the troops in front of Belvedere College, during the Easter Rising, 1916, but the rebellion caused him great heartbreak. Capt. Eugene Sheehy survived active service on the Western Front, but his nationalist background and divided loyalties in the extended Sheehy family contributed to his eventual disillusion with the Allied war effort. He resumed his legal career, which became controversial due to the trials of republicans during the early years of the Irish Free State. Sheehy later served as a circuit court judge.

Fr Willie Doyle, SJ, military chaplain to the Royal Irish and Dublin Fusiliers, was an influential icon for Irish Catholics.[45] From Dalkey, Co. Dublin, his father was a senior official in the High Court. Fr Doyle's final sermon to about 3,000 Irishmen serving in the British forces diplomatically and aptly referred to fighting for Ireland indirectly. The image was heroic and fatalistic, and his death near Frezenberg, Flanders in August 1917 'as a martyr of charity' had an impact in Ireland among diverse traditions.[46] Willie Doyle's connections as student and teacher ensured his special place in Jesuit colleges, including Clongowes and Belvedere.

At Belvedere College from 1900 to 1909, Arthur Cox had a brilliant academic career before attending UCD and becoming a distinguished and influential solicitor. According to Cox's biographer, Eugene McCague,[47] the college rector and co-operative enthusiast, Fr Tom Finlay, SJ,

> ensured that Belvedere was no mere stagnant Catholic version of an English Protestant public school. Indeed, it was not a 'public school' in that sense at all. Fr Finlay's philosophy of voluntarism and co-operation, together with his antipathy to the State – whether England or an independent Irish State – as the sole provider of moral values and economic support, ingrained in Belvedere's students a questioning outlook.

45. Alfred O'Rahilly, *Father William Doyle, S.J.* (London, 1920), especially chapters 9 and 10, pp. 214–335; 'Belvederians killed in wars and conflict of 20th century', exhibition in Dublin, 2003, featured Fr W. Doyle.
46. A.P. (Tony) Quinn, 'The chaplain in the war trenches, in memoriam Fr Willie Doyle', in *Dun Laoghaire Journal*, no. 4. (1995), pp. 56–58, and further article on Fr Willie Doyle, in that journal no. 12 (2003); see also *Court Service News*, vol. 6. no. 2, July 2003, A.P. Quinn, 'WWI memorial in Four Courts', and N. MacFhionnghaile, (McGinley), *Donegal, Ireland and the First World War* (Letterkenny, 1987), pp. 75–87.
47. Eugene McCague, solicitor, *Arthur Cox 1891–1965* (Dublin, 1994), p. 16.

Although the above summary of Belvederian philosophy was linked to an economic context, it has wider application to assertions of an independent outlook in politics and war. Arthur Cox, unlike his brother and many other Belvederians and lawyers, did not join in the war effort but spent his time as an apprentice and junior solicitor.

The impact of the Great War on Belvedere College, described in school annuals at the time, was later analysed by Fr F.X. Martin in anniversary portraits of the college:[48]

> Belvedere reflected the prevailing opinion among the leading Catholic colleges in supporting the Allied war effort, rather than extreme nationalism. National volunteers, following the Redmondite enlistment policy, drilled in Belvedere Park. School diaries of Belvedere pupils indicated enthusiasm for John Redmond and the British Prime Minister, Asquith, although the Easter Rising was also mentioned. Over a hundred past pupils served, mainly as officers, in diverse branches of the British forces. Six military chaplains, including the 'saintly' Fr Willie Doyle, had taught at Belvedere. Four of its past pupils, including Gerald Plunkett were killed in Gallipoli in 1915. (Belvederians, including members of the Plunkett family, were on opposing sides in 1916 and during the subsequent conflicts.)

Kevin Barry, executed in 1920 by the British after court martial following an IRA ambush in Dublin, had been a pupil at Belvedere but that does not demonstrate the existence of significant revolutionary attitudes within the college. Changing loyalties and political trends, however, gradually influenced colleges such as Belvedere which adapted to the political realities of nationalist Ireland. Dr Garret FitzGerald, former taoiseach, speaking on 15 November 2003 at the remembrance ceremonies to Belvederians (including Herbert Tierney and Gerald Plunkett) killed in twentieth-century military conflicts, recalled his own time at Belvedere College. Its ethos during the 1940s reflected the prevailing attitude of amnesia about the Irish role in World War One, and during World War Two ambivalence towards the Allies and also some pro-German attitudes.

48. F.X. Martin, 'Did Belvedere change, 1916–1922', in J. Bowman and R. O'Donoghue, (eds.), *Portraits, Belvedere College, 1832–1982* (Dublin, 1982), pp. 49–62; *The Belvederian, 1915–22*; Kevin Barry's memory evoked controversy because of the State funeral on 14 October 2001, before the re-burial of remains of Barry and other republicans; see Damien Kiberd, 'Belvedere boy who did not like royalty', *Sunday Business Post*, 30 September 2001, p. 15 of Agenda; Paddy Murray, 'Why venerating our own killers is wrong', *Sunday Tribune*, 23 September 2001; Kevin Myers, 'An Irishman's diary', *Irish Times*, 3 October 2001; T. Carey, *Hanged for Ireland* (Dublin, 2001), especially chap. 1.

Nationalists of more radical and separatist views, such as Patrick Pearse, criticised what they regarded as Anglo-Irish upper class schools where foreign games were played. To counteract such influences, leaders of the Easter Rising supported native games and Pearse, educated by the Christian Brothers, had been chairman of the Leinster Colleges branch of the Gaelic Athletic Association.[49] Pearse also founded Scoil Eanna/St Enda's, to educate youths according to the nationalist ethos. That idealistic initiative could be criticised for propagating militarism based on Irish mythology including Cuchulainn and the Fianna, and for providing recruits for the armed rebellion.[50] (The Irish Army subsequently used the OTC system through the Regiment of Pearse and the Pearse Battalion to cater for college students.)

Another Catholic college, St Vincent's, Castleknock, Co. Dublin was criticised, perhaps unfairly, by one of its past pupils, D.P. Moran, editor of the influential nationalist journal, *Leader*. Moran called the Vincentian College 'Caw-stleknock' because of its perceived West British ethos of 'ping pong and cricket', reflected in Queen Victoria's visit in 1900 to the college.[51] Rugby and soccer were played in the college. It had many links with the nationalist parliamentary tradition. The college supported the war effort and provided refuge for Belgian refugees. Rosaries, Holy Communion and masses were offered for past pupils, serving or dying in the conflict.[52] About 256 past pupils of Castleknock volunteered to serve in the British forces and many were mentioned in dispatches and achieved distinction. *Castleknock College Chronicle, 1918*, listed under 'In Memoriam', Lt. Con (Cornelius) A. MacCarthy (a barrister from Bandon, Co. Cork, serving with the Dublins), as having been 'torpedoed in the Mediterranean'. In accordance with general trends after 1916, Castleknock College became more critical of the war effort and moved in a nationalist direction as Irish language articles appeared in its *Chronicle*.

49. Alan Bairner, 'Ireland, sport and empire', in Jeffery (ed.), *An Irish empire? Aspects of Ireland and the British Empire*, p. 67.
50. See generally, Ruth Dudley Edwards, *Patrick Pearse: the triumph of failure* (London, 1977, Dublin, 1990) and Ulick O'Connor, book review, 'Pearse's high place in the story of our country', *Sunday Independent*, 22 May 1977; 'Pearse-fanatic heart', 'Real lives', Steve Carson, RTE television, 9 April 2001; Elaine Sisson, *Pearse's patriots: St Enda's and the cult of boyhood* (Dublin, 2004).
51. Paseta, *Before the revolution*, pp. 28–29, 37–39; the late Fr Dr Patrick O'Donoghue, CM, archivist, Castleknock, and Vincent Browne, past pupil, information to author; Brian Maye, 'An Irishman's diary', *Irish Times*, 7 January 2002, on D.P. Moran and *The Leader*.
52. James H. Murphy (ed.) and Michael M. Collins (associate ed.), *Nos autem: Castleknock College and its contribution* (Dublin, 1996), pp. 107–08; *The Castleknock College chronicle, 1914–18*, also contained information on past pupils serving, some as chaplains, in the British army and navy; copies of history and chronicles courtesy of the late Dr Patrick O'Donoghue, CM.

Down the social scale from the elite schools run by the Jesuits and Vincentians, were Christian Brothers' schools catering mainly for the lower middle class.[53] The Brothers' ethos was more favourable to Irish nationalism and their schools supplied leaders for the Irish revolution, but it would be simplistic to generalise.[54] Christian Brothers College, Cork (CBC), rated higher up the social scale than the average Brothers' school and rugby was played there. According to the college centenary history:

> CBC catered for the sons of comfortable families and, as such, could hardly be expected to be a hot-bed of revolutionary ideas but peer pressure would have had a significant influence. However, the ethos of the Christian Brothers would have been a moderating influence. School debates on war and conscription included references to 'misrule in Ireland' but a vital thrust was to 'support Britain in her hour of peril'. Past pupils who returned to the school wearing khaki boosted the recruitment drive.[55]

During the First World War, over 300 CBC past pupils served in the Allied forces including: Lt. Martin Michael Lillis, of the 1st/2nd Bns., Royal Irish Regiment. Exceptionally for the listed barristers, he was attached to the Royal Flying Corps. He met his death in action on 11 April 1917, aged 26, while piloting a Morane Parasol, during air combat with German ace flyers, near the Somme, France.[56] Three Stantons, sons of a Cork solicitor, were educated at CBC and two were killed: Capt. George Stanton, RAMC, and a young solicitor, Lt. Robert Stanton, 6th Dublins, who fell near Suvla Bay, Gallipoli, aged 29, in August 1915.[57]

Education conducive to military service was provided by more overt methods at university level, attended by aspirant lawyers, including most of the Irish barristers who died in the war. Dublin University Officers Training

53. Paseta, *Before the revolution*, pp. 37–42.
54. C.S. Andrews, *Dublin made me* (Cork and Dublin, 1979), p. 74; also A.P. Quinn's own recollections of secondary education at the all-Irish Christian Brothers' secondary school, Coláiste Mhuire, Dublin.
55. M.J.R. Hogan, 'The Great War', in *Christians: a celebration of one hundred years of CBC, Cork* (Cork, 1988), pp. 168–79. Included in that book is material from the school annual, *The Collegian*, and specifically from the 1917 issue, a list of 295 past pupils serving in the British army. Extracts courtesy of Jerome O'Donovan, CBC Past Pupils Union, Cork.
56. Hal Giblin, Hightown, nr. Liverpool, and Nigel Wood, Nottingham, members of Western Front Association, to author.
57. Tom Burke, 'The story of Lt. Robert Stanton, 6th Battalion, Royal Dublin Fusiliers', in *The Blue Cap*, journal of the Royal Dublin Fusiliers Association, vol. 4 (March 1997), pp. 1–2.

Corps, DU OTC, played an important role in instruction and recruitment for the army.[58] The DU OTC was formed in 1910 in the receptive atmosphere at Trinity College.[59] A rifle club already existed, and under the Hague Convention members had certain rights to repel invasion. Preliminary military instruction was provided for students while graduates availed of commissions through the War Office. The favourable ethos of Trinity College ensured establishment support for the OTC from the provost. Mr Justice Ross and Brig.-Gen. Edward May of the General Staff at the Irish Command of the British Army were also supportive.

The DU OTC from Trinity College participated with armed OTC units from Queen's University, Belfast and from Campbell College, Belfast, in a battalion under the earl of Arran, KP, commandant of the Irish OTCs. The occasion was a parade in the Phoenix Park, Dublin on 11 July 1911 during the visit to Ireland of King George V and Queen Mary. There were royal salutes and cheers for the king who was dressed in field marshal's uniform. Such events inevitably encouraged militarism and reinforced loyalism.

The question of loyalties at Trinity College is complex, but a brief discussion is relevant to enlistment in the army because many lawyers were educated there. Despite its colonial origins in the late sixteenth century during the reign of Elizabeth I, Trinity evolved into an Irish institution, termed formally as the University of Dublin. It had a distinctive and mainly Protestant ethos. Although the general outlook was favourable to the British imperial connection, some Trinity graduates became prominent Irish patriots. For example, Thomas Davis, barrister and leader of the Young Irelanders in the mid-nineteenth century, argued for a pluralist, inclusive Irish nation.[60] During the period before the First World War, according to Senia Paseta's analysis, 'Trinity College was widely perceived as one last remaining Anglo-Irish bastion, [and] thus became an obvious target for cultural nationalists'.[61] Despite arguments about the college's predominant Protestant Anglican ethos and the agitation for a Catholic university, young men from leading Catholic nationalist families, including the Dillons and

58. Roger Willoughby, *A military history of the University of Dublin and its Officers Training Corps, 1910–1922* (Limerick, 1989); Dr Gerald Morgan, TCD, to author.
59. J.V. Luce, *Trinity College, Dublin, the first 400 hundred years* (Dublin, 1992), pp. 128–32, and 134.
60. Anthony P. Quinn, 'Harmony between diverse traditions may be found in the ideals of Davis', *Sunday Tribune*, 24 September 1995, reproduced in a booklet with foreword by Mary Robinson, President of Ireland, for Thomas Davis National Commemoration, Mallow, Co. Cork, September 1995; John Neylon Molony, *A soul came into Ireland: Thomas Davis, 1814–1845, a biography* (Dublin, 1985); D. Budd and R. Hinds (eds), *The Hist and Edmund Burke's club*, pp. 63–68, on Thomas Davis and Young Ireland.
61. Paseta, *Before the revolution*, p. 19.

Redmonds, studied at Trinity College. A relevant context, which Roy Foster refers to in his book, *Irish story*, is the concept of a sub-culture described as Trinity nationalism. That ethos was reflected in attitudes which were neither unionist nor nationalist but were based on culture rather than territorial claims, a concept which is now fashionable.[62] As an indicator of student opinion, varying attitudes were adopted at the 'Hist.' student debates, which approved a motion in favour of compulsory military service in 1914 but rejected a motion on conscription in 1915.

DU OTC at Trinity College supplied 350 junior officers to the new armies in the early part of the war between August 1914 and March 1915. More than 3,000 people, including lecturers, graduates and undergraduates, joined the armed forces during the war and there were many casualties and military distinctions.[63] As Denman points out: 'The OTC of Trinity College, Dublin was bound to be a major source of young officers; military expediency, not political prejudice dictated this.'[64] On the other hand, according to J.V. Luce's history of Trinity College:[65]

> The Trinity response was in line with Redmond's wholehearted support for the British war effort, though most Trinity men fought as unionists, not home rulers. But constitutional nationalists and unionists alike were united in their condemnation of the 1916 insurrection, and this should be remembered in any consideration of Trinity's involvement (against the rebels) in the fateful events of Easter week.

Members of DU OTC protected Trinity College against attack (during the 1916 Rising). Those members were honoured by the provost on behalf of Dublin's citizens for 'their gallant conduct during the rebellion' as 'defenders of Trinity College', although it is not clear whether the rebels had intended to capture the college.[66] William Wylie, who served in DU OTC against the rebellion, was prosecuting counsel in the courts martial of the rebel leaders. He tried to improve the legal procedures by calling witnesses and opposing the speed and secrecy of the trials. He advised clemency for some rebel leaders, including William T. Cosgrave and Eamon de Valera, and later served the Irish Free State as a High Court judge.[67]

62. Foster, *The Irish story*, pp. 48–50.
63. Luce, *Trinity College, Dublin*, p. 129.
64. Terence Denman, *Ireland's unknown soldiers*, p. 46.
65. Luce, *Trinity College, Dublin*, p. 130.
66. *(Sinn Féin) rebellion handbook, 1916*, pp. 260–61; R. Willoughby, *A military history of the University of Dublin*, pp. 15–19; Michael Foy and Brian Barton, *The Easter Rising* (Stroud, Glos., 1999), pp. 26–27 on the controversial question whether the rebels planned to seize Trinity College.
67. Stephen Collins, 'Ireland's prodigal sons', on Protestants in Ireland, *Sunday*

Trinity students, even if they were not formally in the OTC, helped to defend the college during the Easter Rising which had a traumatic impact. A medical student, Michael Taaffe, son of a Catholic court official who was a barrister in the Parliamentary Party tradition, in his memoirs,[68] recalled:

> On my kind and me the Rebellion had immediate effects. It determined the future … In bringing war closer to our doorstep it had also brought the war in France closer and most of the men in my year, whether they were conscious of it or not, had made up their minds to join one of the Services as soon as they had got credit for the term.

T.C. Kingsmill Moore, later a distinguished judge of the Irish Supreme Court, participated as an OTC cadet in the defence of the college in 1916. According to Kingsmill Moore, auditor of the 'Hist', 1915–19, Trinity volunteers for the British army included 700 past and present members of that society and (in 1914) members represented all grades of political opinion, but the extreme nationalists were few, the great majority being either unionist or Redmondite nationalists, and both of these classes regarded service in the armed forces as a manifest and compulsive duty.[69]

An *Irish Times* editorial in March 1918 outlined Trinity's contribution to the war effort:[70]

> No other university in Ireland and hardly any other in the UK has given such splendid proof of its devotion to the cause of freedom. TCD men fought in every corner of the world and in whatever part of far flung battle lines their fortune lies, they carry with them a deep love of their *alma mater*. (The impact of the war was illustrated by the following statistics: During 1914 to 1917, the number of matriculated students at Dublin University fell from 1,074 to 534).

According to university and King's Inns records, most of the listed twenty-five Irish barristers who died in the war had studied at Trinity

---

Tribune, 17 February, 2002; A.P. Quinn, reply, letters column of that newspaper, 3 March 2002; Delany, *Christopher Palles*, pp. 184–87, appendix II, judges and law officers in Ireland, 1921–60.

68. Michael Taaffe, *Those days are gone away* (London, 1959), p. 182.

69. Budd & Hinds, *The Hist*, p. 185.

70. Editorial, *Irish Times*, 23 March 1918, referring to an Arabian night on 11 September 1917, when many TCD graduates serving in the Allied forces, attended a dinner in Baghdad, and the menu included fellows soup and provost's pudding, with wines called MA's milk and porters' paradise. The guest of honour, Sir Stanley Maude, the only non-TCD man present, had instructed the DU OTC during training, Trinity College Library, Dublin, Samuels Collection, 5/70.

College and were influenced by its ethos. The majority were graduates, but some were undergraduates. A few, notably Tom Kettle, Willie Redmond and Herbert Tierney (and also co-incidentally Patrick Pearse), attended Trinity law lectures with the status of external students during the Bar course at King's Inns.[71] Over a half of the barristers, listed as killed in the war, had participated in the military training and camaraderie provided by DU OTC prior to being commissioned as officers.[72] The background to their commissioning as officers is outlined below.

William Magee Crozier: Aged 40 when he enlisted, he was over the age limit but a prominent unionist, Col. T.E. Hickman, recommended him because he had drilled with the Loyal Dublin Volunteers and was 'quite the right stamp and preferable to a boy from the OTC' where he had trained recruits.[73] A member of the Church of Ireland, William Magee Crozier was commissioned as a lieutenant in the 9th Bn., Royal Inniskilling Fusiliers, Tyrone volunteers, formed from the Ulster Volunteer Force, which became part of the 36th (Ulster) Division.[74] That points to the unionist outlook of Crozier. Although he was from Dublin, Capt. Crozier would have been regarded later as one of the sons of Ulster because he was posted missing on the first day of the Somme, 1 July 1916, when the Ulster Division suffered severe casualties. Another son of Ulster, but in the conventional sense of unionist allegiance and motivation for enlisting, was James C.B. Proctor, a Doctor of Laws, LLD, of Trinity College, and a solicitor who became a barrister. Although not a member of DU OTC, he trained with the South

71. Colum Kenny, *Tristram Kennedy and the revival of Irish legal training, 1835–1885* (Dublin, 1996), pp. 162–71 on arrangements between King's Inns and Dublin University for Bar students to attend lectures at Trinity College.

72. Dr Gerald Morgan, TCD, to author indicating that OTC membership was signified by an asterisk on College War Dead List, 1922. Other records also show OTC membership as included in biographical profiles in appendix 1 of this book.

73. Letter dated 13 October 1914 from T.E. Hickman, Finner Camp, Co. Donegal, to Adjutant General, 36th (Ulster) Division, TNA/PRO, WO 339/21334; Brig.-Gen. T.E. Hickman, MP, CB, DSO, had been Inspector General of the Ulster Volunteer Force (UVF), and a prominent unionist as president of the British League for the Defence of Ulster; Major J. Dunlop, Inniskillings museum, Enniskillen, Brian O'Brien, Co. Limerick and Tom Crozier, Colchester, to author, information about W.M. Crozier.

74. Cyril Falls, *The history of the 36th (Ulster) Division* (Belfast and London, 1922; London, 1996) outlines the origins in Sir Edward Carson's Ulster Volunteers of the battalions which, having joined the Irish regiments, formed the 36th (Ulster) Division. The Irish regiments, mainly but not exclusively, based in the North – the Royal Irish Rifles, Royal Irish Fusiliers and Inniskillings – provided battalions for the 36th (Ulster) Division and also the (10th) and (36th) Irish Divisions; Dr Timothy Bowman, 'The Ulster Volunteers 1913–1914: force or farce?', *History Ireland*, vol. 10, no. 1, spring 2002, pp. 43–47. See also generally Crozier, *A brass hat in no man's land*.

of Ireland Imperial Yeomanry (South Irish Horse) and became an expert marksman and organiser for the Ulster Volunteer Force (Derry Volunteers) which formed the 10th Bn., Inniskillings, 36th (Ulster) Division.

Robert Hornidge Cullinan, educated at the Abbey, Tipperary Grammar School, a member of the Munster circuit, and Joseph Bagnall Lee, from the Northern circuit, were commissioned into the Royal Munster Fusiliers. They both served and died with the 10th (Irish) Division in Gallipoli, during August 1915. Edmond Chomley Lambert Farran trained in the South of Ireland Imperial Yeomanry (South Irish Horse) before joining DU OTC. Lt.-Col. T.V.P. McCammond recommended Edmond Farran for a commission in the 3rd Reserve Bn., Royal Irish Rifles, in September, 1914, after earlier rejection at the start of the war because, although only 34 years old, he exceeded the existing age limit. Capt. Farran was reported missing and presumed dead on 16 June 1915 in Flanders. The Royal Irish Rifles, whose motto was 'Quis Separabit', was formally founded in 1881 but its origins date back to the Anglo–French conflict in the late eighteenth century. The regimental songs, 'Garryowen' and 'St Patrick's Day', symbolised its Irish connections.

Also commissioned into the Royal Irish Rifles, as part of the 36th (Ulster) Division, was Arthur Purefoy Irwin Samuels. Educated at Mr Strangway's School, St Stephen's Green, Dublin, he came from a Church of Ireland family closely connected with Trinity College where he was a distinguished student. In 1909, as treasurer of the 'Hist.', the college debating society, Arthur P.I. Samuels seconded a motion to grant £5 towards the cost of a monument in memory of a former auditor of that society, Theobald Wolfe Tone, barrister, leader of the United Irishmen in 1798 and an Irish republican icon.[75] The 'Hist.' motion was withdrawn after the memorial fund's treasurer absconded with the subscriptions but the incident illustrates an awareness of Irish nationalism.

Arthur P.I. Samuels's father, Arthur Warren Samuels, KC (later Mr Justice Samuels) was solicitor-general for Ireland and unionist MP for Dublin University. Arthur Warren Samuels opposed Home Rule but was a sincere Irishman who worked constructively for his country. Arthur P.I. Samuels was attached to the 2nd Bn., Yorkshire Light Infantry, during spring and early summer, 1914 and trained with DU OTC at Mourne Park, Mallow, Co. Cork. Recommended for a temporary commission in the 6th Bn., Connaught Rangers, he was appointed to the 11th Bn., Royal Irish Rifles. That battalion was formed from the South Antrim Rifles, part of the Ulster Volunteer Force, created by Sir Edward Carson, MP, KC, to uphold the union with Great Britain and oppose the nationalist aim of Home Rule

75. Budd & Hinds, *The Hist*, p. 121.

for Ireland. The motivation for Capt. Arthur P.I. Samuels to serve his country as an outstanding and popular officer in a battalion with unionist origins which became part of the 36th (Ulster) Division, presumably included his family background. His father, although sensitive to nationalist opinion, was a prominent southern unionist. Capt. Arthur Samuels's wife, Dorothy Gage Samuels, née Young, was daughter of George Young, JP, DL, of Randalstown, Co. Antrim, and Culdaff, Inishowen, Co. Donegal.

George Bostall (sometimes spelt Bestall) Jenkinson Smyth (whose American mother had married into a family of linen merchants in Banbridge, Co. Down), after training with DU OTC, was also commissioned into the Royal Irish Rifles, based in Belfast. Three of his cousins served and later died in the Great War and two cousins survived to die as British officers during the War of Independence. Family military connection presumably influenced his decision to volunteer. To illustrate the complex nature of service and loyalties, Capt. George B.J. Smyth served with the 6th Bn., Royal Irish Rifles, which formed part of the mainly nationalist 10th (Irish) Division in Gallipoli in 1915. Surviving that ill-fated campaign, he later served on the Western Front with the 7th Bn., Royal Irish Rifles, part of the 16th (Irish) Division, but absorbed into the Ulster Division. He was killed on 22 October 1918, a few weeks before the war ended.

Two influential Trinity men served and died with the Dublin Pals during the Gallipoli campaign in 1915: Capt. Poole Henry Hickman, and Lt. Ernest Lawrence Julian, Reid Professor of Criminal Law at Trinity College. Julian was elected to a commission by the D Company 'Pals', 7th Bn., Royal Dublin Fusiliers, 10th (Irish) Division. Family military connections may have influenced the enlistment of Lt. Ernest Lawrence Julian, who was a nephew of Lt. Gen. Sir Lawrence W. Parsons, KCB, CB, commander of the 16th (Irish) Division during the crucial period of recruitment and training in 1914–15. Capt. Poole Hickman, educated at the Abbey, Tipperary Grammar School and TCD, became an important figure in the recruitment drive, and was pictured leading his men in a Dublin parade before departure for active service in 1915. The example of those two prominent and popular barristers was an inspiration to their legal colleagues and other young professional and business men.

Some of the DU OTC men were commissioned into medical and engineering units and non-Irish regiments in accordance with wider general patterns. There were no distinct reasons for choosing English and Welsh regiments, which were popular with Trinity graduates generally. Among the motivations were family links, career prospects, regimental depots in Ireland, and the availability of commissions to men who trained with OTCs.

John Henry Frederick Leland, from Blackrock, Co. Dublin was commissioned as 2nd Lt., 5th (Flintshire) Bn. (Territorial), Royal Welch (Welsh)

Fusiliers, part of the 158th brigade of the 53rd (Welsh) Division, and served and died in Gallipoli, August 1915. The son of Sir William Moore, MD, FRCPI, the King's physician in Ireland, Arthur Robert Moore, served with distinction as lieutenant in the 1st/4th City of London Regiment, Royal Fusiliers. For bravery on 12/13 March 1915, King George V awarded him the Military Cross at Buckingham Palace, London, in May 1916, but a few months later he fell on the first day of the Somme.

The second MC winner among the twenty-five listed barristers, Hubert (Hugh) Michael O'Connor, after training with the DU OTC, opted for the King's Shropshire Light Infantry, which had a depot in Tipperary. Dr J. Mahaffy, provost of Trinity College, Dublin certified Hubert O'Connor to be of fine moral character and recommended him for the Hampshire Regiment.[76] Capt. O'Connor also trained at Sandhurst. He visited the Law Library, Four Courts, Dublin where his many friends congratulated him, shortly before his death in action on 17 August 1917.[77] Such visits home by war heroes including Michael O'Leary, VC, Connaught Rangers, from the Western Front, boosted the wider recruitment drive which was declining in vigour.

Gerald Plunkett graduated with honours from New College, Oxford before being called to the Irish Bar. On the outbreak of the war, he joined the DU OTC which was 'open, under the discretion of the university authorities and O.C. units, to gentlemen who, though not members of the university are desirous of gaining certificates of proficiency'.[78] Gerald Plunkett was a keen yachtsman like his brother Oliver who later had a distinguished career as a lawyer in the British colonial service. Gerald was commissioned on 20 October 1914 as a sub-lieutenant into the Royal Naval Volunteer Reserve, Collingwood Bn., Royal Naval Division, which was utilised to supplement the army in Gallipoli, where he was among the many casualties in 1915. Reflecting his Jesuit education, combined with high standards of honour and duty from the Oxford and Dublin university ethos, Gerald Plunkett arranged for the men in his platoon to hear mass and receive their last confession in the glare of the sun before facing mortal battle against the Turks.[79]

76. Letter dated 21 December 1914 from Dr J. Mahaffy, Provost, TCD, TNA/PRO, WO 339/5485; D. Holroyd, member Western Front Assoc., Liversedge, West Yorks., to author. Also on PRO papers are detailed reports of Hubert O'Connor's brave conduct before his death in action on 17 August 1917 during the third battle of Ypres. See plate 23.

77. *ILT&SJ*, li (1917), Hubert O'Connor's obituary, 25 August.

78. TNA/PRO, WO 32/9034, royal warrant founding OTC (1908).

79. Revd Eric F. Green, military chaplain, letter to Patrick J. Plunkett, father of Gerald Plunkett, June 1915, in *The Belvederian, 1916*, pp. 57–58.

Second Lt. James Rowan Shaw, son of James J. Shaw, KC, recorder of Belfast, served with the 75th Company, Imperial Yeomanry during the Boer War when he was awarded the Queen's South African Medal with three clasps. Returning home from Malaya, where he had practised law, Rowan Shaw later joined DU OTC and received his commission into the 9th Bn., Cheshire Regiment, which had a base in Derry. Family factors and military experience may have influenced his decision to volunteer as his only brother, Major William Maxwell Shaw, DSO, also served on the Western Front. Within about a year during 1916–17, both Shaw brothers, and their nephew, Thornley Woods, were killed in action.[80]

The barrister members of DU OTC, profiled above, were older than the typical OTC member, whose average age was nineteen according to a sample in a survey by Laura Dooney at Trinity College.[81] In other respects, the distinctive outlook and social class profile of the barristers fit the conclusions in Dooney's sample: mainly from Protestant upper middle-class families, with business and professional connections. There were also some Roman Catholics who had been educated in exclusive schools. For example, two Catholic barristers and former DU OTC members named above as being killed in the war, Gerald Plunkett and Hubert O'Connor, were educated by the Jesuits.

The Church of Ireland, part of the Anglican communion and closely connected with Trinity College, was perceived as being favourable to the ascendancy and British imperialism.[82] Nevertheless, religion was not a decisive factor in enlistment patterns. The loyalty of Catholics, from north and south, in supporting the British army has been noted by Biggs-Davison and Chowdharay-Best in an analysis of the Irish Catholic unionist tradition, a neglected component of the Irish identity.[83] There was strong unionist influence in the Irish legal profession but it would be simplistic to generalise about the political outlook of lawyers who volunteered for army service. The religious affiliations of the twenty-five barristers who died in the war are among the data in the biographical profiles in appendix 1. In summary, there were fourteen from the Church of Ireland (Anglican) tradition, two Presbyterians, one Methodist and eight Roman Catholics.

Commissioned into the Cheshire Regiment was Herbert Tierney, Belvederian and Catholic graduate of the Royal University of Ireland

80. *ILT&SJ*, l (1916), 62 and li (1917), 139; Robert Woods to author.
81. Laura Dooney, 'Trinity College and the War', in D. Fitzpatrick (ed.), *Ireland and the First World War* (Dublin, 1986, 2nd ed. 1988, revised with index), pp. 41–42.
82. David H. Hume, in 'Empire Day in Ireland 1896–1962', in Jeffery (ed.), *An Irish empire? Aspects of Ireland and the British empire*, pp. 153–57.
83. John Biggs-Davison and George Chowdharay-Best, *The cross of Saint Patrick: the Catholic unionist tradition in Ireland* (Abbotsbrook, Bucks., 1984).

(RUI), but not a member of an OTC. The RUI, an examining and degree awarding institution was replaced in 1908 by the National University of Ireland and Queen's University, Belfast. Before the NUI was established, University College, Dublin, a male institution administered by the Jesuits, was among the colleges providing lectures for RUI degrees. Tom Kettle and his future brothers-in-law, Eugene Sheehy and the pacifist socialist Francis Sheehy Skeffington, were involved in nationalist protests, with some anti-Trinity rhetoric, during the early 1900s at Literary and Historical Society (L & H) debates in UCD and during formal events such as RUI degree awarding ceremonies.[84]

The RUI pre-dated the OTC system but an OTC was not formed at the new NUI where Tom Kettle became professor of national economics. Dorothy MacArdle, a republican publicist and historian whose family roots were Protestant and Anglo-Irish, probably exaggerated the difficulties by claiming that 'It was almost impossible for a Catholic to get a commission; the National University (including UCD) was not permitted to have a training corps for officers, although Trinity College had its OTC.'[85] Catholics, especially from leading families such as the Redmonds, Kettles and Healys, with both NUI and Trinity connections, did obtain commissions. Lt. Gen. Sir Lawrence W. Parsons, commander of the 16th (Irish) Division facilitated Willie Redmond to obtain a commission as captain in the Royal Irish Regiment on the basis of previous experience in the Wexford militia and some training with the Leinster Regiment. There were obstacles to nationalists being commissioned. For example, General Parsons resisted political influence for a commission in regiments of the 16th (Irish) Division, on behalf of John Redmond's son, William Archer Redmond, barrister, MP and subsequently a TD in the independent Irish parliament. He became a captain in the Irish Guards and was awarded the DSO.[86]

According to the writer and broadcaster, Myles Dungan:

> The War Office's apparent bias against Irish nationalism by not allowing NUI colleges to establish an OTC resulted in many NUI

84. Paseta, *Before the revolution*, pp. 67–73; Sheehy, *May it please the court*, pp. 19–20; C.C. O'Brien in his *Memoirs*, p. 12 states that such protests were far too advanced for O'Brien's grandfather, and Tom Kettle's future father-in-law, David Sheehy, nationalist MP, who feared that British public opinion would be alienated during the parliamentary campaign for Home Rule.
85. Dorothy MacArdle, *The Irish republic* (London, 1937, 4th ed. Dublin, 1951), p. 121.
86. Tom Johnstone, *Orange, green and khaki: the story of the Irish regiments in the Great War, 1914–1918* (Dublin, 1992, 2001).

students being unable to qualify for commissions without enlisting as privates and rising through the ranks.[87]

It would be simplistic, however, to depict UCD as being radically nationalist or strongly opposed to enlistment in the British army, and about 500 students and graduates enlisted before the threats of conscription. The war list and roll of honour, published by the National University of Ireland (NUI) in 1919, showed the names of many graduates. Members of the well-known families, Tom Kettle and Herbert Tierney and also Joseph and Maurice Healy, William Archer Redmond, MP, and Eugene Sheehy were included on the UCD part of the NUI war lists.

In 1966, on the fiftieth anniversary of the Easter Rising, Fr Francis Shaw, SJ, a professor at UCD, attempted to challenge the prevailing republican perspective by explaining the complex Irish attitudes to the First World War period. According to a revised version of Fr Shaw's controversial and revisionist article, eventually published in 1972:[88]

> Uniquely and rather unacademically, Trinity College voluntarily turned itself into a military barracks, and from its windows machine guns directed their fire at rebel positions in O'Connell Street ... (but) McDonagh and McNeill and the handful of 'rebel' undergraduates from UCD did not enjoy the approval of the authorities or the support of the staff or the student body generally. The rebellion of 1916 took place when tension was high and emotion inflamed at another level, that of the world war, of 'the rape of Belgium', and of general anti-German feeling.

For political and practical reasons, direct commissioning into the British army ceased in February 1916, and subsequently candidates had to participate in officer cadet training units and pass further tests. Most of the barristers killed in the war had enlisted during the early stages.

87. Myles Dungan, *They shall grow not old: Irish soldiers and the Great War* (Dublin, 1997), p. 197, note 10.
88. Francis Shaw SJ, 'The canon of Irish history – a challenge', *Studies*, lxi, no. 242, summer 1972, pp. 115–53, at p. 146. The long article, originally written for the 1916 commemorative issue of *Studies* in spring 1966, was considered inappropriate for that occasion but was published in a revised form in 1972 after Fr Shaw's death in 1970. *College Chronicle*, Castleknock, 1918, lists Francis Shaw, SJ, as a British army chaplain; Joe Lee, analysis of Francis Shaw's controversial article, *Sunday Tribune*, 9 December 2001, and Joe Lee's essay, 'The canon of Irish history – a challenge, reconsidered', in Toner Quinn (ed.), *Desmond Fennell, his life and work* (Dublin, 2001).

There was no OTC at the King's Inns but Irish lawyers and law students had special access to the London-based Inns of Court (IOC) OTC. That corps originated in Queen Elizabeth's reign during resistance to the Spanish Armada when Vice Admiral Drake was a member of the Middle Temple. At the turn of the nineteenth century, when a French invasion was threatened, an Inns of Court Rifle Corps was formalised and acquired the name the 'Devil's Own'. IOC OTC Irish board members included Charles St G. Orpen, solicitor and president of the Incorporated Law Society, and, significantly, Dr Denis J. Coffey, president of University College Dublin, then a constituent college of the NUI, catering mainly for Catholics. Mr Justice (John) Ross, chairman of the IOC OTC Irish selection board, had been involved in founding DU OTC.

The IOC OTC sought 'men of university and public school class, and particularly those of sporting and of outdoor experience ... who were desirous of obtaining commissions in the cavalry and infantry ... upon joining, the usual Army Pay is received, and uniform is provided free.'[89] The Irish selection board sat three days weekly at noon in the Land Judge's Court, Four Courts, Dublin. Membership was also open to non-lawyers of suitable backgrounds such as 2nd Lt. John Samuel Carrothers, a past pupil of Portora Royal School, a Land Commission clerk, killed in action 16 August 1917.[90] The Irish selection board passed other applicants, including: Jeremiah Brennan, Lt., Lancashire Hussars, killed 8 August 1918 in France, referred to as a barrister in *Irish Law Times and Solicitor's Journal* war supplement, Feb. 1916, but a record of his call to the Irish Bar could not be traced. Henry W. Briscoe, 2nd Lt., 3rd Garrison Bn., Royal Irish Fusiliers was drowned at sea from H.T. *Arcadian*, on 15 April 1917, aged 43. He is named on the Mikra memorial, Greece, but not on the Four Courts memorial, presumably because he was not a Law Library member and did not practise at the Bar. That exclusion seems inequitable and his name should be added to the memorial. Henry W. Briscoe is listed in the *Dublin Book of Honour* and the CWGC as a barrister and civil servant in the Irish Land Commission. King's Inns records show that he was called to the Irish Bar in Easter term, 1894.

Also recruited through the IOC OTC were some solicitors including: Hugh Galbraith of the Dublin Fusiliers, later awarded an MC, and Major Ivan Albert Howe of the Royal Garrison Artillery; a solicitor's apprentice, Lancelot J.N. Lloyd Blood, was commissioned as captain in the Dublin Fusiliers. Denis Gwynn, parliamentary nationalist, UCD graduate and

89. *ILT&SJ*, l (1916), war supplement.
90. D.S. Carrothers, compiler, *Memoirs of a young lieutenant, 1898–1917* (Enniskillen, 1992).

author, who served in the Munster and Inniskilling Fusiliers, was also on the IOC OTC list. Overall, however, the London-based IOC OTC did not succeed in attracting many Irish recruits.[91] The relative lack of success of the IOC OTC in recruiting from the Irish legal profession was probably because other avenues to commissions, especially the DU OTC, were more accessible. Almost 14,000 recruits passed through the IOC OTC. Most were commissioned but only a tenth of the candidates interviewed were accepted.

The Irish legal profession was relatively small and there were only a few hundred practising barristers. Nevertheless, by early 1916 the *ILT&SJ* in its war supplement, reported that about 126 barristers, 110 solicitors, 71 solicitors' apprentices, 160 sons of barristers and 175 sons of solicitors, had enlisted in the British army and many were killed.

In summary, the twenty-five listed barrister fatal casualties in the various regiments and units were apportioned as follows: four, Dublins; two, Munsters; one, Connaught Rangers; two, Inniskillings; three, Royal Irish Rifles; two, Royal Irish Regiment (one of these was also attached to the Royal Flying Corps); two, Cheshires; one, Durhams; two, Shropshires; one, Welsh Fusiliers; one, Royal Fusiliers; one, Royal Engineers; one, Royal Naval Division; one, Red Cross; one, Alberta Regiment, Canadian Division. The list was drawn widely and some of the barristers were not in active practice immediately before the war, but had practised at the Irish Bar.

The *ILT&SJ*, reflecting opinion in the legal profession, publicised recruitment efforts. At a crucial time in February, 1916, the journal's war supplement, inscribed with the patriotic motto 'Pro Patria', included messages from: King George V, referring to the 'struggle between my people and a highly organised enemy who has transgressed the Laws of Nations' and expressing pride in 'the voluntary response from my subjects'; Lord Lieutenant Wimborne, director general of recruiting; and Lord Kitchener, Secretary of State for War, who sought 50,000 Irishmen for the armed forces.[92] That target was achieved but estimating the numbers of Irish who joined the British forces during the war can be controversial. Accurate estimates are difficult because the Irish enlisted, not only in Irish regiments, but also in divisions and units based in Great Britain and the wider empire, especially Australia, New Zealand and Canada.

Law students' debates reflected the general support for the Allied war effort in defence of Belgium. In November, 1914, soon after the war started,

---

91. Dr Timothy Bowman, QUB and RDFA, to author information about IOC OTC based on documents in the Guild Hall Library, London. Names listed in F.H.L. Errington (ed.), *Inns of Court OTC during the Great War* (London, 1922), available at the Inns of Court and City Yeomanry Museum, 10 Stone Buildings, Lincoln's Inn, London. Reprinted, Naval & Military Press, Uckfield, East Sussex, n.d.

92. *ILT&SJ*, 1 (1916), war supplement.

Tom Kettle, then a professor at UCD, spoke at the Solicitors' Apprentices' Debating Society inaugural meeting on the subject of Belgian neutrality. The mood at the debate favoured the rights of nations, justice and the rule of international law, and the auditor, Conor A. Maguire (who became chief justice of Ireland in 1946), strongly condemned the German violation of Belgium.[93] Lord Chancellor O'Brien, referring to Ireland as a small nation, said that its isolation from the immediate horrors of war was no excuse for ignoring the reality. Serjeant Sullivan spoke of fighting for civilisation and Christianity which could not be beaten.

The special war supplement of the *ILT&SJ* in February 1916 named those who had joined the IOC OTC, and also included extensive lists of Irish barristers and solicitors. Sons of lawyers, serving in 'His Majesty's Forces', were included in a litany of renowned names such as Campbell, Cherry, Carson, Healy, Ross and Redmond. Hubert D. Walsh, Lt., 6th Bn., Royal Irish Fusiliers, Bernard (Brian) Walsh, Royal Artillery, and Rosemary Walsh who served in the VAD were children of Dr Patrick S. Walsh, KC, of the Donegal recruiting staff, and Mary Afric Walsh (née Harkin). Dr Walsh, who had been a colleague of P.H. Pearse, later became district court president in Cyprus and was appointed chief justice of the Seychelles in 1931.[94]

Included in the general *ILT&SJ* lists were many of the twenty-five listed barristers, not connected with the IOC OTC, who were killed on active service. Lord Chancellor O'Brien, in a message with the *ILT&SJ* war supplement stated that it showed:

> The splendid response of the legal profession to the call of their country and will be most useful at the conclusion of the war, when we shall hope to erect a more permanent memorial to those who have fallen.[95]

As Charles St G. Orpen, Law Society president, pointed out, many other lawyers also served in volunteer detachments, ambulance corps, munition works and auxiliary services. For example, Edmund Richard Meredith, son of the Rt Hon. Richard E. Meredith, educated at Mr Strangway's school,

93. *ILT&SJ*, xlviii (1914), 323; Conor Maguire, SC, to author.
94. Information about Patrick S. Walsh from Deirdre McCormack (P.S. Walsh's great-grand-daughter), Wokingham, Berks.; Mac Fhionnghaile, *Donegal, Ireland and the First World War*, appendix B, pp. 142–43; Patrick S. Walsh appeared with Pearse in one of his few reported court cases, defending a Donegal man, Niall Mac Giolla Bhride (McBride), who was prosecuted for having his name in Irish on a horse cart: *Creeslough-Dunfanaghy guide book* (Donegal, 1987), p. 18; *M'Bride* v. *M'Govern*, [1906] 2 IR at 181–82, analysed by Seamus Ó Tuathail, AS, in lecture at Pearse house, Dublin, 21 March 2002 and in *Gaeilge agus Bunreacht* (Baile Atha Cliath, 2002). Information also from Pat Cooke, curator, Pearse Museum, to author.
95. *ILT&SJ*, l (1916), war supplement.

Dublin, Trinity College and the King's Inns, volunteered for the British Red Cross. He died of dysentery soon after arriving in Italy during August, 1917. Possibly due to conscientious objections, Edmund R. Meredith did not join an OTC or the armed forces, although two of his brothers served as army captains.

As recruitment continued, *ILT&SJ* published further notices about lawyers being commissioned, serving or dying in the war. Information about many of those reports, especially with specific reference to Bar circuits are included in chapter 3 and relevant footnotes.

Mr Justice Molony, Mr Justice Barton and leading lawyers too old for active service gave moral support to the war effort by joining the Irish Association of Volunteer Training Corps, stated to have been a non-political body providing military training for defence purposes. Barristers, solicitors and court officials formed the Four Courts Auxiliary Munitions Association to keep munitions factories going over weekends.[96] The munitions association's chairman, Mr Justice Ross, played a leading role in DU OTC and the IOC OTC's Irish selection board. As a student at Foyle College, Derry and TCD, he was friendly with the entertainer and composer, Percy French, for whom Ross wrote songs including 'Andy McElroe', a mock heroic tribute to an Irish soldier in the Sudan. In the more serious era of the Great War, John Ross was active in the troops' welfare and the Red Cross, and became the last lord chancellor of Ireland in 1921. His son, Major Ronald Deane Ross, MC, MP, served with the North Irish Horse. Like other judges, Cherry as lord chief justice encouraged enlistment and in 1914 he was reported as having presided at a recruitment meeting at Skerries, Co. Dublin.[97] Mr Justice Molony and many prominent lawyers helped in a practical way by arranging a soldiers' club, including dining and other facilities, at the DMP barracks, College Street, Dublin. The lord lieutenant expressed his formal appreciation of that initiative. Those connections illustrate the legal and political establishments nexus supporting recruitment and the war effort.

In accordance with precedent going back to the colourful uniforms of the Barristers' Corps of Volunteers in the late eighteenth century, barristers actively engaged in military service were allowed the option of appearing in court dressed in regimental uniform.[98] There was also an effort to preserve the professional practices of barristers who were absent on active service. Such arrangements were more difficult in Ireland where the English system of formal chambers with clerks did not operate. Henry Hanna, KC, helped

96. *ILT&SJ*, l (1916), 54.
97. Daire Hogan, 'R.R. Cherry, lord chief justice of Ireland', in D.S. Greer and N.M. Dawson (eds), *Mysteries and solutions in Irish legal history* (Dublin, 2001), p. 161.
98. *ILT&SJ*, xlviii (1914), 316.

to maintain morale and encourage recruiting of volunteers through his lectures and publications about the Gallipoli and the Pals of D company, 7th Bn., Dublins, which included barristers and also solicitors such as Robert Stanton from Cork.[99] Swift McNeill, KC, a law professor at King's Inns and UCD, and Irish Parliamentary Party MP for South Donegal, struck an acceptable but perhaps exaggerated note when he said at a recruitment meeting in May, 1915, 'those Irishmen who had gone to the Front are fighting for Ireland as surely as the men of '98 (Rising) fought for her and for so holy a cause'.[100] In that wider context, however, Swift McNeill's approach is now reflected by those individuals who participate in commemorations for their Bar colleagues in respect of both the 1798 Rising and the Great War. Kevin Myers, a journalist who has striven significantly to restore the Irish war contribution to national memory, pointed out that: 'The dissenting voices were few. Political leaders – Carson, Devlin and Redmond – urged the men to go. So did magistrates and judges and mayors ...'.[101] Those who volunteered fought as Irishmen. John Redmond expressed the prevalent mood in his introduction to Michael McDonagh's book about the Irish in the war, written as army recruitment propaganda early in 1916:

> Chivalry is of its essence, and nations who do not want to die, but to live, as Ireland does, must act through their essential qualities. Those brave sons in the field need not fear for the honour they have won for their country. Their brothers are coming to them. Ireland's armies will be maintained.[102]

'The terrible beauty' of violence and death which W.B. Yeats depicted as being born in the Easter Rising, 1916, was conceived and nurtured through wider European militarism in the Great War, in which many Irishmen, including solicitors and the twenty-five listed barristers, died. The Irish mood changed when the leaders of the Easter Rising 1916 were executed and the British government attempted to impose conscription on Ireland.

Reflecting a general pattern of young men who marched to war, with a few notable exceptions such as Tom Kettle, Willie Redmond and Arthur Samuels, most of the twenty-five Irish barristers lost in the conflict of 1914–18 were unmarried. One, John Henry Frederick Leland, 2nd Lt., Royal

99. Hanna, *The pals at Suvla Bay*.
100. P. Cronin, 'South county Dublin and east Wicklow during the 1914–18 war', lecture publication no. 23 (1986), Foxrock Local History Club, Co. Dublin, p. 4.
101. Kevin Myers, 'First to last, Irishmen led the 1914–18 sacrifice', and report of remembrance services for the war dead, *Irish Times*, 15 November 1982.
102. Michael MacDonagh, *The Irish at the front*, introduction by John Redmond, MP (London, New York, & Toronto, 1916), p. 14.

Welsh Fusiliers, returned home to Blackrock, Co. Dublin where he married Florence Mary Leland at Christ Church, Carysfort, Blackrock, on 9 March 1915, in the short period between his enlistment and death in the Dardanelles, in August 1915.[103]

DU OTC pipers led the farewell march of the D Company, Pals, 7th Dublins, on 30 April, 1915, when they left Royal Barracks (now the National Museum, Collins Barracks) to complete their training in England before active service in Gallipoli. It was an occasion of great public demonstration, as described by Hanna in his history of the Dublin Pals:

> In front of the Four Courts a large crowd of barristers, solicitors, and officials gave a cordial send off to the men. Amongst the crowd were judges whose sittings had concluded for the day and they cheered as spontaneously as the others. In the ranks were members of the Bar, who had forsaken excellent prospects to keep the Old Flag flying, and as they were recognised they were cordially cheered.[104]

Like the Pals formed from English public schools alumni, the Dublin Pals were men who had 'left good, comfortable homes ... and had come voluntarily out of a sheer sense of duty.'[105] The Irish Pals, however, differed in scale and background from those in England where young men from closely-knit communities added to the colossal casualty lists which the generals often ignored.[106] Alex Findlater, in the story of his Dublin merchant family, placed enlistment by Irish Protestants in Dublin Pals and other units in the context of self-sacrificing patriotism and loyalty to the empire.[107] Herbert Findlater, a solicitor, enlisted with the Dublin Pals and was killed in Gallipoli.[108]

103. TNA/PRO, WO 374/41658, marriage certificate, extract no. 9/23/188 F3; Dr R. Refaussé, librarian and archivist, Church of Ireland, RCB library, Dublin to author; Cornelius F. Smith, *Newtownpark Avenue, its people and their houses* (Dublin, 2001), pp. 56–58, records that Christ Church, Carysfort, closed during the 1960s, was later demolished to make way for the Blackrock by-pass road.
104. Hanna, *The pals at Suvla Bay*, pp. 28–31.
105. Lt.-Col. C.H. Cobb, 5th Oxfordshire and Buckinghamshire Light Infantry, quoted in P. Simkins, *Kitchener's army: the raising of the new armies, 1914–16* (Manchester and New York, 1988), p. 72, information courtesy of Dr G. Morgan, TCD.
106. Sheffield, *Forgotten victory*, p. 3, quoting foreword by John Prescott, MP, to a book about Hull Pals; B.S. Barnes, *This righteous war* (Huddersfield, 1990).
107. Alex Findlater, *Findlaters: the story of a Dublin merchant family 1771–2001* (Dublin, 2001).
108. Ibid., pp. 258–61, in chapter 8 on Gallipoli. Lance Corpl. (not Lt.-Col. as shown in that book) Herbert Findlater, a TCD graduate and family solicitor, was killed in action on 16 August 1915. His death was described as being in 'a mad-man's charge

Katharine Tynan expressed the prevalent mood of enthusiastic enlistment in her poem, 'Joining the colours':[109]

> There they go marching all in step so gay!
> Smooth-cheeked and golden, food for shells and guns.
> Blithely they go as to a wedding day,
> The mothers' sons.
> High heart! High courage! The poor girls they kissed
> Run with them: they shall kiss no more, alas!
> Out of the mist they stepped – into the mist
> Singing they pass.

---

but on the other hand a very brave one'. Capt. Poole Hickman was killed in the same battle during bayonet attacks which met with machine-gun fire.

109. Katharine Tynan (Hinkson), 'Joining the colours', in James Bentley (ed.), *Some corner of a foreign field, poetry of the Great War* (London, Toronto, Boston, 1992 and 1993), p. 67. The poet married H.A. Hinkson, a magistrate, and their two sons served with the British forces during the war.

CHAPTER THREE

Remembrance

'Let those who come after see to it that his name be not forgotten'
Charles P. Keary

THOSE WORDS BY an historian and novelist, inscribed on the memorial scrolls issued in the name of King George V to the next of kin of those who died in the Great War, evoke a wider continuing call to remembrance.

That mood was echoed in Dublin, when, in response to a decision of the Bar Council, many members of the Irish Bench and Bar met on 27 May 1919. The lord chancellor, Sir James Campbell, bt. (the first Baron Glenavy) presided over the meeting to consider how best to perpetuate the memory of members of the Irish Bar who had fallen in the recent world war. Referring to a sacred trust and a duty to discharge a debt of honour, Campbell paid tribute to 'the dead of professional and commercial classes without distinction of class or creed'.[1] The lord chancellor, focusing on those 'who responded to the call of duty from the ranks of their own (legal) profession who fought and died so nobly', called out the names of the twenty-five 'brave and gallant' men who gave their lives freely for their country. 'As it was impossible to concede a pride of place or honour', the names were read out in alphabetical order, as listed here in our roll of honour and in chapter 1 and appendix 1.[2]

The lord chancellor pointed out that 'twenty-five brave and gallant lives (were) freely given for their country; they died that we might live in liberty and safety. At least one half of those of our departed and glorious dead met their fate in the first year of the war.'[3] Evoking the memory of the dead who were former comrades in the Law Library or on circuit, the lord chancellor

---

1. *ILT&SJ*, liii (1919), 132–33. James Henry Mussen Campbell, lord chancellor, was raised to the peerage as the first Baron Glenavy in 1921. One of his sons had been killed in war action in 1916. A former unionist MP for Dublin University, 1903–16, James H.M. Campbell was a member of the provisional government formed by Sir Edward Carson during the home rule controversy. Campbell/Glenavy adapted to the changing Ireland and served as chairman of the Senate of the Irish Free State.
2. *ILT&SJ*, liii (1919), 132. On the general context of the memorials, see Jane Leonard, 'Lest we forget', in D. Fitzpatrick (ed.), *Ireland and the First World War*, pp. 59–67.
3. *ILT&SJ*, liii (1919), 132–33.

referred to them as 'clean-living gallant young men filled with the highest ideals, and living for their profession, a credit and an ornament to it and their fellows'.[4]

Lord Chief Justice Molony proposed a resolution 'to provide a permanent memorial to the courage, patriotic devotion, and self-sacrifice of their fellow members of the Irish Bar who voluntarily joined His Majesty's forces and nobly fought and died to save our country in the great war'. Molony said that they required no lofty statue, no magnificent design. Their true memorial was in the hearts of those who had dwelt with them and had realised their goodness ... but the required reminder would be best fulfilled by having a quiet and a simple, but a permanent memorial.[5]

At that meeting on 27 May 1919, Molony proposed the resolution with sorrow because he knew many of the dead as: 'men of great promise, with every chance of success in their profession, who at the call of duty, gave up every hope and preferment there, and went forth to fight the battle for everything that they held dear. Their memory would be preserved forever by the Bar of Ireland.'[6]

It was significant that the formal resolution was proposed by Molony, a highly respected Roman Catholic who was 'a Home Ruler of the old stamp, his first loyalty was to the rule of law'.[7]

Serjeant Matheson, seconding the resolution, said that 'now that they had reached the haven of peace, they had time to look back and contemplate the noble courage and self-sacrifice of their brethren of the Irish Bar ... brave Irishmen who gave up everything for their king and country.'[8] William Carrigan, KC, proposed that a committee be appointed, and J.H. Monroe was named as honorary secretary.

Another general meeting of the subscribers to the Bar war memorial was held in the Law Library, Four Courts, Dublin in May 1921. The main

4. Ibid.
5. Ibid. James H.M. Campbell had advised the British prime minister, Lloyd George, to appoint Thomas F. Molony, a suitable Roman Catholic judge, to be lord chief justice in place of Campbell on his promotion as lord chancellor of Ireland in 1918 according to L.W. McBride, *The greening of Dublin Castle: the transformation of bureaucratic and judicial personnel in Ireland, 1892–1922* (Washington, D.C., 1991), p. 249. In 1910, Molony had stood as a Liberal candidate for West Toxteth in Liverpool, a city with strong Irish connections and was appointed solicitor general for Ireland in 1912.
6. *ILT&SJ*, liii (1919), 132–33.
7. Nial Osborough, in *Ir Jur*, ix (1974), 87–98: 'The title of the last lord chief justice of Ireland'. Denis Gwynn in *The Irish Free State, 1922–1927* (London,1928), pp. 168–69, paid tribute to the dignity, firmness and integrity of Lord Chief Justice Molony, during the turbulent years of political upheaval and the transition from British to Irish government.
8. *ILT&SJ*, liii (1919), 132–33.

speaker was Sergeant Hanna, KC, a distinguished lawyer of the Northern Presbyterian tradition, who subsequently served the new Irish state as a High Court judge.[9] Hanna reported on a interview with Oliver Sheppard. He was the sculptor who executed the memorial for the Incorporated Law Society and also the Cuchulainn nationalist memorial. Modelled before the Great War, that memorial was erected in 1936 at the General Post Office, Dublin, to commemorate the Easter Rising. The meeting was informed that the Bar memorial would take the form of a bronze tablet, ten feet by twelve feet in size, with a symbolic figure in relief, and the names of those whom it commemorated embossed underneath. The meeting of May 1921 passed a resolution to commission the memorial at a cost not exceeding £700. From a total of £1,300, the balance of £600 subscribed would be handed over to the Bar Benevolent Fund to help primarily members who had served in the war and their dependants.

The sculptor, Oliver Sheppard, had suggested that the memorial be placed on the wall in front of the staircase leading to the Law Library. The memorial was not formally unveiled until 1924 in Dublin Castle, and there is no evidence that it was erected originally in the Four Courts before they were destroyed in the Civil War. The Law Library was completely destroyed and if the Bar memorial had been erected there, it is unlikely that it would have survived the bombardment.[10]

In the presence of Tim Healy, KC, governor-general of the Irish Free State, Lord Chief Justice Molony performed the formal unveiling ceremony on 27 May 1924 in Dublin Castle, where the Law Library and the superior courts were based temporarily while the Four Courts were being rebuilt.[11]

9. *ILT&SJ*, lv (1921), 186. See A.R. Hart, *A history of the king's serjeants at law in Ireland: honour rather than advantage?* (Dublin, 2000), pp. 132–33, 171, for biographical details of Henry Hanna (1871–1946), author of *The Pals at Suvla Bay* (1917), and later a judge of the Irish High Court, referred to later in this chapter. A.M. Sullivan was called the last serjeant because he was the last living survivor but Henry Hanna was the final appointee in the Irish jurisdiction.

10. *ILT&SJ*, lv (1921), 186; Ronan Keane, later chief justice of Ireland, 'A mass of crumbling ruins, the destruction of the Four Courts in June 1922', pp. 159–68, and Gerald Hogan, SC, FTCD, 'Return to the Four Courts', at pp. 177–219, in Caroline Costello (ed.), *The Four Courts: two hundred years* (Dublin, 1996); Deaglán de Bréadún, 'Damage to Four Courts outlined', report to Michael Collins made available after eighty years in National Archives, feature on State papers, *Irish Times*, 3 January 2002.

11. Turpin, *Oliver Sheppard*, p. 127 suggests that the Bar memorial survived the burning of the Four Courts in the Civil War in 1922 and was later placed in Dublin Castle. Correspondence between the author and John Turpin did not clarify the precise dates of those movements. The speech by Lord Chief Justice Molony at the unveiling ceremony in Dublin Castle in May 1924 implies that the Bar memorial (unlike that for the solicitors) was not originally erected in the Four Courts. That

The memorial, an artistic mural tablet of bronze on a background of polished sheephouse limestone, was placed in the lobby to the right of the grand staircase, near where the State Apartments are now situated. Below the inscription 'In memory of the Irish barristers who fell in the Great War, 1914–1918,' and under a bronze laurel wreath, the names of the twenty-five barristers were listed.

Serjeant Hanna, speaking with emotion, referred to 'the honoured dead … comrades in days of old, who leaped to arms when the call of battle came, and followed whither duty led and fell untimely in the savage strife … the memory of all they did and tried to do will never fade and their names shall live from generation to generation'.[12]

Molony said that 'the memorial was originally designed for the Four Courts but the hand of fate intervened and left Ireland without its great Temple of Justice'.[13] He continued by referring to 'twenty-five gallant young men … who knew no barriers of creed, class or politics, they fought for a great ideal and showed a true unity which should be a hope and inspiration to us all … They fought for justice and we may be sure they found mercy.'[14] That was a reference to the figures of Justice and Mercy on the memorial.

The large and distinguished attendance at the ceremony included Mr Justice (Arthur Warren) Samuels.[15] His son, Arthur P. I. Samuels, named on the memorial, served as Capt., 11th Bn., Royal Irish Rifles, 36th (Ulster) Division, and died after wounds received at Messines/Mesen, Belgium, on 24 September 1916.[16]

Classified as a public sculpture, the Bar memorial includes 'two tall bronze reliefs flanking the lists of the dead. The left relief shows a standing sentinel, a male warrior with bared chest holding a down-turned sword (emblematic of law).'[17] Other distinguishing features include a nude and grieving woman in kneeling position; a crowned female warrior with a

interpretation is supported by minutes of the Bar Council. Due to an editing error, the opposite impression was given in *Court Service News*, July 2003, vol. 6, no. 2.

12. Turpin, *Oliver Sheppard*, p. 127; *Irish Independent*, 28 May 1924; and *ILT&SJ*, lviii (1924), 137–39.

13. *ILT&SJ*, lviii (1924), 139.

14. Ibid.

15. Arthur Warren Samuels, former solicitor-general, attorney-general and unionist MP for Dublin University, was described as 'an undistinguished law officer and judge but a sincere and patriotic Irishman' in Healy, *The old Munster circuit*, new ed. Samuels, a Protestant and unionist formally opposed to home rule, made constructive proposals for the Irish administration, including a council for Ireland, according to McBride, *The greening of Dublin Castle*, p. 239.

16. See biographical outlines of barristers at appendix 1.

17. Turpin, *Oliver Sheppard*, p. 124. See plate 19.

ceremonial two-handed laurel entwined sword, representing justice and carrying an open book inscribed with the King's Inns motto, *nolumus mutari*; oak leaves and acorns ornament the female warrior's hem.

The memorial was described as having 'a hieratic neo-medieval feeling to those standing figures. However, the nude woman is one of the sculptor's most original symbolist conceptions with her gesture of pain and supplication.'[18] The sculptor of the bronze work, Oliver Sheppard, came from the Ulster protestant tradition, but was a friend of Patrick Pearse, the executed leader of the Easter Rising, 1916.[19] The limestone work was undertaken by Sharp and Emery, Great Brunswick (now Pearse) Street, Dublin, near the Pearse family home (now restored) and sculptural workshops.

In parallel with the barristers' memorial, Sheppard conceived the solicitors' memorial which was erected in July 1921 at the Four Courts. The timing suggests that it was completed and installed before the Bar memorial. Although the solicitors' memorial was damaged in the bombardment during the Civil War, it was reported that the 'bronze figure and panels of the memorial were saved, and are in good condition, but the limestone surrounding the bronzes did not escape destruction'.[20] The solicitors' memorial was subsequently installed at the premises of the Incorporated Law Society, 45, Kildare Street, but returned to the Four Courts, and was later transferred to the Law Society's new headquarters at Blackhall Place, Dublin, which were opened in the late 1970s. The memorial returned to a prominent public position in the Four Courts buildings during January 2003. Referring to the solicitors' memorial, Sheppard's biographer, Professor John Turpin, wrote:

> The imagery containing a single standing draped figure with hands resting on a ceremonial sword is much less innovative than the grieving nude woman of the barristers' memorial ... Both memorials were modelled at the height of the War of Independence and are an assertion of the loyalist community to which most of the barristers and solicitors belonged.[21]

18. Ibid.
19. Ibid. and *ILT&SJ*, lviii (1924), 139; Josephine Power, daughter of Albert Power, sculptor and colleague of Sheppard, in conversation with author; Richard Warner (ed.), *Icons of identity* (Belfast, 2000), booklet for a millennium exhibition at the Ulster Museum, Belfast, October 2000 to April 2001, especially pages 3–4 about Cuchulainn; John Turpin, 'Oliver Sheppard and Albert Power, State sculptural commissions,' in *Dublin Historical Record*, journal of the Old Dublin Society, vol. lv. no. 1 (spring 2002), p. 43.
20. Law Society's annual report 1922, courtesy of Daire Hogan, solicitor; Hall and Hogan (eds), *The Law Society of Ireland, 1852–2002*, pp. 66, 286.
21. Turpin, *Oliver Sheppard*, p. 127. See plate 21.

That generalised assertion about loyalist allegiance must be challenged. The legal profession, although mainly upper middle class, contained those who volunteered to serve in the British army during the war from diverse traditions, including Roman Catholic and Protestant, unionist and nationalist. Chief Justice Hugh Kennedy, when seeking government approval in 1924 to erect the Bar memorial at Dublin Castle, wrote to William Cosgrave:

> It had to be remembered that the men who lost their lives were not confined to any particular political or religious section, but were pretty well drawn from all who were represented at the Bar at that particular time.[22]

During the period when the war memorials were conceived, the Irish Bar asserted its independence on 26 March 1921 at a general meeting. It passed unanimously a motion objecting to the Crown forces infringing the privileges of the Bar by seizing counsels' briefs at the office of Mr Noyk, the solicitor engaged in defending IRA prisoners charged with murder after British officers were shot on Bloody Sunday, 21 November, 1920.[23] The Bar motion was proposed by Tim Healy, KC, whose son Joseph, of the Royal Naval Volunteer Reserve, served during the Gallipoli campaign and later became a senior counsel at the Irish Bar.[24] That critical Bar motion was seconded by Tom Kettle's brother-in-law, Eugene Sheehy, who had served on the Western Front as a captain with the 1st and 4th Bns., Dublin Fusiliers and later as an intelligence officer.[25] Copies of the Bar motion were sent to the lord lieutenant and the lord chancellor. In contrast to the barristers' memorial, that commemorating the solicitors was not classified as a public sculpture.[26] It was removed in January 2003 from the Law

22. Letter from Hugh Kennedy, chief justice, to William Cosgrave, president of the Executive Council: National Archives, Dept. of the Taoiseach papers, DTS 3743.
23. *ILT&SJ*, lv (1921), 83. On 14 October 2001, at the State funeral for the 'forgotten ten' including Thomas Whelan, executed on 14 March 1921, for the murder of a British officer, Capt. Baggally, on 21 November 1920; information from the Whelan family to the author suggests that Michael Noyk, solicitor, was engaged to defend Thomas Whelan. The seizing of relevant legal briefs indicates *prima facie* that the legal process was flawed and that trials and convictions of Whelan and others were unfair.
24. Frank Callanan, *T.M. Healy* (Cork, 1996), p. 511; Herbert Tierney, letters home from Gallipoli, copies courtesy of Henry Tierney (appendix 6).
25. E. Sheehy, *May it please the court*, especially ch. 9, 'Futile training for a futile war', and ch. 10, 'Active service', in which Eugene Sheehy, son of David Sheehy, nationalist MP, and brother-in-law of Tom Kettle, was critical of the Great War.
26. *ILT&SJ*, lv (1924), 125, 303. The twenty Irish solicitors and eighteen apprentices who died in the Great War, and listed on the solicitors' memorial, are named at appendix 2; Daire Hogan, solicitor and former president of the Irish Legal History

Society's headquarters, Blackhall Place, Dublin to the Four Courts, where it is now on public display.

There was an impressive remembrance ceremony at the High Courts of Justice, Dublin Castle, on the first Armistice Day after the barristers' memorial was erected there in 1924.[27] Judges and relatives of the men whose memory was being commemorated paid a silent tribute. R.D. Murray, the father of the Bar, laid a wreath of laurel and poppies. Serjeant Hanna placed a similar wreath from the Bar of Northern Ireland. Samuel L. Brown, KC, on behalf of the family of Gerald Plunkett, killed in Gallipoli on 4 June 1915 and named on the Bar memorial, deposited a beautiful wreath of natural red carnations and white chrysanthemums. Frank Lillis laid a wreath 'In proud and loving memory of Lieut. Martin A. Lillis, Royal Irish Regiment, Royal Flying Corps, killed at the battle of Arras, 11 April 1917'.[28]

The barristers' memorial was later placed near the entrance to the Law Library, the traditional base for practising barristers, when the Four Courts had been reconstructed in the early 1930s. On 21 October 1931, the Bar Council unanimously adopted a motion proposed by H.J. Moloney, KC and seconded by P. Lynch, KC:

> That the Board of Works be paid the money expended by them in the removal from Dublin Castle and re-erection in the Four Courts of the Memorial in commemoration of our Brethren who fell in the Great War.[29]

The remembrance ceremonies as reported in the *Irish Law Times and Solicitors' Journal* have continued until the present with some breaks, for example during the Second World War. In recent years special credit is due to the organisers of the annual ceremonies, and especially: the late Gregory Murphy, SC, Daniel Boland and John McCoy. Unfortunately, the trend of recent years to have poetry readings at the commemoration has been reversed. The reason given for the shorter ceremony is to minimise blocking the corridor at lunch hour. The biblical story of the moneychangers in the temple comes to mind as business and professional pressures begrudge a

Society, in correspondence with the author; Daire Hogan, 'Irish lawyers and the Great War', *Law Society Gazette*, xcii, no. 10 (Dec. 1999), 20–21.
27. *ILT&SJ*, lviii (1924), 283.
28. Ibid.; see generally: G.L. Campbell, *Royal Flying Corps, casualties and honours during the war of 1914–1917* (London, 1917); Chris Hobson, *Airmen died in the Great War 1914–1918* (Polstead, Suffolk, 1995).
29. Bar Council minutes, 21 October 1931, copy extracts made available by Jerry Carroll, director, and Jennefer Aston, librarian and archivist. Her trawl through the minutes revealed very few references to the war memorial but supports the view that it was not originally erected in the Four Courts.

relatively short interval for remembrance. Meanwhile in the North, a photograph hung during March 1916 in the Bar room of the Londonderry county courthouse showed sixteen members of the North West Bar 'who answered the call of King and Country, and three of whom (G. Plunkett, W.A. Lipsett and J.B. Lee) have already made the great sacrifice'.[30] Two others included in the photograph, A.W. Samuels and J.B. Proctor, were later killed in action. When the Derry courthouse was being refurbished in the mid-1990s, the photograph was removed to storage in the care of the Court Service of Northern Ireland.[31]

On 18 March 1920, following the initiative of W.M. Whitaker, KC, a brass tablet was placed in the entrance hall at the County Antrim courthouse, Crumlin Road, Belfast to perpetuate the memory of six members of the North-East Bar killed in the war.[32] The Belgian consul conveyed a message from the Bar of Belgium, appreciating the Irish efforts in helping another small nation.

W.F. Coates, JP, lord mayor of Belfast, and corporation members attended the unveiling ceremony, which was performed by Molony, the lord chief justice. He said that while a memorial at the Four Courts, Dublin would commemorate the sacrifices of the Irish Bar as a whole, each circuit should have its own memorial to remember those who fought for truth, freedom and justice. Molony stated that thirty-three members of the North East Circuit responded when 'the call came to fight for the great heritage of their race', and he then specifically referred to the six 'gallant soldiers and gentlemen ... who made the great sacrifice cheerfully because they were fighting for all that humanity held dear'.[33]

In summary, the six members of the North-East Bar were referred to as follows: Two 'Old Contemptibles' killed in Flanders in February 1915 during the early stages of the war – Lt. Rowan Shaw, 9th Bn., Cheshires, son of Judge Shaw, recorder of Belfast (the memory of both father and son would always be held in the highest esteem by the Bar); and Lt. John H. Edgar, 9th Durhams, a native of Dromore, Co. Down; Lt. J.H. Leland, 5th

---

30. *ILT&SJ*, l (1916), 80. There are some inconsistencies between the *ILT&SJ* reports and official records. For example, W.A. Lipsett, who died in Flanders, was shown incorrectly in the *ILT&SJ* as having been killed in Gallipoli, and J.B. Proctor was named as a captain in the Royal Irish Rifles, rather than the 10th Bn., Inniskillings, as noted in the official records.

31. Brian Lowry, Procurement Manager, Northern Ireland Court Service, Belfast, letters to author.

32. *ILT&SJ*, liv (1920), 76; and information from John Creaney, QC, Law Library, Royal Courts of Justice, Belfast, who took the tablet into safekeeping, pending re-erection in a new criminal law courthouse to replace that at Crumlin Road, Belfast.

33. *ILT&SJ*, liv (1920), 76.

(Flintshire) Bn., Royal Welsh (Welch) Fusiliers, a brilliant classical scholar, killed in Gallipoli in August 1915; Capt. R.B. Burgess, Royal Engineers, rugby international and gallant gentleman, fell in Flanders in December 1915; Lt. W.M. Crozier, 9th Inniskillings, 36th (Ulster) Division, killed on the first day of the battle of the Somme, 1 July 1916; Capt. G.B.J. Smyth, Royal Irish Rifles, killed in Flanders, in October 1918, three weeks before the armistice.[34]

A war memorial was placed in 1933 at the newly constructed Royal Courts of Justice, Belfast. At the formal opening ceremony, the duke of Abercorn, the governor of Northern Ireland, spoke about peace and laid a wreath to remember the barristers, solicitors and apprentices from Ulster who died in the war.[35] The following barristers are named on the plaque at the Royal Courts of Justice, Belfast: Robert B. Burgess, Joseph B. Lee, Gerald Plunkett, J. Rowan Shaw, William M. Crozier, J.H. Leland, J.B. Proctor, John H. Edgar, William A. Lipsett, Arthur P. I. Samuels, George B.J. Smyth. Also in Belfast, at St Anne's cathedral (Church of Ireland), there is a regimental chapel which contains various memorials to Irish regiments including the Inniskillings, the Irish Fusiliers and Rifles. There are regimental chapels in Enniskillen, Armagh and Ballymena, Northern Ireland.

In England, at the Temple Church, London, a stone memorial to Inner Temple members lists Gerald Plunkett who is included in the Templars Roll of Honour. Although enrolled as a student at the Inner Temple, he was not recorded as being called to the English Bar.[36] In the Temple Church, John H. Edgar is named on the war memorial to sixty-three members of Middle Temple, where he was called to the English Bar, and he is listed on the Inn's illuminated Roll of Honour.[37] The Middle Temple war memorial was found to be incomplete and a new memorial lists extra names from both the First and Second World Wars. Willie Redmond, as a former student at the Middle Temple, is now included due to the initiatives of the author. There is a war memorial in the great hall of the Royal Courts of Justice, London, to those directly connected with the courts.

34. Ibid.
35. Brian Lowry, Procurement Manager, Northern Ireland Court Service, Belfast, to author; and discussions with John Creaney, QC, who kindly hosted the author's visit to Belfast; *ILT&SJ*, lxvii (1933), 161. See plate 18.
36. Dr Clare Rider, archivist, the Honorable Society of the Inner Temple, London, to author; Roll of Honour list, 'Inner Templars who volunteered and served in the Great War', no date shown; *Temple Church*, Pitkin Guides (Andover, Hants., 1997); *Bar News*, 118, November, 1999 (London), remembrance list includes G. Plunkett and J.H. Edgar.
37. Lesley Whitelaw, archivist, the Honorable Society of the Middle Temple, London, to author; M.T. Archive ref. MT3 ROH / 1.

The twenty-five Irish barristers who died in the war were mentioned and noted in various issues of the *Irish Law Times and Solicitors' Journal*, and are also included among those listed in *Ireland's memorial records, 1914–1918*.[38] The location of, and references to, the known war graves of the twenty-five Irish barristers are noted in the biographical lists at appendix 1. Nine of those graves are in the Western Front area of Belgium and France, where at each cemetery entrance guidebooks facilitate searches and references to named graves.

Exceptionally, Richard Edmund Meredith, who served with the Red Cross, is buried in Italy. As previously noted, only one of the listed barristers was buried in an Irish grave: Capt. Frederick H. Lewin, 3rd Connaughts, killed accidentally during bomb practice at Kinsale, Co. Cork on 8 December 1915. His remains were interred in the Lewin family vault at Kilmaine churchyard, Co. Mayo, and he is also remembered on a memorial at the military cemetery, Blackhorse Avenue, Dublin.

The twelve Irish barristers to whom the fortunes of war denied a known and honoured burial are named on relevant communal memorials maintained by the Commonwealth War Graves Commission (CWGC):[39] 2nd Lt. Cecil Stackpoole Kenny, 9th Bn., King's Shropshire Light Infantry, drowned between Holyhead and Dublin, was buried at sea. He is remembered on the Hollybrook memorial in the cemetery at Chirley Road, Southampton, Hampshire, England. That memorial commemorates 1,868 people lost on transport and other ships around the Irish and British coasts during the Great War: CWGC ref. 40, MR.

The Menin Gate Memorial, in Ypres/Ieper, West Flanders, Belgium, designed by Sir Reginald Blomfield, was built of reinforced concrete faced with Euville stone and red brick. At the unveiling in 1927, Field Marshal Plumer of Messines stated:

---

38. Duchas (now Heritage Section, Dept. of Environment and Local Government) to author re *Ireland's memorial records,1914–1918*, 8 vols. (Dublin, 1923), published under the auspices of the Irish National War Memorial Committee. Copies may be consulted at various libraries, British Legion offices, the War Memorial Gardens, Islandbridge, Dublin 8 and CD-ROM (Dublin, 2005). The memorial there indicates 49,435 Irish war deaths, but that figure has been disputed, for example, by P.J. Casey in 'Irish casualties in the first world war', *Irish Sword*, xx, no. 81 (summer 1997), 193–204, which estimates a total of about 35,000; See also Keith Jeffery, *Ireland and the Great War*, on the Irish National Memorial, and for general background on memorials: Jane Leonard, 'Lest we forget', in D. Fitzpatrick (ed.), *Ireland and the First World War* (Dublin, 1986), pp. 64–67.

39. Author's correspondence with CWGC; and their information sheets and web site, www.cwgc.org.

One of the most tragic features of the Great War was the number of casualties reported missing, believed killed … and now it can be said of each one in whose honour we are assembled: he is not missing; he is here.

The Menin Gate memorial commemorates those from the corps and regiments of the United Kingdom and overseas forces, except those from New Zealand and Newfoundland, who fell in the Ypres salient before 16 August 1917, when the battle of Langemarck began. The names of over 54,000 officers and men are engraved on Portland stone panels, classified in alphabetical order under names of corps and regiments. Two Irish barristers are named at Menin Gate: Capt. Edmond Chomley L. Farran, 3rd Bn., attached to 2nd Bn., Royal Irish Rifles and William Alfred Lipsett, 10th Bn., 1st Canadian Infantry Division, Alberta Regiment.[40] The dead are recalled as heroes at the Menin Gate by many visitors, challenging and contradicting the words about that memorial written by the soldier-poet, Siegfried Sassoon:

Who will remember, passing through this Gate,
The unheroic Dead who fed the guns.

In Northern France, near Albert, the massive multi-arched Thiepval memorial, erected on sixteen legs leading to huge arches, bears witness to the tragic reality that many of those killed in the battle of the Somme in 1916 have no known graves. Many corpses were entirely lost in the pulverised battlefield, while other bodies found after the war could not be identified.[41] The Thiepval memorial was designed by Sir Edwin Lutyens in high empire style and built of brick and portland stone, between 1928 and 1932. The Prince of Wales unveiled the memorial in the presence of the French president in July 1932. Thiepval is also a battle memorial commemorating the Anglo-French offensive on the Somme in 1916. The Thiepval monument represents graves and headstones for over 72,000 named victims (listed according to regiments, mainly British) of the Somme slaughter including three Irish barristers: Lt. William Magee Crozier, 9th Inniskillings,

40. Names on the Menin Gate memorial were restored to make them legible, following the initiative of Pat Hogarty, RDFA. Its members attended the ceremony of the last post sounded by the local fire brigade, at the Menin Gate in September 2000 and remembered the Irish casualties, including Capt. Edmund Chomley L. Farran and William Alfred Lipsett. For reports of visit, see *The Blue Cap*, vol. 8, June 2001; Lipsett was also included in the Canadian Roll of Honour, featured in Christie, *For king and empire – 1*, p. 70.
41. Commonwealth (formerly Imperial) War Graves Commission, *Introduction to the register of the Thiepval Memorial France* (London, 1930); Geoff Dyer, *The missing of the Somme* (London, 1994 & 1995), especially pp. 126–29; CWGC information sheets; and web site, www.cwgc.org.

36th (Ulster) Division, killed on the first day of the Somme battle, 1 July 1916; Lt. Thomas Michael Kettle, 9th Dublins, 16th (Irish) Division, killed in action at nearby Ginchy on 9 September 1916; and Capt. Arthur Robert Moore, MC, 1st/4th City of London Bn., Royal Fusiliers, missing believed killed on the first day of the battle of the Somme, 1 July 1916. Non-fatal casualties at the Somme included Lt. M'Cartan H. Tighe, a barrister serving with the Leinster Regiment, and 2nd Lt. J.R. Moore, Royal Irish Rifles, son of William Moore, KC, MP.

Not far from the Thiepval memorial, the Ulster Memorial Tower was formally dedicated by Field Marshal Sir Henry Wilson on 18 November 1921.[42] The tower was modelled on Helen's Tower, 'a symbol and visible embodiment of filial love and maternal devotion', situated in the Clandeboye estate, near Belfast, where the Ulster Volunteers trained in 1914/15.[43] When the Ulster Tower was rededicated on 1 July 1989, Alice, duchess of Gloucester unveiled a plaque which includes St John's words 'Greater love hath no man than he lay down his life for his friends'. The Ulster Tower, Thiepval, commemorates the 36th (Ulster Division), which included Irish barristers killed in action: Lt. William Magee Crozier; and Capt. James C.B. Proctor, who both served with the Inniskillings; Capt. Arthur P.I. Samuels, 11th Royal Irish Rifles and Capt. George B.J. Smyth, 6th and 7th, Royal Irish Rifles. Near the Ulster Tower, the Mill Road cemetery contains the grave of Capt. James C.B. Proctor, 10th Inniskillings, a member of the Ulster Unionist Council and organiser of the Ulster Volunteers, who was killed on the first day of the Somme slaughter, 1 July 1916.

In Turkey, the Helles memorial, designed by Sir John Burnet, is a high obelisk remembering the Gallipoli campaign, 1915, and the men who died while serving in the British forces (and also some from the wider empire and commonwealth) in that campaign, and whose graves are unknown, or who were lost or buried at sea in adjacent waters.[44] In addition to names of

---

42. Jeffery, *Ireland and the Great War*, at pp. 107–09, explains the controversial background to the Ulster Tower, which is now managed by the Somme Association, Somme Heritage Centre, Newtownards, Northern Ireland; N. McMaster, *Flanders Fields: the 75th anniversary tape of the battle of the Somme* (Belfast, 1991), information about the Ulster Tower and its context.

43. G.F. Savage-Armstrong, *Poems: national and international* (Dublin, 1917), dedicated to Lt.-Col. F.S.N. Savage-Armstrong, DSO, Major W.H.K. Redmond, MP, and other brave Irishmen, at p. 82, 'Helen's Tower', the poet who died in 1906, refers prophetically to ' Love's message from the Living to the Dead.'

44. CWGC information sheet on the Gallipoli Peninsula, Turkey; and web site, www.cwgc.org.and also that of Imperial War Museum, www.iwm.org.uk; Holt, *Battlefield guide to Gallipoli*, pp. 93–101; John Lee, *A soldier's life: General Sir Ian Hamilton, 1853–1947* (London, 2000), which places the Helles memorial in context of the relevant campaign; Anthony P. Quinn, 'Gallipoli – where 4,000 were slaughtered'.

individuals, the names of relevant ships and titles of army units and formations are also inscribed on the Helles monument. It is both a battle memorial and a memorial to the individuals over whose bodies tombstones could not be erected.

On the surrounding walls of the Helles memorial, arranged in panels according to regiments, over 20,000 names are listed including six Irish barristers: Capt. Robert H. Cullinan, 7th Munsters, 10th (Irish) Division, killed in action on 8 August 1915, after the landing at Suvla Bay; Capt. Poole Hickman, D Company (Pals), 7th Dublins, 10th (Irish) Division, killed in action on 16 August 1915, while leading a bayonet charge at Kiretch Tepe Sirti/Kirectepe); Lt. Ernest Julian, also of the Dublin Pals, wounded while leading his men during the assault on Chocolate Hill (Yilghin Burnu), and died on 8 August 1916 on the hospital ship, *Valdivia*; 2nd Lt. Joseph B. Lee, 6th Munsters, killed on 7 August 1915 during an attack led by Major Jephson on Kiretch Tepe, at a peak subsequently known as Jephson's Post; 2nd Lt. John H.F. Leland, 5th (Flintshire) Bn., Royal Welsh (Welch) Fusiliers, killed in action on 10 August 1915 during an advance from Suvla Bay across the dried-up Salt Lake, near Scimatar Hill; Sub-Lt. Gerald Plunkett, Collingwood Bn., Royal Naval Division, shot in the head on 4 June 1915, while laughing and joking, as platoon leader, he gallantly led his men towards the Turkish trenches during the third battle of Krithia/Alcitepe.

Also named at Helles (and on the solicitors' memorial in Dublin) are: Robert Stanton, a solicitor from Cork, killed while serving with the 6th Dublins, and also two solicitors' apprentices who died in August 1915 while serving with the Dublin Pals: Capt. Michael J. FitzGibbon, son of John FitzGibbon, nationalist MP, and Sergeant Arthur C. Crookshank, son of barrister, Charles H. Crookshank. During the RDFA's visit to Gallipoli in August 2001, the author of this book laid a wreath at the Helles memorial to remember the Irish lawyers, including the six barristers, one solicitor and two solicitors' apprentices, named above.[45] Non-fatal casualties in Gallipoli included Capt. T.J.D. Atkinson, 31st Infantry Brigade, formerly a member of the North West Bar, and Lt. F.J.G. Battersby, 4th Royal Irish Fusiliers, son of T.S. Frank Battersby, KC.

Soldiers from both the Allied and Turkish sides are remembered in an inclusive and sensitive way on the Gallipoli peninsula at ANZAC Cove/Ari Burnu. On the Turkish memorial there, the magnanimous words of Kemal Ataturk, the military defender against the Allies in 1915 and later first president of Turkey, are inscribed:

---

45. *Bar Review*, journal of the Bar of Ireland, vol. 7, issue 1 (October/November 2001), p. 56.

Those heroes that (who) shed their blood and lost their lives, you are now lying in the soil of a friendly country. Therefore rest in peace. There is no difference between the Johnnies and the Mehmets (names symbolising soldiers from opposing sides) to us. Where they lie side by side, here in this country of ours. You, the mothers, who sent their sons from far-away countries, wipe away your tears. Your sons are now lying in our bosom, and are in peace. After having lost their lives on this land, they have become our sons as well.

In Iraq, the Allied memorial was originally sited within the Basra war cemetery but was moved by presidential degree in 1997. It was re-erected on the road to Nasiriyah, in the middle of an area which was a major battleground during the Gulf War and the Anglo-American coalition invasion in 2003. The Basra memorial consists of a roofed colonnade of white Indian stone, 80 metres long, and features an obelisk 16 metres high. The memorial records the names of more than 40,000 British, Indian and West African officers and men, killed in Mesopotamia and related areas of operation from 1914 to 1921. Remembered at Basra are two Irish barristers: 2nd Lt. Cornelius A. MacCarthy, 9th Dublins, who was drowned on 19 July 1917 when the *Eloby* was torpedoed and sunk by the Germans near Malta; and 2nd Lt. Herbert Tierney, 8th Bn., Cheshires, formerly of the Pals D Company 7th Dublins, who was reported missing on 9 April 1916, believed to be dead during an attack on Sannaiyat, while attempting to relieve General Townshend in Kut-el-Amara.

In summary, out of a total of twenty-five listed Irish barristers, thirteen, as outlined above, who have no known graves are named on the main collective memorials maintained by the CWGC, as follows: Menin Gate, Ypres/Ieper, two; Thiepval, Somme, France, three; Helles, Turkey, six; Basra, Iraq, two; and one is remembered on the smaller Hollybrook memorial at Chirley Road, Southampton.

Many educational institutions also recall their past pupils and alumni killed in the war. The hall of honour at Trinity College, Dublin was designed by Sir Thomas Deane to remember over 460 college members killed in the Great War who are named on memorial panels. The hall constitutes the entrance to the 1937 reading room which was opened by Eamon de Valera, president of the executive council of the Irish Free State. Recently, that reading room was converted to a postgraduate study area and access to the entrance hall and memorial was restricted.

When the hall of honour at Trinity College was originally opened on 10 November 1928, the orator was the vice-chancellor of Dublin University, Lord Glenavy, the former lord chancellor of Ireland, James Henry Mussen

Campbell KC, who had been involved in the initiatives for the Bar memorial.[46] His son Lt. Commander Philip S. Campbell, RNVR, was wounded in Gallipoli and killed in action in 1916 on the Western Front.

As indicated in chapter 2 on education and training and also in the biographical outlines in appendix 1, with notations and references, most of the Irish barristers who died in the Great War were Dublin University graduates or had connections with Trinity College as students or by military training through DU OTC. The most distinguished was Ernest L. Julian, Reid Professor of Law at Trinity, 1909–14, who is also remembered by the Julian prize which the Law School awards annually to the student achieving second place in the final undergraduate law degree examinations.[47]

The Trinity College War List (WDL), a paper record distinct from the hall of honour panels, also contains the names of most of the twenty-five Irish barristers.[48] Some are not listed, because their connections with TCD were indirect. For example, Tom Kettle, Willie Redmond, and Herbert Tierney, cannot be traced in college records as having been registered for, or awarded, Dublin University degrees. They are shown in King's Inns papers as having attended law lectures as external students at Trinity College during their studies to qualify as barristers. Gerald Plunkett was a graduate of Oxford where he is formally remembered at New College, but he trained with the Dublin University OTC, which gave him a Trinity connection although he is not on its war dead list.

Among the twenty-five Irish barristers who died in the war, only a few had no known affinity with Trinity College. Before studying at King's Inns, Frederick H. Lewin graduated from Oxford, where he is formally remembered at Merton College. John H. Edgar studied at Queen's College, Belfast, graduated from the Royal University of Ireland and London University and is named on the war memorial at Queen's University, Belfast (QUB). The QUB memorial also lists W.H. Davey, Tom Kettle's contemporary at the King's Inns in 1903–06. Presumably this refers to William Hamilton Davey,

46. *ILT&SJ*, lxii (1928), 276–77. On Remembrance Sunday, 9 November, 2003, history was made when the papal nuncio attended the war remembrance service at TCD, in the presence of the provost, Dr John Hegarty. The 1937 Reading Room has recently become a study hall for postgraduate students and the public do not have direct access to the front entrance area to view the Great War memorial.

47. *Dublin University calendar* published annually. Two subsequent Reid professors, Mary Robinson and Mary McAleese, became presidents of Ireland.

48. Information to author from Dr Gerald Morgan, TCD, who takes a very active interest in the *University of Dublin, TCD war dead list* (Dublin, 1922). While that list and the names on the panels in the hall of honour overlap, there are inconsistencies and omissions. For example, Cornelius MacCarthy, who was apparently omitted in error, should have been included because as a TCD student he was a college member, although no record of his graduation can be traced.

Northumberland Fusiliers, Tyneside Irish, who died on 28 September 1920 from a war-related illness. Apparently because that date was outside the usual memorial period, Davey is not listed on the Four Courts memorial, Dublin. Tom Kettle and Herbert Tierney are named in the war list and roll of honour of the National University of Ireland (NUI), University College, Dublin, published in 1919.

Prominent schools through their memorials, rolls of honour, school annuals and other publications have, as outlined below, recorded, to varying degrees, their old boys who 'made the ultimate sacrifice':

Robert B. Burgess and George B.J. Smyth, Portora Royal School, Enniskillen, Co. Fermanagh, which like the other schools in the United Kingdom as listed below, has impressive memorials and rolls of honour.[49] William Magee Crozier, Repton Public School, Repton, Derbyshire, England.[50] John H. Edgar, Campbell College, Belfast.[51] Thomas Michael Kettle, Hubert M. O'Connor, and William H.K. Redmond, Clongowes Wood College, Co. Kildare which, exceptionally for Roman Catholic schools, erected brass plates for remembrance.[52] Ernest L. Julian's name is engraved in stone on the large war memorial at Charterhouse School, Godalming, Surrey, England.[53] Frederick H. Lewin is commemorated at Cheltenham College, Gloucestershire, England.[54]

Martin M.A. Lillis attended Christian Brothers College (CBC), Cork. CBC, which although recording the names of its many past men who enlisted, consciously adopted a relatively neutral approach to protect the college's continuity. Therefore, CBC did not erect physical memorials to its past pupils who participated either in the European conflict or in the Irish

49. R.L. Bennett, MA, Dip.Ed., headmaster, Portora Royal School, Enniskillen, Co. Fermanagh, letters to author; and author's visit to the school through the courtesy of Lt.-Col. (retd.) Mark R.H. Scott, MBE, DL, Portora estate manager and trustee of the Inniskillings Museum, Enniskillen.

50. Russell Muir, Old Reptonian Society, Repton, Derby, England, to author; *The Reptonian*, school magazine, November 1916; and school war register.

51. Keith Haines, archivist, Campbell College, Belfast, to author.

52. Fr John Looby, SJ, archivist, Clongowes Wood College, Co. Kildare, letters to author about memorials in the college; *The Clongownian* (1915, 1917, 1918): articles on, and obituaries of Willie Redmond, Tom Kettle and Hubert O'Connor. The memory of those past pupils was overlooked in 'Clongowes: for the greater glory', True Life series documentary, RTE 1, 30 April 2001, which referred to distinguished alumni but outlined in a confused way John Redmond's connection with Clongowes.

53. Sue Cole, archivist, Charterhouse, Godalming, Surrey, letter to author.

54. Tim Pearce, secretary, the Cheltonian Society, Bath Road, Cheltenham, letters to author; entries in the college register; and extracts from *The Cheltonian*, especially roll of honour in the issue of March 1916; and also brass plates on memorial inside the college chapel cloister; Patrick Lewin, London, and Brigid Clesham, archivist, The Neale, Co. Mayo, to author, information on Lewin family.

struggle for independence.[55] William Alfred Lipsett, St Andrew's College, formerly at St Stephen's Green and Clyde Road, Dublin, now at Booterstown, Co. Dublin, to where the memorial was also moved.[56] Cornelius A. MacCarthy, St Vincent's (Castleknock) College, Dublin, where there is no physical memorial but names were recorded in annuals and history.[57] Gerald Plunkett, Belvedere (Jesuit) College, Dublin.[58] James C.B. Proctor, Reading School, Reading, Berkshire, England.[59] James Rowan Shaw, St Columba's College, Rathfarnham, Dublin.[60] Herbert Tierney, Belvedere (Jesuit) College, Dublin and Prior Park, Bath, England.[61] Sixty-four Belvederians including Gerald Plunkett, Joseph Mary Plunkett and Herbert Tierney, killed in twentieth-century military conflicts, were remembered at the school in November 2003, on a plaque unveiled by Dr Garret FitzGerald, former taoiseach. A book and video were also launched.

There are collective remembrances at various regimental museums, including those of the Inniskillings at Enniskillen Castle, Co. Fermanagh,

55. Jerome O'Donovan, Christian Brothers' College Past Pupils Union, Cork, to author; *The Collegian* (1917), showing a list of 295 past pupils serving at the war front, material republished in *Christians*, a celebration of one hundred years of CBC Cork, 1988, which includes 'The Great War', article by M.J. Cogan.

56. Fitzpatrick, *St Andrew's College, 1894–1994; St Andrew's College Magazine*, especially issue of Easter 1919, including a roll of honour; and memorial board at the college. A stone glass window, by Alfred Child (of An Tur Gloine, the Glass Tower art studio, inspired by the Celtic tradition and Irish revival), part of the original memorial, was not re-erected when the college was moved to Booterstown, Co. Dublin.

57. The late Dr Patrick O'Donoghue, CM, Castleknock College, Dublin to author; Murphy and Collins, *Nos autem: Castleknock College and its contribution*, pp. 106–10; *The Castleknock College Chronicle*, annuals for 1914–18, containing lists of past pupils in the British forces.

58. G. Conran, editor, *The Belvederian*, college annual, Belvedere College, Great Denmark Street, Dublin, to author. The college annual for 1916, at pp. 56–57 includes an obituary of Gerald Plunkett and an account of his career and premature death in the Dardanelles, on 4 June 1915. In contrast, the annual for 1917, while not overlooking the Great War, included appreciations of Gerald's half-nephew, Joseph Mary Plunkett, the mystic and poet who was executed after the Easter Rising. Also included was his mystic poem, 'I see his blood upon the rose', which ensured that his memory survived in independent Ireland where the combination of religion and nationalism was revered. See also Bowman and O'Donoghue (eds.), *Portraits: Belvedere College, 1832–1982*.

59. Kerr Kirkwood, Old Redigensian Association, Reading, Berks., England, to author.

60. Ninian Falkiner, St Columba's College, Rathfarnham, Dublin, to author; Peter Wyse Jackson and Ninian Falkiner, *A portrait of St Columba's College* (Dublin, n.d.).

61. Henry Tierney, Dublin, to author; *The Belvederian* (1917), at p. 68, obituary of Herbert S. Tierney paying tribute to 'his charm of manner and manly bearing reported missing, believed killed April, 1917, universally loved ... he was deeply regretted by a host of friends'; Arthur Crookenden, *A history of the Cheshire Regiment in the Great War, 1914–18* (Chester, 1939).

the Royal Irish Fusiliers in Armagh and the Royal Irish Rifles in Belfast, and in exhibitions, lectures and trips organised by groups such as associations for the Royal Dublin Fusiliers and the Connaught Rangers. The latter are remembered: in Galway in the Roman Catholic cathedral by a stained glass window depicting David and Goliath, in St Nicholas's, Church of Ireland, by memorials, and a museum display in King House, Boyle, Co. Roscommon. The Cheshire Regiment's roll of honour at the cenotaph in the regimental chapel of St George, Chester cathedral, remembers James Rowan Shaw and Herbert Tierney who both served with the Cheshires.[62]

A collective memorial to the Royal Naval Division (RND) (including Sub-Lt. Gerald Plunkett), in the form of a Lutyens fountain, was inscribed with crests of associated regiments including the Dublin Fusiliers. Quoted on the memorial is the first verse of Rupert Brooke's poem grieving lost youth, 'The dead':

> Blow out, you bugles over the rich Dead!
> There's none of these so lonely and poor of old,
> But, dying has made us rarer gifts than gold.
> These laid the world away; poured out the red
> Sweet wine of youth; gave up the years to be
> Of work and joy and that unhoped serene,
> That men call age; and those who would have been,
> Their sons, they gave, their immortality.[63]

Unveiling the RND memorial at the old Admiralty building, Horse Guards, London in 1925, Winston Churchill said that Brooke's words comforted the bereaved who found relief in the noble utterance, as its calm peace rose confidently above tumult and carnage. Churchill, who had been deeply involved in the Gallipoli débâcle, also spoke of the memorial fountain's waters of honour, healing and hope. During the Second World War the RND memorial was removed to the grounds of the Royal Naval College, Greenwich. The RND memorial was restored and returned to Horse Guards, Whitehall, in London's ceremonial centre, where it was rededicated in November, 2003. Winston Churchill, grandson of the former statesman, read Churchill's speech made at the original dedication in 1925. Rupert Brooke's poem was also recited.

62. Alan W. Gregson, Jnr, Western Front Association, Chester, to author.
63. Quoted with information about the RND memorial in Capt. Christopher Page, RN (rtd), 'The Royal Naval Division memorial to return to Horseguards', in *The Gallipolian*, no. 97, winter 2001–02, pp. 12–15; A.P. Quinn, *Seascapes*, RTE Radio 1, 9 January 2003 which mentioned G. Plunkett, radio talk; A.P. Quinn, articles in *Ireland's Own*, July 2003 and St Patrick's Day, 2004.

PLATES

1. William, John and William Archer Redmond at
Clongowes College Centenary, 1914.

2. F.H. Lewin at Cheltenham College, 1894.

3. Capt. F.H. Lewin.

4. Capt. F.H. Lewin's grave at Kilmaine, Holy Trinity churchyard, Co. Mayo.

5. Dr Patrick S. Walsh, KC, Donegal
recruiting staff and later judge in Cyprus
and chief justice of the Seychelles.

6. Lt. John Hammond Edgar.

7. Lt. John Hammond Edgar's grave at Railway Dugouts burial ground, Ieper.

8. Lt. Herbert S. Tierney.

9. Lt. Herbert S. Tierney's medals and scroll.

10. Capt. George B.J. Smyth.

11. Memorial to Tom Kettle, St Stephen's Green, Dublin, sculptor Albert Power.

THOMAS M.KETTLE
1880~1916
BORN IN COUNTY DUBLIN
9TH FEBRUARY 1880.
KILLED AT GUINCHY
9TH SEPTEMBER 1916.
POET. ESSAYIST. PATRIOT

12. The author at Willie Redmond's grave, Loker, Flanders.

13. Somme memorial, Thiepval, France.

14. Ulster Tower,
Thiepval, France.

15. Memorial to 16th (Irish) Division, Flanders.

16. Memorial, Portora Royal School, Enniskillen, Co. Fermanagh.

THESE MEMBERS OF
THE MIDDLE TEMPLE
GAVE THEIR LIVES IN
THE 1914—1918 WAR

G·A·Allan	E·P·Doyle
J·A·J·Baylis	G·C·Dyke
W·H·D·Bell	J·H·Edgar
N·M·Bruce	L·Ekin
J·L·Buckman	F·A·J·Ellicott
H·L·Burgess	E·N·A·Finlay
J·B·Burke	H·P·Fletcher
R·A·Casson	A·K·Gilmour
L·H·Centeno	C·R·Glyn
H·M·Clarke	R·S·Glyn
E·G·Cooper	J·S·Gregory
C·V·P·Cornelius	W·H·Hall
J·E·Crombie	R·H·M·Hands
T·W·David	C·H·Hart
G·B·Davies	A·D·Herbert
C·E·M·Dillon	W·S·Hern

17. Middle Temple memorial, Temple Church, London.

TO·THE·MEMORY·OF·THE·FALLEN
1914-1918
AMONGST·WHOM·WERE·NUMBERED·THE·FOLLOWING·MEMBERS
OF·THE·NORTH-EAST·AND·NORTH-WEST·CIRCUITS·OF·THE·IRISH·BAR

ROBERT·B·BURGESS
ROYAL·ENGINEERS
FLANDERS·9TH·DECEMBER·1915

WILLIAM·M·CROZIER
9TH·ROYAL·INNISKILLING·FUSILIERS
THE·SOMME·1ST·JULY·1916

JOHN·H·EDGAR
9TH·DURHAM·LIGHT·INFANTRY
YPRES·25TH·FEBRUARY·1915

JOSEPH·B·LEE
ROYAL·MUNSTER·FUSILIERS
GALLIPOLI·7TH·AUGUST·1915

JOHN·H·F·LELAND
5TH·ROYAL·WELSH·FUSILIERS
GALLIPOLI·10TH·AUGUST·1915

WILLIAM·A·LIPSETT
10TH·BATT·CANADIAN·CONTINGENT
YPRES·22ND·APRIL·1915

GERALD·PLUNKETT
ROYAL·NAVAL·DIVISION
GALLIPOLI·4TH·JUNE·1915

JAMES·C·B·PROCTOR
10TH·ROYAL·INNISKILLING·FUSILIERS
THE·SOMME·1ST·JULY·1916

ARTHUR·P·I·SAMUELS
11TH·ROYAL·IRISH·RIFLES
MESSINES·24TH·SEPTEMBER·1916

J·ROWAN·SHAW
CHESHIRE·REGIMENT
22ND·FEBRUARY·1915

GEORGE·B·J·SMYTH
2ND·ROYAL·IRISH·RIFLES
FLANDERS·22ND·OCTOBER·1918

NULLA·DIES·UMQUAM·MEMORI·VOS·EXIMET·AEVO

18. Bar memorial, Royal Courts of Justice, Belfast.

ROBERT B BURGESS	MARTIN A LILLIS
WILLIAM M CROZIER	WILLIAM A LIPSETT
ROBERT H CULLINAN	CORNELIUS A MACCARTHY
JOHN H EDGAR	EDMUND MEREDITH
EDMOND C FARREN	ARTHUR R MOORE
POOLE H HICKMAN	HUBERT M O'CONNOR
ERNEST L JULIAN	GERALD PLUNKETT
CECIL S KENNY	JAMES C B PROCTOR
THOMAS M KETTLE	WILLIAM REDMOND
JOSEPH B LEE	ARTHUR P I SAMUELS
JOHN H F LELAND	ROWAN SHAW
FREDERICK H LEWIN	GEORGE B J SMYTH

19. Memorial in Four Courts, Dublin to the Irish barristers who died in the Great War and are named on the bronze panel. Sculptor, Oliver Sheppard. Photo by Godfrey Graham, lighting by Jim Butler.

20. Detail of memorial, Trinity College Dublin.

21. Memorial to solicitors and apprentices, Four Courts,
Dublin, sculptor Oliver Sheppard.

D.U.B.C. Senior Eight 1902

J. Cunningham.   H. B. Mayne.   M. P. Leahy.   W. H. Pim.
(2)   (4)   (3)   (bow)

E. L. Julian.   R. C. Lehmann.   H. A. Emerson.   J. J. Usher.   J. deP. Langrishe.
(5)   (coach)   (Capt., 7)   (stroke)

E. Bate.

22. Ernest L. Julian, rowing at number 5, Dublin University Boat Club,
Senior Eight, 1902.

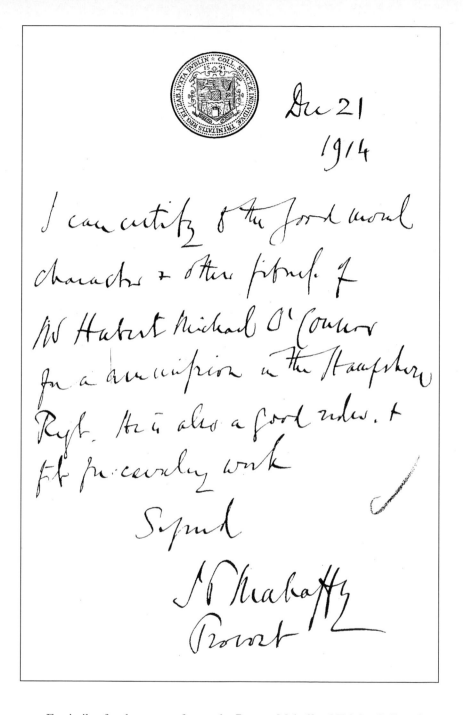

Dec 21
1914

I can certify of the good moral
character + other fitness of
Mr Hubert Michael O'Connor
for a commission in the Hampshire
Regt. He is also a good rider. +
fit for cavalry work

Signed

J P Mahaffy
Provost

23. Facsimile of a character reference by Provost Mahaffy of Trinity College for
Hubert Michael O'Connor.

The Collingwood Memorial is situated on the Downs, beside the A354, east of Pimperne, near Blandford, Dorset. That memorial is in memory of the commanding officer, officers and men of the Collingwood Battalion, RND, who, having trained on the Dorset Downs, fell in action on 4 June 1915 when the battalion was almost completely destroyed in Gallipoli.[64] Among those remembered collectively at the annual service each June at the Collingwood Memorial is Sub-Lt. Gerald Plunkett, baritone singer and musician, who was killed in action on 4 June 1915, while leading his men towards the Turkish trenches.[65] Gerald Plunkett's half-nephew, Joseph Mary Plunkett, poet and insurgency strategist, executed after the Easter Rising, is named on Oliver Sheppard's Cuchulainn memorial in Dublin. Joseph Plunkett is also remembered collectively at the nationalist Garden of Remembrance, Parnell Square, Dublin. Both Gerald and Joseph Mary Plunkett volunteered for military service but their distinct memorials recall their diverse routes to serve Ireland in the way they considered appropriate.

Collective Irish memorials were erected in various former battle-zones, including Wytschaete/Wijtschate, Belgium; Ginchy, Somme, France; Macedonia and Salonika/Thessaloniki in Greece. The 16th (Irish) Division are remembered in Guillemont, France by a Celtic cross and similar memorials at St Martin's cathedral, Ypres/Ieper and Etreux, recall the Munsters.

There are also personal memorials to individuals among the twenty-five Irish barristers who died in the Great War. The CWGC's charter, however, provides for only one official commemoration for each casualty, and additional private memorials or extra inscriptions on standard war graves must be financed by other means.[66] Apparently because of family preference, Willie Redmond's grave was placed just outside the official cemetery at Locre/Loker, Flanders, not far from the Irish Peace Park at Mesen/Messines. The grave is marked by a private memorial in the form of an impressive cross made from local stone and inscribed: Major W.H.K. Redmond, 6th

64. D.R. Saunders, Milford Haven, Pembrokeshire, Wales, to author; *The Gallipolian*, journal of the Gallipoli Association, ed. D.R. Saunders; articles and reports in that journal, especially spring 2000, autumn 2000 and spring 2001; Dr C.J. McCormack, Portlaoise, to author, information on Plunkett family.

65. Stanley Geary, *The Collingwood Battalion, Royal Naval Division* (Hastings, 1919), biographical notes of officers; for information on the Plunkett family, Moira Laffan, *Count Plunkett and his times* (1992); Sinead McCoole, *Guns and chiffon: women revolutionaries and Kilmainham Gaol* (Dublin, 1997), especially pp. 32–33 on Grace Gifford and Joseph Plunkett; Marie O'Neill, *Grace Gifford and Irish freedom: tragic bride of 1916* (Dublin, 2000), especially ch. 2, pp. 18–25, on Joseph Mary Plunkett; Elizabeth, Countess of Fingall, *Seventy years young, memoir* (London, 1937, Dublin, 1991) re Catholic branch of Plunkett family.

66. Barrie Thorpe, *Private memorials of the Great War on the Western Front*, The Western Front Association (Reading, Berks., 1999), pp. 1 and 2.

Bn., Royal Irish Rgt, killed in action, 7–6–17, RIP.[67] Soon after Willie Redmond's death in the methodical Allied victory at Messines, a delegation which included Nicholas Byrne, mayor of Wexford, Myles Keogh, high sheriff of Dublin, and Dr James Ashe, memorial committee secretary, visited the lonely grave at Locre/Loker. There they deposited Wicklow heather and also a sprig of shamrock from Vinegar Hill, Co. Wexford, a place hallowed in Irish nationalist memory since the Rising of 1798. A guard of honour from the Royal Irish Regiment and Inniskillings of the 36th (Ulster) Division reinforced the symbolism of Willie Redmond's blood sacrifice for Ireland and his idealistic, and perhaps over-optimistic aspiration for real unity of the Irish people, and reconciliation between Orange and Green. The grave is not so lonely now as many people visit Loker, Flanders, where Willie Redmond is a local icon and the Irish pub is named Redmonds.[68]

Redmond's death at Messines Ridge on the feast of Corpus Christi, 1917, and his title as chevalier of the Legion of Honour are also recalled by a memorial plaque at St Patrick's Roman Catholic church, Kilquade, near his Delgany home in Co. Wicklow. In Ireland such memorials are fairly rare in Catholic churches, compared with churches of other denominations.

A bronze bust of Willie Redmond, significantly in army uniform, was erected in a public park at Wexford town in 1931. The Wexford project was supported in Dublin at a public meeting in September 1917, at which the lord chancellor, Sir Ignatius O'Brien, presided. He praised Willie Redmond's qualities of personality, charm, ability and eloquence which could have placed him in the forefront of the legal profession.[69] The lord chancellor and the lord lieutenant were patrons of the memorial committee.

The sculptor of the Willie Redmond bust was Oliver Sheppard, who had executed the barristers' memorial at the Four Courts, Dublin and also

---

67. Ibid., pp. 95 and 96; Denman, *A lonely grave*, appendix A. Film and displays at the In Flanders Fields museum, and museum guide (1998), Ieper/Ypres, Belgium; Ian Passingham, *Pillars of fire: the battle of Messines ridge, June 1917* (Stroud, Glos., 1999), ch. 6, pp. 94–133, re phase one of battle, 7 June 1917, and pp. 107, 132–33 re death of William Redmond; Ian Passingham, lecture on Messines, RDFA, 2001; Tony Spagnoly and Ted Smith, *Salient points: cameos of the Western Front, Ypres, 1914–1918* (London, 1993), pp. 26–33. See plate 12.

68. Kevin Myers, 'An Irishman's diary', *Irish Times*, 14 March 2001 and A.P. Quinn's letter, 24 March 2001, in response to that column; A.P. Quinn, 'Remembering the Irish in World War One is relevant to peace and reconciliation', in *The Blue Cap*, vol. 8 (June 2001); see also Jeffery, *Ireland and the Great War*, pp. 63–64 and, specifically, the reference to Willie Redmond, remaining as an 'iconic figure for those who still profess faith in the reconciling power of war service'; on icons generally in that context, see L.W. McBride (ed.), *Images, icons and the Irish nationalist imagination* (Dublin, 1999).

69. Turpin, *Oliver Sheppard*, pp. 128–31; *ILT&SJ*, li (1917), 216–17.

nationalist monuments to the Risings of 1798 and 1916. At the unveiling of the Redmond bust on 31 May 1931, the all-Ireland dimension was symbolised by a park seat presented by the Ulster Division. Parliamentary nationalism and the Irish contribution in the Great War were the dominant themes of that formal occasion. It concluded with the participants singing the patriotic anthem, 'A nation once again', written by Thomas Davis (1814–45), the visionary of an inclusive, pluralist Ireland.

In the south aisle of St Ann's church, Dawson Street, Dublin, a stained glass window featuring St George and the archangels, by Wilhelmina Geddes, is inscribed:

> In memory of Ernest Lawrence Julian, 7th Dublin Fusiliers and of Robert Hornidge Cullinan, 7th Munster Fusiliers, who died for their country at Suvla Bay in August 1915. Both were members of the Irish Bar. This window was erected by some of their friends.[70]

The annual ANZAC Gallipoli commemorative service is held at St Ann's church, Dublin, in memory of Australian and New Zealand casualties in Gallipoli. Near St Ann's church, in the University and St Stephen's Green Club, there is a plaque recalling former members of the University Club killed in the war, including William M. Crozier, Arthur R. Moore, and James Rowan Shaw.

A bust of Tom Kettle, by the sculptor Albert Power, and cast in Brussels, was placed in the Royal Hibernian Academy in 1921 and later transferred to the National Gallery.[71] Due to controversy and fear of political repercussions about the proposed words 'killed in France' on the plinth, the bust in St Stephen's Green, Dublin was not erected until 1937. There was no formal unveiling ceremony. The eventual achievement of the memorial project's aim was mainly due to the determined efforts of Tom Kettle's fellow barrister and friend, William Fallon.[72] The inscription below the bust omits

70. Information leaflets about St Ann's church (Church of Ireland, Anglican), and visits to church, courtesy of Canon C.A. Empey. Wilhelmina Geddes (1887–1955) was a member of the distinguished art studio, An Tur Gloine, the Tower of Glass. Her works include the Duke of Connaught's war memorial window in St Bartholomew's church, Ottawa. Cf. A.P. Quinn, 'Anzac Day in Dublin', in *The Gallipolian*, autumn, 2002, pp. 17–18.
71. Lyons, *The enigma of Tom Kettle*, pp. 304–07; Myles Dungan, *Irish voices from the Great War* (Dublin, 1995), and *They shall grow not old: Irish soldiers and the Great War*, generally, and for more information about Tom Kettle and Willie Redmond.
72. A.P. Quinn, 'Wigs and guns', *Irish Law Times*, xviii, no. 6 (2000), pp. 90–92; Sighle Bhreathnach-Lynch, 'Commemorating the hero in newly independent Ireland', in McBride (ed.), *Images, icons and the Irish nationalist imagination*, pp. 159–60; OPW file, NA 2007, memorandum 14 July 1936, and National Library of Ireland, W.G. Fallon

to explain the Great War context but includes some of Kettle's enigmatic words from the renowned sonnet which he wrote to his daughter, Betty, shortly before his death in September 1916 near Ginchy, France, about dying 'not for flag, nor King, nor Emperor, but for a dream born in a herdsman's shed and the secret scripture of the poor'.[73] Betty Kettle, known as Mrs Elizabeth Dooley, who survived until December, 1996, aged 83, was the only offspring of any of the twenty-five barristers, listed as killed in the Great War, who could be traced from available knowledge. Most of those listed were not married. Another of the few married men, Willie Redmond, had no children.

That final poem of Tom Kettle, about dying for idealistic reasons, and religious rather than political motives, was a prime exemplar of the Christian perspective of war. It was also included in a memorial book, *Poems and parodies*, depicting the tragic hero, Kettle, in terms of John Milton's poetry: 'For Lycidas is dead, dead ere his prime Young Lycidas, and hath not left his peer'.[74] Lt. T.M. Kettle, Royal Dublin Fusiliers, was sensitive to the criticism that he would be remembered only as dying in a British Army officer's uniform while the leaders of the Easter Rising 1916 would become heroes and martyrs. Although critical of British military repression after the Rising, which resulted in the death of his brother-in-law Francis Sheehy Skeffington, T.M. Kettle, poet, professor and former MP for East Tyrone at Westminster, considered that the Irish rebels had spoiled his 'dream of a free and united Ireland in a free Europe'.[75]

T.M. Kettle is also included among the Irish officers and soldiers named on a bronze plaque in St Mary's Roman Catholic parish church, Haddington Road, Dublin. A new stained glass window in the Garrison Chapel, Cathal Brugha barracks, formerly Portobello barracks, Dublin by

Papers, MS 22,589; Josephine Power, daughter of Albert Power, sculptor, in conversation with author. See plate 11.

73. T.M. Kettle, *The day's burden and other essays*, p. 47; A.P. Quinn, *Irish Times*, 25 Sept. 2000, letter about the Kettle memorial in St Stephen's Green, Dublin, and criticising Duchas – the Heritage Service – for misquoting on a display stand the final line of Kettle's poem as 'the sacred scripture'.

74. Tim Cross, *The lost voices of World War I* (London, 1998), pp. 41–43; T.M. Kettle, *Poems and parodies*, preface by William Dawson (Dublin, 1916); Keith Jeffery, 'The great war in modern Irish memory' in T.G. Fraser and Keith Jeffery (eds), *Men, women and war*, (Dublin, 1993), p. 141

75. Denis Gwynn, 'Thomas M. Kettle 1880–1916', in *Studies*, lv, no. 220 (1966), pp. 384–91; current (2001) graduation literature at UCD names Francis Sheehy Skeffington as a famous past pupil but ignores his brother-in-law Tom Kettle; Eilis Ní Dhuibhne, 'Sources – Family values: the Sheehy-Skeffington papers in the National Library of Ireland', *History Ireland*, vol. 10, no. 1 (spring, 2002), pp. 14–18; Tom Burke 'In memory of Tom Kettle', pp. 3–10, in *The Blue Cap*, vol. 9 (Sept. 2002), includes extensive research from UCD archive LA 34.

the Royal Dublin Fusiliers Association in honour of the Dublin Fusiliers remembers Tom Kettle. The memory of Kettle also survives in the character, Hughes, and Mary Sheehy Kettle as Emma Clery in *Stephen Hero*, James Joyce's evocation of growing-up in Dublin.

Both Kettle and Willie Redmond are included in literary remembrance by the pacifist and poet George Russell, known as Æ. His poem connected the leaders of the two apparently opposing traditions, Irish participation in the Great War and involvement in the Easter Rising. In an accompanying letter to the *Irish Times*, Æ expressed concern at the increasing bitterness, 'a welter of hate', between the diverse steams of Irish life, and hoped that those 'who mourned their dead would not have to endure to hear scornful speech of those they loved'.[76] In an expanded and inclusive version of his eloquent poem 'Salutations', Æ paid tribute in alternate verses to the memory of those who fought for their country, both at home and abroad, outlined with relevant extracts as follows:[77]

> Here's to you, Pearse, your dream not mine,
> You who have died on Eastern Hills
> Or fields of France as undismayed …
> Thomas McDonagh, you paid the price
> You who have fought on fields afar,
> That other Ireland did you wrong
> Who said you shadowed Ireland's star,
> Nor gave you laurel wreath nor song …
> Equal your sacrifice may weigh,
> Dear Kettle, of the generous heart
> Oh, gallant dead
> This wreath, Will Redmond, on your clay

76. George Russell (Æ), letter to the *Irish Times*, 17 December 1917. The author was familiar with this material of Æ but an unexpected connection with one of the twenty-five listed barristers, Arthur Samuels, was provided by a copy of the relevant extract from the *Irish Times* in Trinity College Library, Dublin, Samuels Collection, papers 2/58. A.P. Quinn, ed. with additional material, *The golden triangle: the Æ commemorative lectures*, the Society for Co-operative Studies in Ireland (Dublin, 1989), pp. i–ii, iv, v, 11–20.

77. H. Summerfield, *That myriad minded man: Æ* (Gerards Cross, Bucks., 1975), pp. 186–87; D. Kiberd, *Inventing Ireland, the literature of modern Ireland* (London, 1995), ch. 13, 'The Great War and Irish memory', p. 240, quoted Æ's verses. M.O Dubhghaill, *Insurrection fires at Eastertide* (Cork, 1966), p. 332, published on the Easter Rising's 50th anniversary, quoted from 'Salutations' by Æ, ignoring his inclusive views towards diverse traditions. Colin Smythe Ltd, on behalf of Diarmuid Russell's estate, acknowledged for quotations here.

> Here's to you, men I never met,
> Yet hope to meet behind the veil …
> And sees the confluence of dreams
> That clashed together in our night,
> One river, born from many streams,
> Roll in one blaze of blinding light.

It was fashionable to dedicate books to the memory of personalities who died in the Great War. Some such volumes included the writings of the deceased, published posthumously. For example, *Trench pictures from France*, mainly consisted of articles which Willie Redmond had contributed to the *Daily Chronicle* under a pseudonym, and also contained a foreword by his widow, Eleanor Redmond, and a poem 'In memoriam' with a biographical introduction by E.M. Smith-Dampier.[78] Also included in that book of reflections from the trenches is Willie Redmond's last speech to the House of Commons on 7 March 1917. Dressed in a trench-stained army uniform, Redmond referred to past mistakes by the British authorities when justice was denied to Ireland. He pleaded for reconciliation between 'Ulstermen and Nationalists' and Home Rule for Ireland, on equal basis with Canada, Australia and New Zealand within the British Empire.[79]

Arthur P.I. Samuels, who was mortally wounded when shot through the head at Messines on 24 September 1916 while serving as a captain with the 11th Bn., Royal Irish Rifles (South Antrim Volunteers), kept extensive war diaries. They were published posthumously as a book, formally dedicated to the people of Ulster, 'in remembrance of those who gave their lives for their King and Country'. The book was inscribed as a written memorial to Arthur P.I. Samuels, formerly of Howth, Co. Dublin.[80] The book's editor and co-author was Arthur's widow, Dorothy Gage Samuels, née Young, from Culdaff, Co. Donegal, and Millmount, Randalstown, Co. Antrim.[81] After Arthur's death, and in memory of him, Dorothy Samuels served as a nurse in France until the end of the war.

The Pals at Suvla Bay, by Henry Hanna, KC, published in 1917, was dedicated as a 'memorial to our brave dead of D Company of the 7th Royal Dublin Fusiliers'.[82] That book, 'beautifully produced, and enriched by photographs and illustrations in colour', contains a Who's Who of the Pals with photographs and sketches, including those of Ernest L. Julian, Poole

---

78. Major William Redmond, *Trench pictures from France*.
79. Ibid., appendix, pp. 173–85.
80. Samuels, *With the Ulster Division in France*, quoted in Orr, *The road to the Somme*.
81. Samuels, ibid., dedication and preface.
82. Hanna, *The Pals at Suvla Bay*.

Hickman, both of D Company, Pals, 7th Dublins (both died in Gallipoli in 1915); and Herbert S. Tierney, formerly of the Pals, who was gazetted as 2nd Lt., 8th Bn., Cheshires in November 1914. Surviving Gallipoli, he was reported missing and presumed dead in Mesopotamia, April 1916.[83] The Pals of D company, the Footballers Company, mainly recruited from friends and colleagues in offices and in the Irish Rugby Football Union clubs, were also commemorated in a stone tablet at Lansdowne Road, Dublin.

A memorial book, published in 1923 on the distinguished graduate of Trinity College, Dublin, and Middle Temple student, Edmund Burke, was based on research by Arthur P. I. Samuels.[84] An introduction by his father Judge Samuels, of the Irish High Court, refers to Arthur as a talented scholar, barrister and army officer: terms which could aptly describe the other Irish barristers who died in the war –

> He was but one of the Innumerables – but one, too, of the many, many of his class-fellows and companions in Trinity College who fell in the Great War. The devoted generation of young Irishmen, such as he, trained and educated like him, and with aspirations such as his, has been almost exterminated. Whether there was to be left any longer a place for such as they in their native land is a question they have not had to solve. Perhaps this volume may be taken as some surviving service to his Country by one of them, who had tried in his time to serve her, and had hoped to serve her more.[85]

Irrespective of whether 'his country' is construed in nationalist terms of Home Rule or complete Irish independence, or in a wider European and imperial context, that tribute provides reasons to recall the memory of a generation of lost leaders. The full flowering of their talents was denied to Ireland because of their premature deaths.

Our heroes, a supplement to the magazine *Irish Life*, included photographs and biographical notes of Irish officers in both Irish and British regiments, who fell in action or who were mentioned for distinguished conduct.[86] Included are some Irish barristers listed among the twenty-five

83. *ILT&SJ*, li (1917), 168; Henry Tierney, speaking at Bar remembrance service, Four Courts, Dublin, 9 November 2001; O. Fallon, 'An Irishman's diary', re battles in Mesopotamia and siege of Kut-el-Amara, *Irish Times*, 22 March 2003; Major-General Sir Charles V.F. Townshend, *My campaign in Mesopotamia* (London, 1920).
84. Samuels, *Early life, correspondence and writings of Edmund Burke*.
85. Ibid., introduction, p. xi.
86. *Our heroes, Mons to the Somme*, originally published as a supplement to the magazine, *Irish Life*, Dublin, in 1916, reprinted no date shown, London Stamp Exchange Co., London, and Naval & Military Press, Uckfield, Sussex. Some subsequent issues of

dead: R.B. Burgess, R.H. Cullinan, J.H. Edgar, Poole H. Hickman, E.L. Julian, C. Stackpoole Kenny, J.H.F. Leland, J.C.B. Proctor, A.P.I. Samuels, Rowan Shaw, and also some barristers who survived the war, such as Lt. Samuel Spedding John, MC, 9th Bn., Cheshires. Increased interest by local historical societies throughout Ireland, from Dublin to Donegal, is expressed in exhibitions, research and publications, some containing information on lawyers.[87]

As outlined above, there is an impressive range of memorials which, often in the role of surrogate graves, record the names of the Irish barristers who died in the Great War. Most of the various memorials date from the immediate post-war period. The extent to which the Irish war casualties were remembered in the wider context has been subject to much analysis and re-evaluation in recent years by historians, the media and politicians.[88]

The memorial and roll of honour at St Andrew's College, Dublin is an example of the effect of history on attitudes and practices. That college memorial, which had been covered with Union flags, was unveiled during an uneasy Anglo-Irish truce on St Andrew's Day, 30 November 1921, when Revd John Bernard, provost of Trinity College Dublin, linked imperial service and citizenship with the concept of the Irish identity.[89]

Within a few years, however, public ambivalence towards the Irish victims of the Great War influenced the mood at St Andrew's College. Its annual remembrance service continued, but became more private and circumspect to avoid provocation to republicans or to provide a platform for imperialists; but some pacifist and nationalist sentiments were expressed at later commemorations.[90] In general, Roman Catholic schools in Ireland did not sustain much interest in commemorating their past pupils who served in the Great War. The mood contrasted with that in Britain where, according to a

Irish Life also contained pictures and biographies of Irish officers who served with distinction or died in the Great War. Included also were solicitors, such as Capt. William Reeves Richards, 6th Bn., Dublins, Law Society gold medallist, killed in action at the Dardanelles, 15 August 1915. Extracts from *Irish Life* were received by author from Gerald O'Brien, Skibbereen, D. Byrne, Dublin (who found copies of that magazine discarded as rubbish in a skip), and Frank Liston, Wirral.

87. See, for example, *Dun Laoghaire Journal*, and especially no. 9 (2000), 'Wigs and guns', article by A.P. Quinn, pp. 43–49, outlining the local connections of six Irish barristers from the list of twenty-five dead: R.B. Burgess, W.M. Crozier, J.H.F. Leland, J.B. Lee, M.M.A. Lillis, and W.A. Lipsett; Cronin, 'South county Dublin and east Wicklow during the 1914–18 war'; Dermot Kennedy, 'Local heroes of the 1914–1918 war', lecture publications no. 23 (1986) and 41 (1999) respectively, Foxrock Local History Club, Co. Dublin.

88. See, for example, Keith Jeffery, *Ireland and the Great War*, especially p. 135, quoting speech by Sean Lemass, as taoiseach, at King's Inns, Dublin in February, 1966, in which he re-evaluated Ireland's engagement with the Great War.

89. Fitzpatrick, *St Andrew's College, 1894–1994*, pp. 67–68.

90. Ibid.

recent critical analysis, 'public schools, universities and aristocratic families all maintained a cult of the dead'.[91]

Remembrance is also expressed by relevant families and the wider public who collect British army service medals. Everyone serving in a war zone received both the war and victory medals. They were sent to the appropriate surviving family members of those killed in battle, together with circular bronze next-of-kin plaques inscribed with 'He died for Freedom and Honour'. Accompanying letters from King George V stated simply: 'I join with my grateful people in sending you this memorial of a brave life given for others in the Great War.' Those who fought in 1915 also received the 1914 Star, and men of Kitchener's army in the early months of the conflict received the 1914 Star, sometimes called erroneously the Mons Star.[92] The earlier mood of national amnesia, neglect and antagonism towards Irish memories of the war has been overtaken in recent years by more positive and mature attitudes, expressed by national and other leaders, including two barristers in their role as president of Ireland, Mary Robinson and Mary McAleese, and also by Bertie Ahern, TD, as taoiseach. All three are honorary benchers of the King's Inns.

The barristers with Ulster connections are remembered at the annual armistice day service in the Royal Courts of Justice, Belfast. Irish barristers are also remembered annually at collective ceremonies: the National Day of Commemoration each July, and in November at the Irish War Memorial Gardens, Islandbridge, Dublin; and at the ecumenical service at St Patrick's cathedral, Dublin; and each June at the wreath-laying parade for the Irish regiments at the Cenotaph, Whitehall, London. Visits by Irish groups, for example, by the RDFA and the Connaught Rangers Association to the battle sites of the Great War and the Irish Peace Park at Mesen/Messines, on the Western Front and to Gallipoli provide remembrance opportunities.[93]

The twenty-five dead barristers from Ireland are remembered specifically at the annual ecumenical ceremony at the Bar memorial in Dublin's Four Courts. That remembrance occasion adopts an inclusive perspective of reconciliation. It recalls diverse religious, political traditions which include barristers who died in the Great War from opposite sides of the spectrum,

91. Richard Vinen, *A history in fragments: Europe in the twentieth century* (London, 2000), p. 85.
92. Patrick J. Casey, Blackrock, Co. Dublin, and R.W. O'Hara, Kew, to author.
93. On the RDFA visit to Flanders and the Somme, September 2000, in which the author participated, Willie Redmond, Tom Kettle, and James C.B. Proctor were specifically named and remembered. Speech by An Taoiseach, Bertie Ahern, TD, at State reception in honour of the RDFA, Dublin Castle, 26 April 2001 and article by A.P. Quinn, 'Remembering the Irish in World War One is relevant to reconciliation and peace', *The Blue Cap*, vol. 8, June 2001, pp. 27–28.

such as James C.B. Proctor, a Protestant Ulster unionist-organiser, and the poet-patriot, Tom Kettle, a Roman Catholic Irish nationalist of the constitutional parliamentary tradition.

Lines from Laurence Binyon's poem, 'For the fallen', quoted on remembrance occasions, are particularly apt for the Irish lawyers cut off in the prime of life during the Great War:

> They shall grow not old, as we that are left grow old:
> Age shall not weary them, nor the years condemn.
> At the going down of the sun and in the morning
> We will remember them.[94]

---

94. Laurence Binyon, 'For the fallen', originally published in *The Times*, London, 21 September 1914, included in Robert Giddings, *The war poets* (London, 1988), pp. 16–19. Verses from that standard epitaph are quoted at military funerals and remembrance events, occasionally in an Irish language translation. Vera Brittain called the poem, 'Binyon's direful dirge for the fallen' in her letter to Roland Leigton, quoted in A. Bishop and M. Bostridge (eds), *Letters from a lost generation*, p. 177.

EPILOGUE

Vindication and reconciliation

HISTORICAL REVISIONISM takes different forms. After the Great War, British reaction to massive losses and millions of casualties led to inevitable disillusion. Soldiers were praised for their bravery, generals were blamed for incompetence and the term, 'lions led by donkeys', became a cliché.[1] The first of July was remembered, not only as the anniversary of the start of the Somme battle, but also because of Field Marshal Haig's incompetence as 'the butcher of the Somme'. In recent years, the pendulum has swung back in the other direction. In particular, Gary Sheffield, a military historian, concluded that although the Great War was a tragic conflict, it was neither futile nor meaningless.[2] Sheffield refutes assumptions about the futility of war and justifies the Allied war effort and eventual victory as essential in defence of democracy. Some of his arguments are convincing, but the jury of public opinion is still out on definitive conclusions and attitudes fluctuate.

In Ireland, enlightened attitudes have restored the Great War to national memory. The Belfast agreement and the peace process provided a fresh start for relations between differing traditions in Ireland and Britain, North-South and East-West. In that context, the inclusive ideals and aspirations expressed in writings and speeches of Willie Redmond and Tom Kettle find a new resonance in current Anglo-Irish relations.

History illustrates that there were faults and wrongs on all sides at personal and national levels. Redmond's final speech as an MP in the Westminster parliament before he died on Flanders fields in 1917, although made in the context of Home Rule and the Great War, is still relevant:[3]

1. Alan Clarke, *The donkeys* (London, 1961, Pimlico ed., 1991), quoting from Field Marshal von Falkenhayn, *Memoirs*, refers to the German General Erich Ludendorff saying 'The English soldiers fight like lions' and Hoffman replying 'True. But don't we know that they are led by donkeys.'
2. Sheffield, *Forgotten victory: the First World War, myths and realities* (London, 2001).
3. Major Willie Redmond, MP, final speech at Westminster, 7 March 1917, quoted in Denman, *A lonely grave*, pp. 106–11; Redmond, *Trench pictures from France*, pp. 173–85.

> I represent the wishes nearest to the hearts of Irishmen who went with me and their colleagues to France, many of whom will never return. Mistakes – dark, black, and bitter mistakes – have been made (in Anglo-Irish relations). A people denied justice, the redress of which has been long delayed. A newer and better chapter with Great Britain was about to be opened. There is nothing (we) most passionately desire than there should be an end of this old struggle between the North and the South. We all desire to make our country happy and contented.

Tom Kettle, in a final plea for reconciliation, wrote that if he lived he intended to call his next book, 'The two fools: a tragedy of errors'.[4] Kettle visualised harmony between soldiers of diverse traditions in a free Ireland. Later, during the official celebrations in 1966 for the fiftieth anniversary of the Easter Rising, the climax of Brian Boydell's musical tribute, 'A terrible beauty is born,' included lines from Kettle's poem, 'Cancel the past':

> Bond, from the toil of hate we may not cease,
> Free, we are free to be your friend.[5]

In the new millennium, detailed research has provided definitive proof of German atrocities in Belgium at the beginning of the Great War.[6] Therefore, vindication has been provided retrospectively for the attitudes and actions of Willie Redmond and Tom Kettle and also the other Irish who donned the khaki in defence of Belgium against German aggression.

In 1998, An Taoiseach, Mr Bertie Ahern, TD, unveiled a plaque at the Four Courts, Dublin in memory of the barristers involved in the 1798 Rising. Reflecting inclusive attitudes, the same people often participate in the annual remembrance ceremonies for both the '98 Rising and First World War. Particularly relevant is the poet Æ's theme of inclusive commemoration in 'Salutations,' examined in chapter 3, and summarised as follows:

> One river, born from many streams,
> Roll in one blaze of blinding light.

4. Kettle, *The day's burden* (Dublin, 1968), p. 21.
5. Jeffery, *Ireland and the Great War*, p. 136; Dept. of Foreign Affairs, *Cuimhneachán* (Dublin, 1966), p. 47.
6. John Horne and Alan Kramer, *German atrocities 1914 – a history of denial* (New Haven, CT, 2001), and review by Kevin Myers, *Irish Times*, 'Weekend', 1 December 2001 and comment by Dr Gerald Morgan, 'The legacy of Tom Kettle', letter, *Irish Times*, 11 December 2001; 'Crucified soldier', TV documentary, Channel 4, showing proof of German atrocities in Belgium and France.

The mood is now opportune to commemorate formally at the Four Courts other barristers of the Irish nationalist tradition, including Daniel O'Connell but especially the three Ds: Thomas Davis, John Blake Dillon and Charles Gavan Duffy.[7] Over a century and a half ago, Davis and his Young Ireland colleagues had a remarkable vision of an inclusive Irish nation. In the traditional republican context, the Irish Bar should remember Patrick Pearse, leader of the Easter Rising, 1916. A co-ordinated approach is necessary to commemorating Irish lawyers of various strands and traditions, including those killed in the Great War.

Diverse and apparently conflicting Irish legacies were linked during 2001 at ceremonies for the reburial of a republican executed by British authorities during the War of Independence. In his graveside oration, John O'Donoghue, TD, then Minister for Justice, Equality and Law Reform, asserted:[8]

> Patrick Maher and his comrades (including Kevin Barry) chose an honourable path to fight for the right of Ireland to be free. We remember too, the many Irishmen who choose another courageous path, whose motives are summed up in the enigmatic words of another Irishman, Thomas Kettle:
>
> > Know that we fools, now with the foolish dead,
> > Died not for flag, nor King, nor Emperor,
> > But for a dream, born in a herdsman's shed,
> > And for the secret scripture of the poor.

The Justice Minister continued:

> Thomas Kettle died at the battle of the Somme along with thousands of Irishmen, many of them Nationalists and Volunteers, who fought together for the rights of small nations. We do not belittle the memory of those brave men by honouring a comrade, a fellow countryman, who followed his own conscience and who fought to defend the liberty of this small nation.

7. Brendan O'Cathaoir, in *John Blake Dillon, Young Irelander* (Dublin, 1990) describes at p. 11 a meeting between Davis, Dillon and Duffy at the Four Courts in spring 1842. The three young men took off their Bar gowns and strolled to the Phoenix Park to discuss their New Ireland projects, specifically a newspaper, the *Nation*. See generally, Richard Davis, *The Young Ireland movement* (Dublin and Totowa, NJ, 1987).

8. John O'Donoghue, TD, then Minister for Justice, Equality and Law Reform, graveside oration at Ballylanders, Co. Limerick, 19 October 2001, during the reburial of the remains of Patrick Maher, one of the 'Forgotten Mountjoy ten', notably Kevin Barry, executed by the British authorities during the War of Independence, 1920–21, quoted in Carey, *Hanged for Ireland*, pp. 204–13; A.P. Quinn, letter, *Irish Times*, 28 March 2002.

In June 2004, representatives of diverse traditions attended a conference at the International School for Peace Studies in Mesen (Messines), Belgium. At the associated remembrance service in the Irish Peace Park to honour the Irish from North and South who were killed alongside each other in Flanders during the First World War, President McAleese referred to 'a shared memory that we didn't share, forgot to share for almost 90 years'. The sacrifice of nationalists who fought in the British Army had not been properly respected, said the President.[9] She spoke on the 7th of June, the anniversary of Willie Redmond's death in 1917 at the battle of Messines.

This book should help to remember the Irish role, especially of lawyers, in the First World War.

9. *Irish Times*, report by Tim King, 8 June 2004. Representatives of the RDFA, including the author, attended the service.

Barristers' biographies

Biographical information on Irish barristers who died in the Great War.

Robert (Bobbie) Balderston Burgess

Born 25 December 1891.

Parents Henry Givens Burgess, Irish Manager of LMS Railway Co., and Agnes Burgess.

Address Eglinton House, Eglinton Park, Kingstown/Dun Laoghaire, Co. Dublin; 6R Bickenhall Mansions, Gloucester Place, Portman Square, London.

Religion Church of Ireland.

School Portora Royal School, Enniskillen, Co. Fermanagh, 1905–09, where he played rugby for the unbeaten Portora team, 1908/09, recalled by photographs on display in that school.

University Dublin, TCD. BA, Aestiva 1913.

Legal career King's Inns, Dublin. Admitted as student: 1910. Called to Bar: Hilary term, 1914.

Legal practice North East circuit but had a limited time to practise because he enlisted soon after being called to Bar.

Army career Enlisted: November, 1914. Unit: Inland Water Transport, Royal Engineers. Rank: Captain. Service: Western Front, France. At the outbreak of the Great War, he undertook special work for the French government. Served in casualty depot, North Wall, Dublin, during mobilisation in 1914 and was a second lieutenant in Army Service Corps.

Died 10 December 1915, aged 24, in no. 2 casualty clearing station after a shell burst as he was cycling through rue de Dunkerque at Armentiers, France.

Grave Bailleul communal cemetery extension, Nord, France, CWGC ref. CR 285, II.B.63, near the Belgium border, 14.5 km. south of Ypres/Ieper.

Memorials Named: Four Courts, Dublin; TCD, WDL no. 55; IMR; Royal Courts of Justice, Belfast; *Our heroes*, p. 178; roll of honour for Rugby internationals, London, 1919; roll of honour and memorial at Portora Royal School, Enniskillen, Co. Fermanagh; PRO, WO 339/14609; *Dublin Book of Honour*, 2003

Remarks Bobbie Burgess played rugby for Portora School, the Barbarians, DU and Ireland. Of splendid physique, he was one of 130 Rugby internationals, including ten Irishmen, who died in the Great War. He played cricket and was also a salmon angler, a good shot and keen rider to hounds.

Publications Mentioned in Solomons, *One doctor and his time*, pp. 96 and 172.

William Magee Crozier

Born 5 December 1875.

Parents Francis Rawdon (also shown as Rawton) Moira Crozier, solicitor and Catherine Sophia Magee. There was a family connection with patriot William Smith O'Brien (1803–64).

Address Carrickbrennan, Monkstown, Co. Dublin; and 19 St Stephen's Green, Dublin.

Religion Church of Ireland.

School 1886–92 attended Repton, a public school in Derbyshire, England, where he gained an entrance exhibition and had a very successful career. He played cricket and football, got a cap of honour and 1st XI colours. Loyal to his school, he was a founder member of Irish branch of Old Reptonian Society.

University Dublin, TCD. Exhibition winner and scholar, played cricket and soccer for DU. BA, Verna 1897.

Legal career King's Inns, Dublin. Admitted as student: 1895. Called to Bar: Michaelmas term, 1898.

Legal practice North East circuit.

Army career Enlisted: August 1914 as second lieutenant. Unit: 9th Bn., Royal Inniskilling Fusiliers (Tyrone volunteers), 36th (Ulster) Division, 109th Brigade. Rank: Lt. from 10 October 1914. Service: Western Front, France, 1915–16. Crozier was aged 40 when he enlisted but was recommended because he had drilled with the Loyal Dublin Volunteers and was regarded as 'a gentleman of quite the right stamp ... an active keen man preferable to a boy from the OTC'. He also had been a member of DU OTC, TCD.

Died 1 July 1916, aged 42, at Thiepval, posted missing on first day of the Somme offensive, when the 36th (Ulster) Division suffered severe losses.

Grave No known grave.

Memorials Named at: Four Courts, Dublin; TCD, WDL no. 96; Kildare Street and University Club, St Stephen's Green, Dublin; IMR; Royal Courts of Justice, Belfast; Repton School memorial and magazine, November, 1916; Thiepval, France, ref. M 21, 4D, 5B. PRO, WO 339/21334; *Dublin Book of Honour*, 2003.

Remarks Played golf at Foxrock, Dublin and won tankards.

Robert Hornidge Cullinan

Born 9 August 1881.

Parents John Cullinan, solicitor, and Martha Frances Faris, daughter of the Revd. Francis Faris.

Address 6 Bindon Street, Ennis, Co. Clare.

Religion Church of Ireland.

School The Abbey, Tipperary Grammar School.

University Dublin, TCD. Senior Erasmus Smith exhibition; prizeman and gold medallist in history and political science; Senior Moderator, BA, 1903; record secretary of the College Historical Society (the Hist debating society); member of DU Rugby Club.

Legal career King's Inns, Dublin. Admitted as student: 1901. Called to Bar: Trinity term, 1904.

Legal practice The Cullinans were an influential family in Co. Clare where Robert's father was a solicitor and his uncle a prominent barrister. Robert practised on the Munster circuit.

Army career Enlisted: November, 1914 and commissioned as captain. Unit: C Company, 7th Bn., Royal Munster Fusiliers, 30th Brigade, 10th (Irish) Division. Service: Sailed with the 7th (Service) Bn., from Liverpool to Malta. Disembarked from the *Rowan*, 6 August 1915 at Suvla Point, Gallipoli. Member of DU OTC, TCD. He was regarded as an outstanding officer in the Munster Fusiliers.

Died 8 August 1915 (War Diary shows 9 August), aged 34, in action after the landing in Suvla Bay, killed almost instantaneously from bullet wounds in an advance during important reconnaissance on eastern side of Kiretch Tepe/Kirectepe ridge when C Company was unable to make headway against severe fire from the Turkish trenches.

Grave No known grave.

Memorials Named at: Four Courts, Dublin; TCD, WDL no. 97; IMR; *Our heroes*, p. 116; stained-glass window by Wilhelmina Geddes, and plaque commemorating R.H. Cullinan and E.L. Julian in St Ann's church (Church of Ireland), Dawson Street, Dublin ; roll of honour, Free and Accepted Masons of Ireland, lodge 60, Ennis, Co. Clare; Helles Memorial, Turkey, CWGC ref. MR 4.4. Munsters' panels 185–190; roll of honour, in R.W. Walker, *To what end did they die: officers died at Gallipoli*; PRO,WO 339/18517.

Remarks 2nd Lt. F.E. Bennett, a Corkman, was killed aged 19, when he stood up to help Capt. Cullinan. According to Major Hendricks, Capt. Cullinan 'died, as he had lived, a noble hero, thinking of his men rather than himself'.

John Hammond Edgar

Born 23 October 1879, Belfast.

Parents Robert Smyth Edgar, merchant, and Eliza Jane Jardine.

Address 15 Cliftonville Avenue, Belfast and Dromore, Co. Down; 4 Powis Gardens, Bayswater, London.

Religion Presbyterian.

School Campbell College, Belfast, register no. 273, 1895–97 and played on cricket XI, 1897.

University Queen's College, Belfast, Royal University of Ireland (law, history and political science), and London University. BA (Hons & Exhib) RUI, 1900, MA (Hons & Studentship) 1900; Law scholar, Queen's College, Belfast; LLB London University 1904; read a paper on 'The depopulation of Ireland' at the British Association, 1902; exceptionally for the twenty-five listed barristers who died in the war, he had no known connection with TCD.

Legal career King's Inns, Dublin; admitted as student 1901; called to Irish Bar, Michaelmas term, 1904, 2nd place and exhibition in final examination. Middle Temple, London; admitted as a student 1902; called to the English Bar, 26 January 1905, 3rd place and honours in final examination.

Legal practice Brooke scholar at King's Inns, 1904; Murphy prizeman, Middle Temple; member of Irish and English Bars, practised on North East circuit, Ireland,

and at Newcastle-on-Tyne, England where he was a member of the Pen and Palette Club and a capital oarsman at the Tyne Rowing Club.

Army career Volunteered on outbreak of war. Unit: 9th Bn. (Territorial), Durham Light Infantry (battalion history, Harry Moses, *Gateshead Gurkas* (Durham 2001)). Rank: Lt. Commissioned as second lieutenant on 3 November 1914 and promoted lieutenant shortly afterwards. Service: Western Front, France and Belgium. Went to France, May 1915. Survived bomb explosion at the end of 1915. According to Lieut.-Col. Henderson, John H.Edgar 'was a good and kindly officer, kind to his men, greatly respected by all'.

Died 24 February 1916, aged 36, of shell wounds in the back of neck, after the 9th Bn., Durham Light Infantry had relieved the 8th Bn. in the front line trenches 37–41, Hill 60, Ypres salient. It was very cold and snow fell.

Grave Railway Dugouts Burial Ground (Transport Farm), Zillebeke, Ypres/Ieper, West Flanders, Belgium, CWGC ref. I.M.27.

Memorials Named at: Four Courts, Dublin; IMR; Royal Courts of Justice, Belfast; Temple Church, north side, London and on Middle Temple roll of honour, London, (archive ref. MT 3/ROH/1); Queen's University, Belfast; Campbell College war memorial, Belfast, and photograph in Central Hall of that college; *Our heroes*, p. 198; de Ruvigny roll of honour; PRO, WO 95/2840, 9th Durhams' war diary.

Remarks John H. Edgar was the only one of the twenty-five barristers listed on the memorial at the Four Courts, Dublin who was called to both the Irish and English Bars. Two others, Gerald Plunkett and Willie Redmond, enrolled as students at the Inns of Court, London (Inner Temple and Middle Temple, respectively) but there are no records of their call to the English Bar.

Edmond Chomley Lambert Farran

Born 2 October 1879.

Parents Edmond Chomley Farran, gentleman and Anne Hume Ryan.

Address Knocklyon House, Templeogue, Co. Dublin.

Religion Church of Ireland.

School Dr Benson's, Rathmines School, Dublin.

University Dublin, TCD. Prizewinner in law; BA, Aestiva 1902; LLB, Hiemalis 1902.

Legal career King's Inns, Dublin. Admitted as student: 1901. Called to Bar: Hilary term, 1904.

Legal practice Certificate of Honour, King's Inns, 1903. Munster circuit. Co-author of *The law relating to purchase of land* (Dublin, 1903–4, and supplement, 1906) with R.A. Walker.

Army career Enlisted: September 1914, on recommendation of Lt.-Col. T.V.P. McCammond, commander 3rd reserve Bn., Royal Irish Rifles, after earlier rejection due to being considered too old at 34. Unit: 3rd Bn., attached to 2nd Bn., Royal Irish Rifles. Rank: Captain. Service: Western Front, Belgium. He had been a member of South of Ireland Imperial Yeomanry and DU OTC, TCD. Reached France on 28 April 1915 and was attached to the Northumberland Fusiliers when serving in Belgium.

Died 16 June 1915, aged 35, killed in action while serving with C & D companies, 2nd Bn., Royal Irish Rifles, during bombardment at Bellewaarde Spur, near Hooge and Ypres/Ieper, Belgium. After an assault under Capt. Farran and Lt. C.H.H. Eales, the companies had re-organised and withdrawn but again attacked. Capt. Farran, a gallant leader, was wounded and reported missing, presumed dead. Reports to his family from colleagues suggest that he was shot by German machine gun fire while returning to the trenches and was found dead by two men who went looking for him. There were over 300 Allied casualties in the action, including dead and wounded (2nd Bn., Royal Irish Rifles, War Diary, extracts courtesy of James Taylor, Wexford).

Grave No known grave.

Memorials Named at: Four Courts, Dublin; TCD, WDL no. 133; IMR; Menin Gate, Ypres/Ieper, Flanders, Belgium, panel 40, CWGC ref. MR 29. Lectern at St Maelruan's church (Church of Ireland), Tallaght, Co. Dublin; PRO, WO 339/58010; *Dublin Book of Honour*, 2003.

Remarks A keen trout and salmon fisherman, he returned from fishing at Bandon, Co. Cork, to enlist in the army at the outbreak of the Great War. The surname is incorrectly spelt on the Four Courts memorial, Dublin, as Farren.

Poole Henry Hickman

Born 8 June 1880.

Parents Francis William Gore Hickman, deputy lieutenant, gentleman, and Elizabeth O'Brien.

Address Family: Kilmore, Knock, near Kilrush, Co. Clare. Self: 25 South Frederick Street, Dublin, Vaughans Hotel, 29 Rutland (now Parnell) Square, and 23 Earlsfort Terrace, Dublin.

Religion Church of Ireland.

School The Abbey, Tipperary Grammar School.

University Dublin, TCD. BA, Hiemalis, 1902.

Legal career King's Inns, Dublin. Admitted as student: 1906. Called to Bar: Easter term, 1909.

Legal practice Awarded an exhibition at King's Inns, and medal for legal debate at the Law Students' Debating Society. Some of his extended family were solicitors, practising as Kerin and Hickman, Ennis. He was honorary secretary and treasurer of the Munster Bar. 'His short legal career was full of promise and he was highly esteemed by his colleagues', according to *Our heroes; Mons to the Somme*, supplement to *Irish Life* (24 September 1916).

Army career Enlisted: September 1914. Unit: D Company (Pals), 7th Bn., Royal Dublin Fusiliers, 10th (Irish) Division, 30th Brigade. Rank: Captain. Service: Gallipoli. Member of DU OTC, TCD; gazetted as lieutenant, 7th Dublins and promoted captain in January, 1915. As commanding officer of D company, Pals, 7th Dublins, he led them as they marched from Royal (Collins) Barracks to the ferry at North Wall, Dublin on 30 April 1915 en route to Gallipoli. His brothers, Thomas and Norman, also served with the Dublin Pals.

Died Killed in action on 16 August 1915, aged 35, in Gallipoli when leading a bayonet charge at Kiretch Tepe/Kirectepe ridge during the gallant stand and subsequent fall of the Dublins. Well out in front of his wavering men, waving his revolver he shouted, 'On, Dublins!', according to Michael McDonagh, *The Irish at the front* (London, 1916), p. 95.

Grave No known grave.

Memorials Named at: Four Courts Dublin; TCD, WDL no. 212; IMR; Helles memorial, Turkey, CWGC ref. MR 4.6, Dublins' panels 190–96 ; *Our heroes*, p. 126; roll of honour, Free and Accepted Masons of Ireland, lodge 60, Ennis, Co. Clare; roll of honour, in R.W. Walker, *To what end did they die: officers died at Gallipoli*; Hanna, *The Pals at Suvla Bay*; PRO, WO 339/12366; *Dublin Book of Honour*, 2003.

Ernest (Ernie) Lawrence Julian

Born 28 July 1879.

Parents John Julian, crown solicitor for King's County, and Margaret Parsons. Her brother, and Ernest's uncle, was Lt.-Gen. Lawrence W. Parsons, KCB, whose distinguished career included commanding the 16th (Irish) Division, 1914–15, during its crucial recruitment and training period.

Address Dundrum, Co. Dublin and Drumbane, Parsonstown, King's County (now Birr, Offaly), seat of the Parsons, earls of Rosse.

Religion Church of Ireland.

School Strangway's School, Dublin, and Charterhouse, Godalming, Surrey, 1884–87, where he was a senior and junior scholar, winning prizes in mathematics and French.

University Dublin, TCD. Classical scholar, senior moderator, BA Hiemalis 1901; rowed in DU Boat Club, 1st VIII, 1900–02, captain 1901, continued to row and coach after graduation. He won the Emerald Sculls competition in 1914, using name E.L. Souspierre, as he felt circumscribed by his position as Reid Professor of Law at TCD (cf. R. Blake, *In black and white: a history of rowing at Trinity College, Dublin* (Dublin, 1991), pp. 101–04).

Legal career King's Inns, Dublin. Admitted as student: 1900, Brooke prizewinner. Called to Bar: Michaelmas term 1903.

Legal practice Popular member of Connaught Bar. Reid Professor of Law, TCD, 1909–14.

Army career Enlisted: 1914. Unit: D Company (Pals), 7th Bn., Royal Dublin Fusiliers, 10th (Irish) Division, 30th Brigade. Rank: Lt. He was commissioned following election by members of D Company, gazetted October 1914. His men considered him rather prudish but that attitude may have been due to class distinctions. Service: Gallipoli, Dardanelles. Member of DU OTC, TCD. After his death, his personal belongings were saved and sent to his mother.

Died A young officer of great promise, he was wounded when leading his men in Gallipoli during the assault on Chocolate Hill/ Yilghin Burnu, 7 August 1915, dying the following day, aged 36, on the hospital ship, *Valdivia*.

Grave Buried at sea.

Memorials Named at: Four Courts Dublin; TCD, WDL no. 231; IMR; stained-glass window by Wilhelmina Geddes, and plaque commemorating R.H. Cullinan and E.L. Julian in St Ann's church, Church of Ireland, Dawson Street, Dublin; named carved in stone on Charterhouse School memorial; Helles memorial, Turkey, CWGC, ref. MR 4/13, Dublins' panels 190–96; *Our heroes*, p. 128; roll of honour in Walker, *To what end did they die: officers died at Gallipoli*; Hanna, *The Pals at Suvla Bay*; PRO, WO 339/20466; *Dublin Book of Honour*, 2003; following a bequest from the mother of

Ernest Julian, the Julian prize is awarded by the Law School, TCD, to the student achieving second place in the final examination for the undergraduate law degree

---

Cecil Stackpoole Kenny

Born 20 October 1891 (also shown as 1888), Limerick.

Parents Thomas Hugh Kenny, solicitor, and Louise Stacpoole/Dunne, author of fiction and hagiography.

Address 55, George Street, Limerick, and Indiaville, Corbally.

School Private study.

University Dublin, TCD. Scholar; BA, Hiemalis, 1912.

Legal career King's Inns. Admitted as student: 1909. Called to Bar: Michaelmas term, 1912.

Legal practice No available information.

Army career Enlisted: August 1915. Unit: 9th Bn., King's Shropshire Light Infantry, no. 3 (b),Young Officers' Company. Rank: 2nd Lt. He left his regiment on leave, pending resignation, apparently due to trauma or mental illness. While travelling back by troopship, SS *Greenore*, he fell overboard and was drowned. Pte. McDonnell, 5th Bn., Connaught Rangers, who was travelling on furlough to Brook Street, Ballina, reported the tragic incident; the body could not be found.

Died Accidentally drowned at sea, between Holyhead, Wales, and Kingstown/Dun Laoghaire, Co. Dublin, 11 November 1915, aged 25.

Grave No known grave.

Memorials Named at: Four Courts, Dublin; TCD WDL no. 235; IMR; Hollybrook Memorial, in cemetery at Shirley, Southampton, Hants., England, CWGC ref. MR 40; *Our heroes*, p. 216; PRO, WO 339/38456.

Remarks His military kit was retrieved from the troopship. John W. de Courcy, Dublin, wore 2nd Lt. Cecil Kenny's Sam Browne belt and shoulder strap while serving in the Irish Local Defence Force (LDF) during the Second World War, the Emergency.

Thomas (Tom) Michael Kettle

Born 9 February 1880, County Dublin.

Parents Andrew (Andy) Joseph Kettle, farmer, one of the Land League's founders and influential supporter of Charles Stewart Parnell, and Margaret McCourt.

Address Newtown, St Margaret's, Co. Dublin.

Religion Roman Catholic.

School O'Connell's School, Christian Brothers, Dublin and Clongowes Wood (Jesuit) College, Co. Kildare (1894–97) where he played rugby, soccer and cricket and won many academic awards, including a gold medal for English.

University University College, Dublin (UCD) which under the Jesuits' guidance prepared young men for examinations of the Royal University of Ireland (RUI), the degree-awarding institution. He attended law lectures at TCD as an external student while reading for the Bar at the King's Inns. Auditor of the revived Literary and Historical Society (the L & H debating society), 1898–99, winner of gold medal for oratory; editor of student magazine, *St Stephen's*; BA, mental and moral science, 2nd class honours, RUI, 1902. Professor of national economics at the new National University of Ireland, a federated body, which included UCD, 1909, where he is remembered.

Legal career King's Inns, Dublin. Admitted as student: 1903. Called to Bar: Easter term, 1906.

Legal practice Victoria prizewinner at King's Inns but his early promise in Dublin courts was not pursued due to his own sensitivity and concentration on other interests, especially politics and public affairs. First president of the Young Ireland Branch of the United Ireland League, he was elected MP for the Irish Parliamentary Party at Westminster, for East Tyrone, 1906–10. Active in the nationalist Volunteers. War correspondent in Belgium where he was appalled by German atrocities and reported on them.

Army career Enlisted November 1914. Unit: 9th Bn., Royal Dublin Fusiliers, 16th (Irish) Division, 48th Brigade. Rank: Lt. Service: he used his oratorical powers during the recruitment campaign for the British Army; Western Front, Belgium, July–September, 1916.

Died 9 September 1916, aged 36, at Ginchy, Somme, France.

Grave No known grave.

Memorials Named at: Four Courts, Dublin; bust in St Stephen's Green, Dublin; IMR; NUI, UCD, roll of honour; bronze plaque on south west wall of St Mary's Roman Catholic parish church, Haddington Road, Dublin; plaque near students' chapel, Clongowes Wood College; *The Clongownian*, college annual, 1917, p. 24, included his obituary (quoted from the *Freeman's Journal*) and *The Clongownian*, 1918, detailed account of his career, pp. 148–50; Milltown Golf Club, Dublin, roll of honour; rugby club, in North County Dublin, Fingal, named after him; PRO WO 339/13445; UCD, Kettle archive, LA 34/413–423; Thiepval memorial, Somme, France, CWGC ref. MR 21, panel 16C; *Dublin Book of Honour*, 2003; the Irish Peace Park, Mesen, Flanders, includes a stone plinth inscribed with verse from his renowned poem to his daughter, Betty, 'Died not for flag, nor King nor Emperor, but for a dream …'

Remarks Tom Kettle was an outstanding man of his distinguished generation which included James Joyce; Patrick Pearse and Thomas McDonagh (executed by the British after the Easter Rising, 1916); and Eoin McNeill, in whose favour he gave evidence at a court-martial. As reported in *In re Kettle*, 40 ILTR 234, section 1 of the Corrupt and Illegal Practices Act, 1895, was pleaded in 1906 when the *Northern Whig* alleged that Tom Kettle was part of a gang of 'hobbledehoys' who created a disturbance during a Royal University conferring by objecting to 'God save the King' being played.

Although he had been involved in the volunteers, Tom Kettle was critical of the Rising which he considered to have 'spoilt his dream of a free united Ireland in a free Europe'. He married, in 1909, Mary Sheehy, BA, RUI, daughter of David Sheehy, nationalist MP and Land League veteran. Another daughter, Hanna Sheehy, married the pacifist Francis Sheehy Skeffington, who was shot after the Easter Rising in controversial circumstances on the orders of Capt. J.C. Bowen-Colthurst, 3rd Bn., Royal Irish Rifles, in Portobello Barracks, Dublin, when the commander, Lt.-Col. McCammond, was on sick leave.

A royal commission of inquiry consisting of Sir John A. Simon, KC, MP, Lord Justice Molony, and Denis Henry, KC, MP, reported in September 1916, that Sheehy Skeffington and two others were in no way connected with the rebellion. Capt. Bowen-Colthurst was found guilty of murder, but regarded as insane. Tom Kettle was deeply affected by the death of his brother-in-law.

Tom Kettle was an author and poet whose works included: *The day's burden* (Dublin, 1910 and revised edition 1965); *Poems and parodies* (Dublin, 1916), in which William Dawson in his preface referred to Kettle as 'a genial cynic, a pleasant pessimist, an earnest trifler, … made up of contradictions'.

'Politics', Kettle says in *The day's burden*, 'is not as it seems in clouded moments, a mere gaggle and squabble of selfish interests: it is the State in action … and the foster-mother of the arts, of love, of comradeship, of all that redeem from despair that strange adventure we call human life'. Kettle's political philosophy inspired many people including James M. Dillon, 1902–86, barrister and politician, and son of John Dillon, who succeeded John Redmond as leader of the Irish Parliamentary Party in 1918 (cf. Maurice Manning, *James Dillon, a biography* (Dublin, 1999)).

Biography: Lyons, *The enigma of Tom Kettle* (Dublin, 1983); Burke, 'In memory of Tom Kettle', with focus on UCD aspects; *The Blue Cap*, RDFA, vol. 9, Sept. 2002.

Joseph Bagnall Lee

Born 3 May 1888.

Parents Edward Lee, JP, of Lees, prominent Dublin drapery stores, former chairman of Bray Urban District Council, and Annie Shackleton.

Address The Grange, Stillorgan, Co. Dublin; Bellevue, Blackrock, Co. Dublin and Bray, Co. Wicklow.

Religion Church of Ireland.

School Educated privately.

University Dublin, TCD. Academic distinctions/degrees 1st class honours and gold medal in moderatorship, legal and political science; BA, LLB, Hiemalis, 1908; LLD Aestiva, 1914.

Legal career King's Inns, Dublin. Admitted as student: 1905. Called to Bar: Trinity term, 1909.

Legal practice Auditor, Law Students Debating Society, King's Inns, 1910; he read paper on 'Law and problems of poverty' and won prize for legal composition. North East and North West circuits. Wrote, with Henry John Moloney, *The law relating to compensation for criminal injuries to person and property* (Dublin, 1912). Author of *Shops Acts, 1912, and Irish regulations, notices and forms* (Dublin, 1912).

Army career Enlisted: September 1914, as private in 6th Bn., Royal Munster Fusiliers, 10th (Irish) Division, 30th Brigade. Rank: 2nd Lt. Service: Gallipoli. Both Joseph B. Lee and his brother, Lt. Alfred T. Lee, were commissioned through DU OTC, TCD, of which they had been members. (Information courtesy of Michael Lee, RTE and Glenageary, Co. Dublin.)

Died Killed in action on 7 August 1915, Gallipoli, aged 27, in an attack led by Major J.N. Jephson which gained and consolidated the position on Kiretch Tepe/Kirectepe, later known as Jephson's Post.

Grave No known grave.

Memorials Named at: Four Courts, Dublin; TCD WDL no. 247; IMR; Lee family grave at Deansgrange cemetery, Dublin; named with his brother, Capt. Robert Ernest

Lee, RAMC, on marble plaque in St Philip and St James Church of Ireland church, Blackrock, Co. Dublin; Royal Courts of Justice, Belfast; included in photograph of sixteen enlisted members of North West Bar, which was placed in Bar room of the County Courthouse, Londonderry, in 1916; Helles memorial, Turkey, CWGC ref. MR 4/7, Munsters' panels 185–90; roll of honour, in Walker, *To what end did they die: officers died at Gallipoli*; PRO, WO 95/3496, 6th Munsters' war diary; *Dublin Book of Honour*, 2003.

John Henry Frederick Leland

Born 17 September 1884.

Parents Henry Leland, and Laura Leland.

Address 6 Idrone Terrace, Blackrock, Co. Dublin.

Religion Church of Ireland, apparently.

University Dublin, TCD. Classical scholar, Moderator; BA, Hiemalis, 1907.

Legal career King's Inns. Admitted as student: 1907. Called to Bar: Easter term, 1911.

Legal practice North East circuit. His petition for call to the Bar was signed by Arthur Warren Samuels, KC, bencher of King's Inns, later unionist MP for Dublin University and attorney-general for Ireland, and judge, whose son Arthur Purefoy Irwin Samuels, is also listed among the twenty-five Irish barristers who died in the Great War.

Army career Enlisted August 1914. Unit: 5th (Flintshire) Bn. (Territorial), Royal Welsh (Welch) Fusiliers, part of 158th brigade of 53rd (Welsh) Division. Rank: 2nd Lt. Service : Gallipoli.

Died Killed in action in Gallipoli, 10 August 1915, aged 30, during 158th Brigade's advance across Salt Lake under heavy shrapnel and rifle fire. Penetrated to within a few hundred yards of Scimitar Hill and opened fire. Further attempts to take enemy positions failed due to lack of maps and confusion.

Grave No known grave.

Memorials Named at: Four Courts, Dublin; TCD WDL no. 249; IMR; Mount Jerome cemetery, Dublin; Royal Courts of Justice, Belfast; Helles Memorial, Turkey, CWGC ref. MR 4.7, Welsh (Welch) Fusiliers' panels 77–80; *Our heroes*, p. 124; Roll of honour, Free and Accepted Masons of Ireland, lodge 329, Dublin, shown as Lt., RDF; roll of honour, Walker, *To what end did they die: officers died at Gallipoli*; PRO, WO374/41658; *Dublin Book of Honour*, 2003.

Remarks Trained with DU OTC, TCD. One of the few married men among the twenty-five listed barristers (apart from Tom Kettle and Willie Redmond, who were older than the average). John H. Leland's wedding to Florence Mary Leland, took place at the Church of Ireland, Christ Church, Carysfort, Blackrock, Co. Dublin, on 9 March 1915, when he was home on leave, five months before his death, after which his widow was granted an annual pension of £100. Christ Church was later demolished to make way for the Blackrock by-pass road.

Frederick Henry Lewin

Born 26 August 1877.

Parents Frederic(k) Thomas Lewin, DL, JP, high sheriff, Co. Mayo, 1886, and Co. Galway, 1892, and Lucy Emma Corrie. According to family tradition, Frederic is spelt without a 'k', but the 'k' is shown in F.H.Lewin's name in King's Inns and other formal records.

Address Cloghans, Co. Mayo, and Castlegrove, near Tuam, Co. Galway; town residence, 6 Merrion Square, Dublin.

Religion Church of Ireland.

School Cheltenham College, Glos., England, 1891–95, boarder at Christowe House there; excellent forward on school rugby team. Following family tradition, he also enjoyed horse-riding and hunting.

University Oxford, Merton College, 1896–99. Rowed in Merton's successful crews, 1898. Member of Myrmidon Club, a dining society at Merton. BA, Oxford, 4th class honours in jurisprudence. In contrast to most of the twenty-five listed barristers who died in Great War, F.H. Lewin had no known connection with the University of Dublin, TCD.

Legal career King's Inns, Dublin. Admitted as student: 1899. Called to Bar: Trinity term, 1902.

Legal practice Connaught Bar and circuit.

Army career Mobilised: 4 August 1914. Unit: a former lieutenant in the East Surrey Regiment Special Reserve, he was commissioned as 2nd Lt., 3rd Bn., Connaught Rangers and promoted captain on 2 February 1915. Service: Ireland

Died 8 December 1915, aged 38, at Cork from injuries to skull and neck from accidental explosion of bomb during trench practice involving a demonstration of a wooden catapult for throwing bombs at Pregane Rifle Range, Kinsale, Co. Cork on

10 November 1915. Capt. Lewin was caught in the full blast of the explosion and seriously injured.

There is a conflict of evidence about the date and place of his death. Capt. Brett's report (filed in the Imperial War Museum, London) claims that there were no first aid arrangements and that Capt. Lewin was dead on admission to the barracks hospital, Kinsale, on 10 November 1915.

Family and official correspondence at the National Archives (PRO), Kew, clearly show that Capt. Lewin did not die until 8 December 1915. There was a dispute between the Lewin family and military authorities about medical and funeral expenses.

Grave Lewin family vault, Kilmaine, Holy Trinity (Church of Ireland) churchyard, Co. Mayo, beside the ruined church on the road between Tuam, Co. Galway, and Ballinrobe, Co. Mayo. See plate 4.

Memorials Named at: Four Courts, Dublin; IMR; Grangegorman memorial, military cemetery, Blackhorse Avenue; Dublin, CWGC ref. CR Ireland 14; collectively remembered by Connaught Rangers' memorial window, Roman Catholic cathedral, Galway; Cheltenham College, roll of honour in *The Cheltonian*, March 1916, and on the brass plated memorial in the chapel cloister at the college; Oxford University roll of service; Merton College, Oxford, war memorial; PRO, WO 339/23219; *The New Ranger*, Connaught Rangers Assoc. Journal, vol. 1, no. 1, (2003), article by A.P. Quinn.

Frederick H. Lewin was the only one of the twenty-five listed barristers to die and be buried in Ireland.

Additional family background The Lewins were a distinguished family with a military tradition which included the battles of Hastings, Fontenoy and service in the Napoleonic wars, India and Africa. Frederick's brother Arthur had a remarkable career: Brig.-Gen. Arthur Corrie Lewin served in Gallipoli; Lieutenant-Colonel in Connaught Rangers, 1913–1919, he defended family house, Cloghans, against republicans; he was reputedly offered a command in the Irish army; he was ADC to British monarchs, and became a celebrated aviator at an advanced age. Arthur Corrie Lewin, as a professional soldier, was so ashamed of the behaviour of the British auxiliary forces, the 'Black and Tans', in meeting 'savagery with savagery' that he emigrated to Kenya.

Remarks The Lewin family were included in Burke's *Landed gentry of Ireland*. The Lewins were landlords whose property extended to both sides of the Mayo and Galway border. Cloghans was built onto the ruins of Lewin castle; Castlegrove House, a hospitable mansion near Tuam, was so described in an article by Mrs Power O'Donoghue (1894), reprinted in John A. Claffey (ed.), *Glimpses of Tuam since the Famine* (Tuam, 1997). Castlegrove House was burnt down during the Irish Troubles in the 1920s. In reaction to that and to the controversial tactics of the Black and Tans, British auxiliary forces, during the War of Independence, members of the

Lewin family left Ireland. The Lewin family was reputedly renowned for the beauty of its women and the bravery of its men (information courtesy of Patrick T.C. Lewin, London).

Martin Michael Arthur Lillis

Born 21 September 1890, baptised on 27 September 1890 in St Patrick's Roman Catholic church, Monkstown, Co. Dublin.

Parents Thomas Barry Lillis, managing director, Munster and Leinster Bank, and Annie Victoria Goggin.

Address Glenville, Monkstown, Co. Dublin; Janeville, Ballintemple, Cork; and Carrig, Queenstown/Cobh, Co. Cork.

Religion Roman Catholic.

School Christian Brothers, Cork, entered 1st year class in 1904, aged 14.

University Dublin, TCD. BA, Hiemalis, 1913; LLB, Aestiva, 1914.

Legal career King's Inns. Admitted as student: 1911. Called to Bar: Trinity term, 1914.

Legal practice Munster.

Army career Enlisted: September, 1915, having attended Sandhurst. Unit: 1st/2nd Bn., Royal Irish Regiment, attached to Royal Flying Corps, 3rd squadron, in February, 1916. The only one of the twenty-five listed barristers to be killed in air combat. Rank: Lt. Service: Western Front.

Died Killed in action during air combat, near Lagnicourt, 11 April 1917, aged 26, while flying on artillery observation control in Morane Parasol, A 6722, with Alexander Fyffe, as observer. It was the 19th confirmed victory, out of an ultimate score of 27 for German ace, Ltn. Fritz Otto Bernert of Jasta 2, who, for his achievement on 11 April 1917, was awarded the Blue Max. Ironically, that German award's official title, Pour le Mérite, is in French deriving from the French-speaking Frederick the Great, king of Prussia, 1740–86.

Grave Heilly station cemetery, Mericourt l'Abbé, south west of Albert, Somme, France, ref. VI E 25. Alexander Fyffe was also buried there.

Memorials Named at: Four Courts, Dublin; TCD WDL no. 255; IMR; listed as killed in school annual *The Collegian*, 1917, among 295 past pupils who served in the

Great War, material republished in *Christians: a celebration of one hundred years of CBC Cork*; PRO, WO 374/41658; *Dublin Book of Honour*, 2003.

Remarks To quote W.B. Yeats on Lady Gregory's son, Robert, Martin Lillis also met his 'fate somewhere among the clouds above, a lonely impulse of delight, drove to this tumult in the cloud'. The wheel turned full cycle as Martin Lillis, baptised in a French-style church, was buried in a French grave. His personal effects included a prayer book, rosary and other devotional items in addition to the usual items such as military badges, regimental crests, personal letters and photographs.

William Alfred Lipsett

Born 29 January 1886.

Parents Robert Lipsett, merchant, and Martha Elizabeth Bowker/Booker.

Address Main Street, Ballyshannon, Co. Donegal.

Religion Church of Ireland.

School St Andrew's College, Dublin, on rugby team.

University Dublin, TCD. BA, Verna, 1908.

Legal career King's Inns. Admitted as student: 1904. Called to Bar: Trinity term, 1907.

Legal practice North west, Ireland; emigrated to Canada in the spring, 1914 and engaged in legal work in Calgary, Alberta.

Army career Enlisted: August 1914. Unit: 10th Bn. (Alberta Regiment), known as the Canadians, 2nd Brigade, 1st Canadian Infantry Division. Rank: Private/grenadier, no. 20330. Service: Western Front. Exceptionally for the barristers who enlisted, William Lipsett was not ranked as an officer, and he refused a commission.

Died On night of 22/23 April, 1915, aged 29, at the second battle of Ypres/Ieper, in a hand grenade attack during the charge of the 10th and 16th Canadian Bns. and the Canadian Scottish, on a wood west of St Julian/Sint-Juliaan. William Lipsett, one of the Canadian Divisions's many casualties, was described by his adjutant as an excellent and gallant soldier. He was killed within 10 or 15 yards of the German redoubt and his body could not be recovered.

Grave No known grave.

Memorials Named at: Four Courts, Dublin; TCD WDL no. 258; IMR; Royal Courts of Justice, Belfast; roll of honour, *St Andrew's College Magazine*, Easter, 1919 and memorial board at St Andrew's College, originally at St Stephen's Green, Dublin, now at Booterstown, Co. Dublin; grave 178, St Anne's, Church of Ireland, Ballyshannon, Co. Donegal, as noted in *Donegal Annual*, 1978; roll of honour, Grand Lodge of Free and Accepted Masons of Ireland, lodge 287, Ballyshannon; Menin Gate, Ypres/Ieper, Flanders, Belgium, CWGC ref. 24,28,30. Canadian roll of honour, copy extract in Christie, *For king and empire: the Canadians at Ypres, 22–26 April 1915*; *Donegal Book of Honour*, 2002.

Remarks William's brother, Capt. Lewis Lipsett, OBE, barrister, Army Service Corps, was appointed counsel to the Irish attorney general in 1920. A cousin, Major-Gen. Louis J. Lipsett, MC, CBE, formerly Royal Irish Regiment, commanded the 8th Bn., Canadian Infantry, during the second battle of Ypres/Ieper, and became GOC, 3rd Canadian Division. Killed in action, 16 October 1918, just before end of war. Another cousin, Sarah Margaret Lipsett, married George Corscadden. Their daughter, Hazel, was mother of Tony Blair, MP, British prime minister, who therefore had a grandmother named Lipsett.

Cornelius (Con) Aloysius MacCarthy, sometimes shown as McCarthy

Born 15 June 1889.

Parents Patrick J. MacCarthy, solicitor, and Charlotte Mary Moynihan.

Address Kilbrogan, and South Main Street, Bandon, Co. Cork.

Religion Roman Catholic.

School Castleknock College (Congregation of the Mission, Vincentians), Co. Dublin, 1902–05, where he was good at games and study. He played soccer for the college team in 1904 and achieved honours at the intermediate exams. He also attended Mungret Jesuit College, Co. Limerick.

University Queen's College, Cork and Dublin, TCD. Undergraduate of junior sophister level at TCD, but no graduation record can be traced.

Legal career King's Inns. Admitted as student: Michaelmas term, 1910. Called to Bar: Trinity term, 1913.

Legal practice Munster. His father, who practised as a solicitor in Bandon and Clonakilty, Co. Cork, had great expectations for Cornelius's career at the Bar and it was hoped that it would financially benefit his sisters, Maria and Kathleen.

Army career Enlisted: 2nd Lt. 1916. Unit: 6th Bn., Royal Dublin Fusiliers, 10th (Irish) Division, 30th Brigade which served in the Middle East in 1917, but records also indicate that he was attached to 9th Bn., Royal Dublin Fusiliers, 16th (Irish) Division, 48th Brigade. Rank: Lt. Service: Greece, Macedonia and Mesopotamia. His parent battalion was the 9th but he was attached to the 6th Bn., when drowned.

Died 19 July 1917, aged 28, reported missing, drowned at sea when the ship, *The Eloby*, sank immediately after being torpedoed by the Germans after leaving Malta.

Grave No known grave.

Memorials Named at: Four Courts, Dublin; omitted, apparently in error, from TCD WDL; IMR; and in memorial list, *Castleknock College Chronicle*, 1917/18. Named on restored family headstone in St Patrick's cemetery, Bandon, Co. Cork as 'Corlis A. McCarthy, BL, lost in the Great War, June 19th 1917', but official records show date of death as 19 July. Recollected on Remembrance Days in Bandon, Co. Cork; named on Basra memorial, on the road to Nasiriyah, Iraq, CWGC ref. panel 41, which suggests that he had been assigned to operations in Mesopotamia, now Iraq; PRO, WO 339/53232.

Remarks King's Inns records show the surname as MacCarthy.

Richard Edmund Meredith

Born 5 March 1884.

Parents Richard Edmund Meredith, barrister, 1879, QC, 1892, judge of the High Court of Judicature in Ireland, Judicial Commissioner of the Irish Land Commission, 1898 and Master of the Rolls in Ireland, 1906–1912, and Annie Pollock.

Address 31 Fitzwilliam Square, Dublin.

Religion Church of Ireland.

School Mr Strangway's, Dublin.

University Dublin, TCD. Senior Moderator, Legal and Political Science, BA, 1906.

Legal career King's Inns. Admitted as student: 1904. Called to Bar: Trinity term, 1907.

Legal practice Secretary to Master of the Rolls in Ireland.

Army career Unit: 1st British Red Cross Unit, according to CWGC, but record of his service could not be traced by the Red Cross. Rank: Chauffeur. Service: Italy. Edmund's elder brother, Major W.R. Meredith, was wounded at Gallipoli and a younger brother, Major J.C. Meredith, served in France.

Died 20 August 1917, aged 33, from dysentery contracted shortly after his arrival in Italy where the Italians and the other Allied forces fought against the Austro-Hungarian and German troops, north of Venice.

Grave Ravenna War Cemetery, CWGC ref. 6.AA.3, Italy, on road 1 km. south of road SS 16 from Ravenna to Ferrara, near the village of Piangipane, Ravenna, on the Italian coast south of Venice.

Memorials Named at: Four Courts, Dublin; TCD WDL no. 289; IMR.

Remarks The Meredith family were prominent in the legal profession in Ireland and Canada. During his father's term as Master of the Rolls, Richard Edmund Meredith's uncle, F.W. Meredith, solicitor, was president of the Incorporated Law Society in 1911. Two close relations were judges in Canada: Sir Richard Ralph Meredith was chief justice of the Common Pleas of Ontario, and R.M. Meredith was a puisne judge of the Chancery Division in Ontario.

Arthur Robert Moore

Born 22 July 1883.

Parents Sir John William Moore, Kt, MD, FRCPI, physician to H.M. the King in Ireland, and Louisa Emma Armstrong.

Address 40 Fitzwilliam Square, Dublin.

Religion Church of Ireland.

School St Stephen's Green School, Dublin.

University Dublin, TCD. BA, Hiemalis, 1904; MA, Hiemalis, 1907.

Legal career King's Inns. Admitted as student: 1903. Called to Bar: Michaelmas term, 1906.

Legal practice Leinster Bar.

Army career Enlisted: August 1914. Unit: 1st/4th City of London Regt., Royal Fusiliers, Territorial Force. Rank: 2nd Lt. Service: Western Front. Wounded in

France, March 1915. Mentioned in dispatches, May 1915. MC, May 1916. Awarded the MC by King George V at Buckingham Palace, London, on 20 May 1916 for bravery on 12/13 March, 1915. *ILT&SJ*, xlix, 20 March 1915, p. 72, reported that he was wounded at St Eloi, near Ypres. He was injured in the leg while his battalion came under heavy shell fire when taking over trenches during relief operations at Richebourg. He declined to go to the field ambulance but continued to lead his platoon into the trenches. On 13 March, 1915, during a march to Vieille Chapelle he was limping and in great pain but he remained with his platoon to arrange billets. He reluctantly went to the field ambulance. His conduct was considered to have had an inspiring effect on the soldiers who were under fire for the first time.

Died Missing, believed killed, 1 July 1916, aged almost 33, near Hebuterne, in the advance on the first day of Somme battle. When he was within sixty yards of the first German trench, a bullet hit his left elbow and passed into his left side.

Grave No known grave.

Memorials Named at: Four Courts, Dublin; TCD WDL no. 296; IMR; Thiepval memorial, Somme, France. CWGC ref. 9 D and 16B; University and Kildare Street Club, St Stephen's Green, Dublin; PRO, WO 3741/48507; *Dublin Book of Honour*, 2003.

Remarks Arthur R. Moore and Hubert M. O'Connor were the two MC awards winners among the twenty-five barristers who died in the Great War.

Hubert (Hugh) Michael O'Connor

Born 22 January 1887.

Parents Charles Joseph O'Connor, medical doctor, medical advisor to Clongowes Wood College, and Mary Anne Lynch.

Address Simmondstown and the Grove, Celbridge, Co. Kildare.

Religion Roman Catholic.

School Clongowes Wood College, Co. Kildare (1898–1904), where he excelled academically and also at games; he played on the cricket and rugby teams.

University Dublin, TCD. Undergraduate of senior freshman status TCD in 1905, but a record of his graduation cannot be traced.

Legal career King's Inns. Admitted as student: 1905. Called to Bar: Hilary term, 1910.

Legal practice Leinster Bar. Shortly after being awarded the MC in 1916, he revisited the Law Library, Four Courts, Dublin, where his many friends and colleagues congratulated him.

Army career Enlisted: September 1914. Cadet DU OTC, and applied for commission, which was granted early in 1915. Unit: 6th Bn., King's Shropshire Light Infantry, KSLI, BEF. Rank: Captain. Service: Western Front. Dr J. Mahaffy, provost of TCD, certified him to be of fine moral character and recommended him for service in the Hampshire Regiment (plate 23). Later commissioned as 2nd Lt. in the King's Shropshire Light Infantry. Awarded Military Cross for conspicuous bravery at the start of the Somme battle when commanding and leading a raiding party on 29/30 June 1916 with great courage. Promoted captain. Attended advanced course at Sandhurst and was in line for further promotion.

Died 17 August 1917, aged 30, at no. 4 casualty clearing station, Dozinghem, Flanders, Belgium, from gunshot wound in the groin when the KSLI attacked Langemarck/Langemark during the third battle of Ypres/Ieper.

Grave Dozinghem Military Cemetery, Westleteren, Flanders, Belgium, CWGC ref. 542.10.IV.B.1.

Memorials Named at: Four Courts, Dublin; TCD WDL no. 320; IMR; plaque near students' chapel, Clongowes Wood College; *The Clongownian*, 1918, p. 199; PRO, WO 339/5483.

Remarks Contested East Limerick as an independent nationalist candidate for Westminster Parliament, 1910. After his death in 1917, the inventory of his personal effects included: spectacles, pince-nez, cracked monocle, pipe cleaner, rosaries, crucifixes, religious badges, books and medallions. He bequeathed £157 to his mother and £4 to his servant, Pte H.G. Cornelius.

Gerald Plunkett

Born 11 August 1887.

Parents Patrick Joseph Plunkett, builder, property owner and alderman, and Helena O'Sullivan. Patrick's first wife, Elizabeth Noble, who had died, was mother of George Noble (Count) Plunkett, the father of Joseph Mary Plunkett. Count Plunkett was half-brother of Gerald, whose half-nephew, Joseph Mary Plunkett, was executed after the Easter Rising, 1916.

Address 14 Palmerston Road, Dublin.

Religion Roman Catholic.

School Belvedere (Jesuit) College, Dublin. Honours at each year of Intermediate examinations.

University Oxford, New College, 1906–08. He did not attend TCD as a student but was connected with TCD when training with DU OTC. BA, Honours, Oxford, 26 November 1908, 3rd class honours in Jurisprudence.

Legal career King's Inns; Inner Temple, London. Admitted as student: 1907. Called to Bar of Ireland: Michaelmas term, 1910; he kept some terms at Inner Temple but there is no record of his call to English Bar.

Legal practice North East and North West. Unusual at the time for a Catholic, he was a member of Rathmines Urban Council, Dublin. When he was posted to the Dardanelles, his resignation was announced at the council meeting on 2 June 1915, and at the next meeting on 18 June, his death was reported (S. Ó Maitiu, *Dublin's suburban towns 1834–1930* (Dublin 2003), quoting minutes of Rathmines Council, 2 and 18 June 1915, Dublin City Archives, UDC/1/min 1/7a/ pp. 500, 501).

Army career Enlisted: at the outbreak of war, he joined the DU OTC, TCD, and from there he received his commission on 20 October 1914, into the Royal Naval Division and gazetted to HMS *Victory*. Unit: A company, Collingwood Bn., Royal Naval Division, Royal Naval Volunteer Reserve, Mediterranean Expeditionary Force. The only one of the twenty-five listed barristers killed while serving with a naval unit. Rank: Sub-Lt. Service: Gallipoli and Dardanelles. On 4 June 1915, after the French retired, the Collingwood Bn. advanced during the third battle of Krithia/Alcitepe, not far from Helles. The Collingwoods were massacred by hidden Turkish machine-guns. Observers referred to 'a field of corn under the reaper' and 'a ship sinking, with all hands', quoted in Michael Hickey, *Gallipoli*, p. 205. The Collingwood battalion ceased to exist after that encounter, and the few survivors were dispersed to other battalions.

Died 4 June 1915, aged 27, during third battle of Krithia/ Alcitepe in Gallipoli while as platoon leader, laughing and joking he gallantly led his men towards the Turkish trenches. He was shot in the head and killed instantly (*London Gazette*, 3rd supplement, 17 September 1915; information courtesy of Peter Plunkett, London, and a letter from one of Gerald's colleagues to his brother, Oliver, also a barrister).

Grave No known grave.

Memorials Named at: Four Courts, Dublin; IMR; not on supplementary DU WDL although a member of DU OTC; Royal Courts of Justice, Belfast; *The Belvederian*, Dublin, 1916, pp. 56–57 and in school's list, plaque and book, *The cruel clouds of war*, on the Belvederians killed in conflict during twentieth century (Dublin 2003); Inner Temple memorial at South Wall of the Round in Temple Church, London; death noted as 7 June 1915 (but service records show 4 June) in *Inner Templars who volunteered and died in the Great War* (London, no date given); roll of service, Oxford University and memorial in the chapel of New College, Oxford; Helles memorial, Turkey, CWGC ref. MR 4/1, panels 8–15 of Royal Naval Volunteer Reserve; roll of honour, in Walker, *To what end did they die: officers died at Gallipoli*; listed in D. Jerrold, *The Royal Naval Division* (London, 1923), p. 339; *Dublin Book of Honour*, 2003.

Remarks The distinguished Plunkett family included St Oliver Plunkett, martyr, 1625–81; Sir Horace Plunkett, co-operative leader, 1854–1932; and Lord Dunsany, 18th baron, 1878–1957, patron of the poet Francis Ledwidge who was also killed in WW1. In his poem 'To Mrs Joseph Plunkett Grace Gifford', Ledwidge referred to Plunkett as 'a noble and a splendid name'.

Gerald was related to the Roman Catholic Fingall branch of the Plunkett family through his grandfather, Walter Plunkett, of Bayna House, Co. Meath.

Gerald's father, Patrick, married young, and had a son George Noble Plunkett; Patrick re-married years later after his wife's death and had four more children, who were of the same age range as his grandchildren. Gerald was Patrick's youngest son. Gerald's half-brother Count George Noble Plunkett, called to the Bar in 1886, was elected Sinn Féin MP for North Roscommon in a historic by-election, 1917, and later took the anti-Treaty side.

Three of the count's sons participated in the Easter Rising 1916, and one son, the mystical poet Joseph Mary Plunkett, was known by a code name, James Malcolm, on his secret missions to Germany. One of the seven signatories of the Proclamation of the Irish Republic in 1916, just before his execution he married Grace Gifford, artist and daughter of a Dublin solicitor. Gerald's father Patrick was Joseph's grandfather. Both Gerald and his half-nephew Joseph were born in 1887 and attended Belvedere College, Dublin, where they were remembered in the school annual, *The Belvederian*, 1916–17. Each volunteered to follow different paths to serve their country and to die prematurely.

James Claude Beauchamp Proctor

Born 21 June 1885, Limavady, Co. Londonderry.

Parents James Edwin Proctor, solicitor, and Frances Jenkinson Orr.

Address Limavady, and Tullydoey House, Moy, Co. Tyrone.

Religion Methodist.

School Reading School, Berks., England, distinguished in sport, athletics and studies.

University Dublin, TCD; Queen's College, Cork. Honours in Ethics and Logic. Prizeman in Legal and Political Science at TCD. TCD: BA, LLB, Hiemalis, 1907; MA, LLD, Hiemalis, 1910; legal scholarship, Queen's College, Cork.

Legal career King's Inns. Called to Bar: Michaelmas term, 1913.

Legal practice Auditor, Solicitors' Apprentices Debating Society. Previously solicitor, admitted 1907 and worked in his father's practice at Limavady. Barrister, North West.

Army career Enlisted: September 1914. Unit: 10th Bn., Royal Inniskilling Fusiliers (Derry volunteers, formed from the Londonderry Ulster Volunteer Force), OC of C company, 36th (Ulster) Division, 109th Brigade. Rank: Captain. Service: went to France in October, 1915 and served on Western Front. He spent three years before the Great War as a trooper in the South of Ireland Imperial Yeomanry (5th, later South, Irish Horse) and became a first-class marksman. According to his CO, he was a gallant and favourite officer.

Died 1 July 1916, aged 31, the first day of the Somme offensive, France, when the 36th (Ulster) Division suffered severe losses. Killed in action, while gallantly leading his C company near Thiepval at Schwaben Redoubt, towards the crucifix; a German officer shot him. Capt. Proctor was carried back to 'A' line, where he died. Proctor's men refused to accept the German's surrender and avenged their officer's death.

Grave Mill Road Cemetery, CWGC ref. IX.D.9, Thiepval, Somme, France, near Ulster Tower commemorating the 36th (Ulster) Division.

Memorials Named at: Four Courts, Dublin; TCD WDL no. 340; IMR; Royal Courts of Justice, Belfast; Mill Road Cemetery, Thiepval; *Our Heroes*, p. 234; de Ruvigny roll of honour; PRO, WO 339/21332.

Remarks James C.B. Proctor, a unionist in politics, was organiser and secretary of the Limavady Unionist Club, member of Ulster Unionist Council, county organiser and secretary of the Ulster Volunteer Force (UVF). Siblings served also: Major G. Norman, Kashmir Rifles; Lt. Edwin, Australian forces, Egypt; and a younger sister was a military nurse.

William (Willie) Hoey Kearney Redmond

Born 13 April 1861, Liverpool.

Parents William Archer Redmond, MP, for the Home Rule Party at Westminster, and Mary Hoey.

Address Parents: Ballytrent House, on south east coast, Co. Wexford. Self: Glenbrook House, Delgany, Co. Wicklow; 9 The Chase Clapham and Palace Mansions, Kensington, London.

Religion Roman Catholic.

School St Mary's Preparatory School, Knockbeg; Carlow College, now St Patrick's College; Clongowes Wood College, Co. Kildare, 1873–6, where he was not especially distinguished intellectually, being over-shadowed by his more brilliant brother, John, who became leader of the Irish Parliamentary Party.

University Dublin, TCD, as external student when attending Bar course at the King's Inns.

Legal career King's Inns: admitted as student 1887; called to the Irish Bar 1891; Middle Temple, London, student, 1887, but no record of call to the English Bar. Kept two terms at the Middle Temple where he attended the chambers of Arthur O'Connor, Irish nationalist MP and barrister. That gave Redmond access to legal cases in the areas of chancery and criminal law. He lived at Clapham, as it suited him to spend time in London during the late 1880s because of his interest in the controversy about Parnell and the forged Pigott letters. During the Bar course at the King's Inns, he attended lectures on constitutional and criminal law at TCD.

Army career Commissioned as temporary captain 22 February 1915, aged 54. Exceptionally old when he enlisted but was facilitated by Lt.-Gen. Sir Lawrence Parsons, commander of the 16th (Irish) Division during crucial recruitment period. Unit: Following some experience in 7th Leinsters, served in 6th (Service) Bn., Royal Irish Regiment (18th Foot), part of the 47th Irish Volunteer Brigade of the 16th (Irish) Division. Rank: captain, promoted to major. Service and career: as a young man, following a family tradition of military service, he joined the Royal Irish Regiment, Wexford Militia. He was promoted lieutenant in 1880 but he resigned on becoming involved in nationalist politics. During the land agitation, he spent his 21st birthday with Parnell in Kilmainham gaol, Dublin and, following further agitation and outspoken speeches, he returned there during Christmas 1902. An eloquent orator for the causes of nationalism, and specifically Home Rule and peace between Orange and Green and also for Irish recruitment in the British army, he gave preference to his own military duties.

During his service on the Western Front, he was mentioned in dispatches by Sir Douglas Haig. Chevalier of the Legion of Honour/Légion d'Honneur, France.

Although Willie Redmond had served as a young man in the Wexford militia, at 54 he was exceptionally old when commissioned during the Great War but insisted on serving on the Western Front.

Died 7 June 1917, the feast of Corpus Christi, aged 56, at the battle of Messines/ Mesen, an Allied victory, which was a prelude to the third battle of Ypres. Stretcher bearers of the 36th (Ulster) Division brought his wounded body back to Locre but he died soon afterwards. Buglers from the Irish Guards sounded the last post at a requiem mass in St Mary's Roman Catholic church, Clapham, London, S.W., 23 June 1917.

Grave Near Locre/Loker, Flanders, Belgium, just outside the official Hospice Cemetery, ref. no. B.183. That cemetery is under the control of the CWGC which is now also the official guardian of Willie Redmond's lonely grave, tended traditionally by the local community. A stone cross marks the private memorial.

Memorials Named at: Four Courts, Dublin; IMR; Redmond memorial park and sculptured bust in Wexford town; plaque at St Patrick's Roman Catholic church, Kilquade, near Delgany, Co. Wicklow (where the Redmonds lived); plaque beside students' chapel, Clongowes Wood College; *The Clongownian*, college annual, various issues, especially, 1917 and 1918, special souvenir; stone cross at grave in Loker, Belgium as indicated above, listed in Thorpe, *Private memorials of the Great War*; exhibit, in Flanders Fields museum, Ieper; PRO, WO 95/1970, 6th Royal Irish Regiment's war diary; PRO, WO 339/19182. Name added to Middle Temple roll of honour and memorial in Temple Church following correspondence from A.P. Quinn in 2000/01, drawing attention to Redmond's membership of that Inn as a student.

Remarks During a tour to Australia promoting the nationalist cause, he met his future wife, Eleanor Dalton, from an eminent Irish-Australian family, but they had no children. His older brother, John Redmond, MP, and leader of the Irish Parliamentary Party, also married into the Dalton family.

Willie Redmond was MP at Westminster for: Wexford (1883), North Fermanagh (1886), and finally East Clare (1892) until his death in 1917. Eamon de Valera won the consequential historic by-election for Sinn Féin, defeating Patrick Lynch, KC.

Publications: *Trench pictures from France*, writings of William Redmond, with foreword by his widow, Eleanor Redmond, Glenbrook, Delgany, Co. Wicklow (London, 1917); T. Denman, *A lonely grave: the life and death of William Redmond* (Dublin, 1995).

Arthur Purefoy Irwin Samuels

Born 14 February 1887.

Parents Arthur Warren Samuels, KC, Leinster Bar, appointed solicitor-general for Ireland, and elected as unionist MP for Dublin University, 1917, re-elected in the general election, 1918, later judge of the King's Bench Division until his retirement in 1924; and Emma Margaret Irwin.

Address 80 Merrion Square, Dublin and Cloghereen, Howth, Co. Dublin.

Religion Church of Ireland.

School Mr Strangway's, St Stephen's Green, Dublin.

University Dublin, TCD. Gold medallist, senior moderator in history, economics and political science, treasurer and auditor of College Historical Society (the Hist.). BA, 1909, MA, 1912.

Legal career King's Inns. Admitted as student: 1907. Called to Bar: 1910.

Legal practice North West circuit

Army career Enlisted: June 1914. Unit: Territorial Force, unattached unit; C Company, 11th Bn., Royal Irish Rifles (South Antrim Volunteers), 36th (Ulster) Division, 108th Brigade. Rank: Lt; promoted Captain. Service: Western Front. A member of DU OTC, TCD, he was attached to the 2nd Bn., Yorkshire Light Infantry, during spring and early summer, 1914, and recommended for temporary commission in 6th Bn., Connaught Rangers but was appointed to 11th Bn., Royal Irish Rifles. Wounded at Thiepval on 26 June 1916, just before start of the main offensive at the Somme, he recovered and served in the fighting line until mortally wounded on 24 September 1916. Shortly before his death he was observed reading the *Irish Times*.

Died 24 September 1916, aged 29, in Belgium of wounds received during action at Messines/Mesen.

Grave Ration Farm (La Plus Douve) Annex, Ploegsteert, Heuvelland, West-Vlaanderen, Flanders, Belgium, CWGC ref. 11.B.25.

Memorials Named at: Four Courts, Dublin; TCD WDL no. 367; IMR; Royal Courts of Justice, Belfast; grave at Ploegsteert, as outlined above; PRO, WO 339/13357; *Dublin Book of Honour*, 2003.

Remarks Married, 16 December, 1913, Dorothy Gage Young of Millmount, Randalstown, Co. Antrim, only daughter of George Lawrence Young, JP, DL, and

Annie Young, of that Antrim address and also of Culdaff, Inishowen, Co. Donegal. There were no children of the marriage and, after Capt. Samuels's death, his widow served as a nurse in France until the end of the war.

His wife's brother, Lt. George Young, 2nd Bn., Leinster Regt., MC, killed 25 July 1915, aged 23, was buried at Wimereux Communal Cemetery, Pas de Calais, France, 111.0.4 (*Donegal book of honour*, 2002, p. 173).

The Youngs of Culdaff House became a well-known family in Inishowen after Sir Arthur Chichester, lord deputy of Ireland in the seventeenth century, acquired lands there following the defeat of the old Irish and Sir Cahir O'Doherty's death.

Publications in memory of A.P.I.Samuels Samuels, *With the Ulster Division in France* (Belfast, n.d. *c.* 1920), quoted in P. Orr, *The road to the Somme* (Belfast, 1987); A.P.I. Samuels, edited with foreword by his father, Arthur W. Samuels, *The early life, correspondence and writings of Rt. Hon Edmund Burke*. After a favourable review in the *Dublin Magazine*, February 1925, Mr Justice Samuels wrote to the editor, Seamus O'Sullivan (J.S. Starkie), expressing thanks, especially for 'the high estimation it expressed for that portion of the book which was my dear (only) son's work' (TCD, O'Sullivan MSS. 4633/634). While training with the DU OTC at Mourne Park, Mallow, Co. Cork, A.P.I. Samuels had researched local connections with Edmund Burke.

James Rowan Shaw

Born 20 May 1880.

Parents James Johnston Shaw, KC, later county court judge of Kerry and recorder of Belfast, and Mary Elizabeth Maxwell.

Address 69 Pembroke Road, Dublin.

Religion Presbyterian.

School St Columba's College, Rathfarnham, Co. Dublin.

University Dublin, TCD. BA, Aestiva, 1904.

Legal career King's Inns. Admitted as student: 1901. Called to Bar: Michaelmas term, 1904.

Legal practice Christopher Palles, last chief baron of the exchequer, a distinguished Roman Catholic judge, signed his memorial form for entry to King's Inns. North East circuit, where he was held in high esteem. Rowan Shaw was also an advocate and solicitor in the Federated Malay States where he practised for over seven years.

Army career Enlisted: April 1915. Unit: 9th Bn., Cheshire Regiment. Rank: 2nd Lt. Service: Western Front. He served previously in the Boer War with the 75th

Company, Imperial Yeomanry. Awarded the Queen's South African Medal with three clasps and was later a member of the DU OTC, TCD.

Died 22 February 1916, aged 35, killed in action in France.

Grave Pont-du-Hem Military Cemetery, CWGC ref. I.D.5, La Gorgue, Nord, France, on the main road, D 947, from La Bassée to Estaires.

Memorials Named at: Four Courts, Dublin; TCD WDL no. 371; IMR; Royal Courts of Justice, Belfast; University and Kildare Street Club, St Stephen's Green, Club, Dublin; St Columba's College, Dublin; roll of honour of Cheshire Regiment at the cenotaph in Regimental Chapel of St George, Chester cathedral; grave at La Gorgue, France, as outlined above; *Our heroes*, p. 182; PRO, WO 339/28638.

Remarks Major William Maxwell Shaw, DSO, RFA, his only brother, who was younger than Rowan, was killed in action in France on 28 May 1917, aged 35. Within one year, both brothers and their nephew, Thornley Woods, were killed.

George Bostall Jenkinson Smyth
(sometimes shown as Bestall and Smythe)
named after his maternal grandfather from Newark, USA

Born 23 July 1890.

Parents James Davis Smyth, linen merchant, and Charlotte Jenkinson.

Address Milltown House, Banbridge, Co. Down.

Religion Church of Ireland.

School Portora Royal School, Enniskillen, Co. Fermanagh, 1903–8.

University Dublin, TCD. Entered college, 1908, but apparently did not graduate and no record of graduation can be traced.

Legal career King's Inns. Admitted as student: 1909. Called to Bar: Trinity term, 1913.

Legal practice North East, where he was known as Hellfire Smyth.

Army career Enlisted: August 1914. Unit: 6th Bn., Royal Irish Rifles, 10th (Irish) Division, 29th Brigade; 7th Bn., Royal Irish Rifles, 16th (Irish) Division, 48th and 49th Brigades and later transferred to the 36th (Ulster) Division. In November 1917, the 7th Bn. was absorbed by the 2nd Bn., Royal Irish Rifles, posted to the 108th Brigade. Rank: Captain. Service: Dardanelles, severely wounded in ankle, August, 1915, when serving as 2nd Lt. with 6th Bn., Royal Irish Rifles; out of action, August 1915–spring 1916. On board *Letitia*, he returned from Alexandria, Egypt to Southampton. While recovering in the Belfast area, his request for reassignment in that area was rejected as he was certified to be fit for general service. Served on Western Front as Captain and survived until the final push for victory near the end of the war. He had been a cadet member of DU OTC, TCD. He was also wounded at Cambrai, 1917. After service as 2nd lieutenant and lieutenant, he was promoted acting captain, 31 August 1917.

Died 22 October 1918, aged 28, killed in action in Flanders three weeks before the war in Europe ended.

Grave Harelbeke/Harlebeke New British Cemetery, CWGC ref. VII.B.17, Harelbeke, near Courtrai/Kortrijk, Belgium. Re-buried there in 1920 in accordance with the British agreement with the French and Belgian authorities to remove all scattered graves and small cemeteries.

Memorials Named at: Four Courts, Dublin; TCD WDL no. 382; Royal Courts of Justice, Belfast; IMR; Harelbeke New British cemetery, ref. VII.B.17; roll of honour and memorial at Portora Royal School; roll of honour, Free and Accepted Masons of Ireland, lodge 18, Newry; named also at family grave in cemetery at Banbridge, Co. Down and plaque in Seapark parish church, Banbridge (*Banbridge Chronicle*, 10 May 1924); cf. Paul McCandless, *Smyths of the Bann* (Newcastle, Co. Down, 2002); PRO,WO 339/11541.

Remarks Horseman, popular sportsman, leading member of Banbridge hockey, cricket and other sports clubs. Three of his cousins, Major R.S. Smyth, RAMC, Major E.F. Smyth, Royal Irish Rifles, and Capt. W.H. Smyth, Royal Irish Rifles, were also war casualties. Another relative, Daniel M. Wilson, KC, who served in the 9th Bn., Royal Inniskilling Fusiliers (Tyrone Volunteers), was elected unionist MP for West Down. He was solicitor-general for Ireland during the turbulent years, 1919–1921, recorder of Belfast (June-October 1921) and then a High Court judge in Northern Ireland until his death in 1932.

Two other cousins of George B.J. Smyth were assassinated during the Irish War of Independence, 'the Troubles': Lt.-Col. Gerald Brice Ferguson Smyth, DSO, was commissioned in the Royal Engineers and served in France where he lost his left arm. In June 1920, he became RIC Divisional Commissioner in Munster but due to the short period in the post, he did not receive any police rank but retained his army title of Lt.-Col. He claimed that he would not tolerate reprisals by the crown forces but his Sinn Féin opponents alleged that he had 'a shoot to kill policy' and the IRA assassinated him in Cork on 17 July 1920, aged 34. His murder caused widespread revulsion in Banbridge, Co. Down, where his large funeral was controversial.

Gerald Smyth's brother, Capt. Brevet-Major George Osbert Stirling Smyth, MC, DSO, Royal Field Artillery, served in 1920 in Dublin Castle with British Military Intelligence, which the Irish republican side called 'The Cairo Gang' or 'The Murder Gang'. The IRA assassinated Capt. Smyth on 12 October 1920 in Drumcondra, Dublin, aged 30, when the suspected gunmen included Dan Breen and Sean Treacy. See McCandless, *Smyths of the Bann* (2002).

For a republican perspective on the above incidents, see Tim Pat Coogan, *Michael Collins* (London, 1991), pp. 149–51, and generally Tom Barry, *Guerilla days in Ireland* (Dublin, 1949; Cork, 1955; Dublin 1989 & 1991).

Herbert (Bertie) Stanislaus/Joseph Tierney
King's Inns' admission papers show Stanislaus
but family and army records show Joseph as second name.

Born 13 November 1888.

Parents Christopher Tierney and Frances Healy, from Co. Clare.

Address 14 Rostrevor Terrace, Rathgar, Dublin.

Religion Roman Catholic.

School College of SS Peter and Paul, Prior Park, Bath; Belvedere College, Dublin.

University RUI. BA. Also attended TCD, as an external student when pursuing Bar course at the King's Inns.

Legal career King's Inns. Admitted as student: 1907. Called to Bar: Hilary term, 1910.

Legal practice Popular and promising member of Munster Bar, practised for four years on the Munster circuit, in the Kerry, Limerick and Clare areas.

Army career Enlisted: Joined D company (the Pals), Royal Dublin Fusiliers as a private, but was commissioned as 2nd Lt., 8th Bn., Cheshire Regiment, November 1914. Career marked by many acts of gallantry and bravery. Unit: 8th Bn., Cheshire Regiment, 40th Brigade, 13th Division Indian Expeditionary Force. Rank: 2nd Lt. Service: served in Gallipoli, Suvla, wounded and evacuated to hospital in Alexandria, Egypt, and served in Mesopotamia (now Iraq). The 8th Bn., Cheshire Regiment was the first part of the 'New Army' raised at the Castle, Chester, and later became part of the 13th Division. It is not clear why Herbert Tierney joined the Cheshire Regiment. Possible reasons include an English connection as he had been educated in England, and the availability and assignment of a commission to him in the Cheshires. There was a family tradition of service as medical doctors in the RAMC. A family connection and colleague, Henry Blackall, also joined the Cheshires, and later had a distinguished career in the British colonial service, including service as chief justice of Hong Kong. Sir Henry Blackall was conferred with an honorary LLD by Dublin University.

Mesopotamia, or 'Mespot' the soldiers called it, was of strategic importance to the British imperial strategy, especially that of the Royal Navy, because there were oil interests in the Persian Gulf area. The 8th Bn., Cheshires participated in the evacuations from Suvla and Helles, Gallipoli, and were assigned with the 13th

Division to Mesopotamia in an ill-fated and wasteful attempt to relieve the arrogant Major-General Sir Charles Townshend in the besieged Kut-el-Amara.

During that attempt, in an attack on Sannaiyat, 2nd Lt. Tierney was one of the few to reach the Turkish trenches but he was shot. Herbert Tierney's parents were reluctant to accept his death and hoped that he had survived as a prisoner of war.

See generally, A. Crookenden, *The history of the Cheshire Regiment in the Great War* (Chester, 1939); and Major-General Sir Charles Townshend, *My campaign in Mesopotamia* (London, 1920).

Died Missing 9 April 1916, aged 27, believed dead in an attack on Sannaiyat, Mesopotamia, while acting in a more senior capacity than his official rank, in the attempt to relieve General Townshend in Kut-el-Amara.

Grave No known grave.

Memorials Named at: Four Courts, Dublin; IMR; NUI, UCD, roll of honour; *The Belvederian*, Dublin, 1917, pp. 68–9 and on school plaque, video and in *The cruel clouds of war*, listing Belvederians killed in conflict during the twentieth century, 2002/03; Basra memorial, Iraq; roll of honour of Cheshire Regiment on cenotaph in regimental chapel of St George, Chester cathedral; Hanna, *The Pals at Suvla Bay*. *Dublin Book of Honour*, listed with NCOs and ordinary soldiers.

Remarks Tim Healy, KC, nationalist politician and later first governor general of the Irish Free State, signed memorials for entrance and call to the Bar at the King's Inns for Herbert Tierney. Tierney's cousin and fellow Belvederian, Capt. James O'Shaughnessy Beveridge, RAMC, twin son of John Beveridge, barrister and Dublin town clerk, was killed in France, November 1917.

When Herbert Tierney was in Gallipoli in 1915, he corresponded with his family in Dublin and with Patrick Lynch, KC, of the Irish Parliamentary Party, who was subsequently defeated by Eamon de Valera in the Clare by-election in 1917 caused by the death of Willie Redmond in Flanders. Lynch became attorney-general during de Valera's government in the 1930s.

See letters from Herbert Tierney in appendix 6.

Tom Barry, in *Guerilla days in Ireland* (Dublin, 1949; Cork, 1955; Dublin 1989), recalled that during his own service in the British army in 1916, when Kut-el-Amara was under siege, he heard about the Easter Rising, an event which awakened his sense of Irish nationality. Herbert Tierney had been killed a few weeks before Easter 1916.

Alphabetical list of solicitors

and solicitors' apprentices who died in the Great War and are
named on the Law Society memorial, Four Courts, Dublin

SOLICITORS

Francis Ahern
Thomas Joyce Atkinson [1]
Louis Barron
James S. Boal
Edward Ellard Brady
William Purefoy Bridge [2]
John Valentine Dunn
Herbert S. Findlater [2]
Brendan Joseph Fottrell
Robert Clifford Orr

John Geoffrey Persse
William Reeves Richards
W. Howard Sanderson
Richard Talbot Scallan
Alfred George F. Simms
William Alan Smiles
Robert Stanton
Richard Cooke Wallace
Samuel Cecil Webb
William Whaley

APPRENTICES TO SOLICITORS

Hugh Montgomery Baillie
Vincent Connell Byrne
Arthur Nickson Callaghan
Arthur Chichester Crookshank [2]
James John (Jack) Davidson [2]
Frederick E.B. Falkiner [2]
Michael J. Fitzgibbon [2]
Philip James Furlong
Ivan Harold Garvey

J. Kenneth MacGregor Greer
Thomas O.J. Kavanagh
Henry Irwin Mahaffy
Daniel O'Rorke
Robert Kelly Pollin
Marcus Ralph Russell
John Hartley Schute
Samuel Lee Tolerton
Alexander M. Turnbull

1 Previously a barrister.
2 They served in Gallipoli in 1915, and are listed with brief biographies and photographs in
   Hanna, *The Pals at Suvla Bay*.

APPENDIX THREE

Chronology

1910

Dublin University Officer Training Corps founded following initiatives from the British War Office to train students who would be suitable for commissioning as officers.

1912

March. Home Rule rally in Dublin attracts about 200,000 people.

September. Nearly half a million people sign Ulster's Solemn Covenant, and its parallel women's declaration.

1913

January and July. Home Rule for Ireland Bill passed in House of Commons, Westminster, but defeated in House of Lords. Ulster Unionist Council organises Volunteer Force. Opposition to Home Rule intensifies in the north of Ireland under the leadership of Sir Edward Carson, KC.

September. The Palace of Peace, endowed by Andrew Carnegie, opens in the Hague, amid hopes that international law would be the arbiter to resolve disputes between nations.

November. Irish Volunteers founded at meeting in Rotunda, Dublin; chairman Eoin MacNeill, a clerk in the Dublin law courts, and scholar of early Irish law and history, who became a professor at UCD.

1914

July. After the assassination of Archduke Franz Ferdinand and his wife, Sophie, Austria-Hungary declares war on Serbia. In the complex European alliances, the central powers of Germany and Austria-Hungary align against the allied states of the United Kingdom of Great Britain and Ireland, France and Russia.

August. In executing its Schlieffen Plan, Germany invades France and Belgium, where Germans perpetrate atrocities. As the invasion of Belgium violated its neutrality guaranteed under the Treaty of London, 1839, Britain declared war on Germany. Consequently, Ireland, as part of the United Kingdom, and also Australia and other dominions within the British empire were involved in the war.

When the Great War started, Tom Kettle, barrister and professor of national economics at UCD, was buying rifles for the Irish Volunteers. Having reported on the German atrocities in Belgium for the *Daily News*, he enlisted in the British army and used his gifts of oratory to encourage Irish recruitment.

September. The Home Rule Act, amended to allow exclusion of Ulster counties, is suspended for the duration of the war. John Redmond, leader of the Irish Parliamentary Party, at Woodenbridge, Co. Wicklow, calls for the Irish Volunteers to fight on the British side during the war. His speech causes a split and the Redmondite section becomes the National Volunteers. Traditional patterns of recruitment of Irishmen to the British forces were boosted by exhortations from John Redmond and Lord Kitchener, Secretary of State for War. The Officers' Training Corps at Trinity College, Dublin and Inns of Court, London, through its Irish selection board facilitated voluntary enlistment of Irish lawyers.

'For the fallen', by Laurence Binyon, English poet and dramatist, published in *The Times* on 21 September 1914, destined to become the standard cenotaph poem, included the poignant lines :

'They shall grow not old, as we that are left grow old'.

October. Turkey, the core of the crumbling Ottoman empire, enters the war on the side of the Central Powers.

1915

April–May. The second battle of Ypres, during which the Germans use a new weapon, poison chlorine gas. During that battle, the Canadian division fought with great bravery and distinction. Among their 2,000 dead was Private/Grenadier William Alfred Lipsett, the first Irish barrister killed in the Great War.

April. 7th Bn., D Company, the Pals, Royal Dublin Fusiliers, headed by the pipers of Dublin University OTC, leave the Royal (later renamed Collins) Barracks, Dublin, to complete their training. In front of the Four Courts, a large crowd of judges, barristers, solicitors and officials, cheered the marching men, including many lawyers, on their way to active service.

May. Sir Edward Carson, KC, as attorney general, included in British government, but John Redmond declines office.

June. Capt. Edmund Chomley Farran, a barrister serving with the 2nd Bn., Royal Irish Rifles, killed in action during attack on Bellewaarde, near Ypres.

April–August. Allied naval and military forces attacked the Dardanelles and Gallipoli, in an attempt to reach Constantinople/Istanbul and relieve Russia. Allies repulsed by Turkish defenders with German assistance. The 10th (Irish) Division were deeply involved. In the worst disaster in modern British military history, the heavy death toll included six Irish barristers, who are named on the Helles memorial in Gallipoli: Capt. Poole Hickman, and Lt. Ernest Julian, both of the Pals, D Company, 7th Bn., Dublins; Capt. Robert H. Cullinan and 2nd Lt. Joseph B. Lee, both of the Munsters; Lt. John H.F. Leland, 5th (Flintshire) Bn., Royal Welsh (Welch) Fusiliers and Sub-Lt. Gerald Plunkett, Collingwood Bn., Royal Naval Division. Also named at Helles is Lt. Robert Stanton, a solicitor from Cork.

In the bitter recriminations after the Gallipoli fiasco, Winston Churchill, First Lord of the Admiralty, resigned from the British government, and Lloyd George was demoted from his post as Chancellor of the Exchequer.

November. 2nd Lt. Cecil Stackpoole Kenny, a barrister serving with the 9th Bn., King's Shropshire Light Infantry, no. 3(b), Young Officers' Company, was drowned after falling from a ship between Holyhead and Kingstown/Dun Laoghaire.

December. Action continues on the Western Front. Sir Douglas Haig replaces Sir John French as the British commander in chief. Irish rugby international and barrister, Capt. Robert (Bobbie) Burgess, of the Royal Engineers, aged 24, is killed by a shell while cycling at Armentiers, France. Capt. Frederick H. Lewin, 3rd Bn., Connaught Rangers, dies from wounds when shell explodes during military practice at Charles Fort, Kinsale, Co. Cork. He was the only one of the twenty-five Irish barristers killed in the Great War to die and be buried in Ireland.

1916

For most of the year, the deadly battle of Verdun continued between the French and Germans, leaving over half a million casualties.

February. 2nd Lt. James Rowan Shaw, a barrister serving with the 9th Bn., Cheshire Regiment, was killed in action on the Western Front, France. Lt. John Hammond Edgar, a member of the Irish and English Bars, who served with the 9th Bn., Durham Light Infantry, died aged 36 from neck wounds in the Hill 60 sector, Ypres salient.

April. Easter Rising against British rule in Ireland. Signatories of proclamation of Irish Republic include Patrick Pearse, barrister, and also Joseph Mary Plunkett, poet and mystic, half-nephew of Gerald Plunkett, who had been killed in Gallipoli in 1915. DU OTC assists in defending Trinity College against the rebels. In the aftermath of the rebellion, the leaders were executed and a British officer was held responsible for murdering Francis Sheehy Skeffington, brother-in-law of Tom Kettle. News of the Easter Rising reached the 16th (Irish) Division on the Western Front, where they suffered heavy casualties. The general negative reaction reflected that of Tom Kettle, who was disappointed that the Easter Rising had occurred.

April. Relief forces under Irish VC winner, General Sir Fenton J. Aylmer, had failed to reach Kut-el-Amara, besieged by the Turks. British advance in Mesopotamia, but casualties include Irish barrister, 2nd Lt. Herbert Tierney, 8th Bn., Cheshires, formerly of the Pals, D Company, 7th Dublins. He was reported missing, believed dead, during attack on Sannaiyat, while attempting to relieve Kut-el-Amara and Major-General Sir Charles Townshend. That arrogant commander of British and Indian troops surrendered after a tragic waste of resources with little Allied gain. Townshend's detention by the Turks in Constantinople was comfortable but Herbert Tierney was among the 21,000 Allied casualties.

July–November. The battle of the Somme, a Franco-British offensive during which the British began to use tanks and the Allies made only small territorial gains at great cost. The high numbers of fatal casualties on the first day, 1 July 1916, included three Irish barristers: Lt. William Magee Crozier, 9th Bn., Inniskillings; Capt. James C.B. Proctor, 10th Bn., Inniskillings, former Unionist organiser, who both served with the 36th (Ulster) Division which included many Ulster Volunteers; also killed was Capt. Arthur Robert Moore, MC, 1/4 City of London Bn., Royal Fusiliers. Lt. Tom Kettle, former nationalist MP and UCD professor, died in action at Ginchy on 9 September 1916 while serving with the 9th Dublins, 16th (Irish) Division.

September. Continuous fighting on the Western Front claimed many fatal casualties, including barrister, Capt. Arthur P.I. Samuels, 11th Bn., Royal Irish Rifles (South Antrim Volunteers), 36th (Ulster) Division, who died of wounds received at Messines/Mesen, a place renowned for the battle that took place there in June 1917.

Controversy continued over proposed exclusion of north-eastern counties from Home Rule regime and regarding conscription in Ireland.

1917

March. Major Willie Redmond, MP, made his most famous speech at Westminster. War-worn and grey-haired, as an Irish soldier he pleaded with parliament for Home Rule for his beloved country and for peace and reconciliation between Orange and Green.

April. U.S.A. enters war. Lt. Martin M.A. Lillis, a barrister serving with the 1st/2nd Bns., Royal Irish Regiment, attached to the Royal Flying Corps, 3rd squadron, is killed during air combat with the German ace, Lt. Fritz Otto Bernert.

June. *The Pals at Dublin Bay, being the record of D company of the 7th battalion of the Royal Dublin Fusiliers*, by Henry Hanna, KC, published in Dublin.

June–July. Douglas Haig starts new offensive, the Big Push, on the Western Front, leading to the third battle of Ypres, ending in November at Passchendaele which symbolised that battle and the horrors of war. The prelude at Messines included successful mining of German positions but the casualties included Major Willie Redmond, MP. He was mortally wounded while serving with the 6th Royal Irish Regiment, on the flank of the 16th (Irish) Division where it joined up with the 36th (Ulster) Division.

July. After Willie Redmond's death, in the consequential by-election in East Clare, Eamon de Valera, the Sinn Féin candidate, defeated Patrick Lynch, KC, Irish Parliamentary Party, who stood for Home Rule. The result heralded a new era in Irish politics and indicated more critical attitudes to Irish participation in the war. Francis Ledwidge, poet and soldier, was killed in action in Flanders. 2nd Lt. Cornelius A. MacCarthy, a barrister serving with the 9th Bn., Dublins, was drowned aged 28 when *The Eloby* was torpedoed by the Germans near Malta.

August. During the third battle of Ypres, in the attack on Langemarck, Capt. Hubert (Hugh) M. O'Connor, MC, barrister, serving with the 6th Bn., King's Shropshire Light Infantry, died from a gunshot wound. The padre in the trenches, Fr Willie Doyle, SJ, son of Hugh Doyle, an Irish High Court official, was killed while ministering as chaplain to the 16th (Irish) Division, including his beloved Dublin Fusiliers.

The 16th (Irish) and 36th (Ulster) suffered heavy casualties and the Irish brigades were virtually wiped out.

August–November. Peripheral to the Western Front, there was fierce fighting during the battles of Isonzo and Caporetto in north-eastern Italy, between the Italians, aided by British and French troops, and the Austro-Hungarians assisted by the Germans. On 20 August, Richard Edmund Meredith, a barrister serving with the British Red Cross, died aged 33 from dysentery shortly after arriving at Ravenna in Italy.

November. The Italian army was demoralised. The Allies gained territory and an armistice was signed with Austria.

December. Following the Bolshevik revolution, Russia signs a peace accord with Germany and withdraws from the war.

1918

March. John Redmond, barrister and Irish Parliamentary Party leader, dies and John Dillon becomes leader. The Sinn Féin challenge to John Redmond's Waterford seat was repulsed by his son, Capt. William Archer Redmond, barrister, who had served with distinction in the Irish Guards and was later elected a TD in the Dáil, the Irish parliament.

April. The controversial Military Service Act applied conscription to Ireland but was strongly opposed by John Dillon, Sinn Féin and the Roman Catholic hierarchy. The Irish national consensus against proposals to extend conscription resulted in their withdrawal but voluntary enlistment still continued in Ireland.

August–September. General Haig's offensive at Amiens pushed the Germans back to the Hindenberg Line.

September–October. Finale on the Western Front. Allied forces stormed the Hindenberg Line, breaking through at many points. Within a month before the end of the war, George Bostall Jenkinson Smyth, a barrister serving with the 7th Bn. (absorbed by the 2nd Bn.), Royal Irish Rifles, was killed in action, aged 28, near Courtrai in Belgium. He was the last Irish barrister to die in the Great War.

November. The Allies gain territory on the Italian Front and an armistice is signed with Austria on 3 November.

Kaiser Wilhelm II of Germany abdicates and flees to the Netherlands.

November 11. Armistice between the Allies and Germany; the Great War ended in Europe at 11 a.m. but continued in other places including Mesopotamia. When Prime Minster Lloyd George announced the armistice to the House of Commons at Westminster, he hoped in vain that 'thus, and this fateful morning, came to an end all wars'. That memorable armistice day provided a basis for future Remembrance Days in the Allied tradition to honour the millions who died during the war. Almost half a million Irish had served in Irish regiments and other units, including the Canadian division and the ANZAC forces from Australia and New Zealand. The Irish fatal casualties were about 35,000.

December. The poet, pacifist and co-operative leader, George Russell, Æ, in a letter to the *Irish Times*, expressed concern at the increasing bitterness between diverse traditions. His accompanying poem, an expanded version of 'Salutations', links the Irish dead of the Great War with the executed leaders of the Easter Rising, as facets of the same ideal: 'One river born from many streams.'

In the general election, the Nationalist Irish Parliamentary Party, which had pinned its hopes on Home Rule, was decisively defeated by Sinn Féin, which was pledged to abstaining from attending Westminster. Outside of Ulster, among the few unionists elected was Arthur Warren Samuels, KC, MP for Dublin University, whose son, Capt. Arthur P.I. Samuels, died in action in Flanders in 1916.

1919

May. Lord chancellor of Ireland, Sir James Campbell, presides at meeting of Irish Bench and Bar, which initiated a project to erect a memorial to the barristers who died in the war.

May–June. Treaty of Versailles negotiated and signed.

1920

March. Brass tablet placed at entrance hall of the Co. Antrim courthouse, Crumlin Road, Belfast, to perpetuate the memory of six members of the North-East Bar killed in the war.

November. Bloody Sunday: British forces kill 12 people during football match at Croke Park, Dublin after an IRA squad under Michael Collins killed 14 British officers, suspected of being secret agents. The Black and Tans ordered shops and factories in Athlone to be closed for Armistice Day and threatened to destroy the premises of traders who did not comply.

1921

March. The Irish Bar asserts its professional independence by unanimously passing a critical resolution proposed by Tim Healy, KC, whose son Joseph had served in the British forces. The resolution, seconded by former British army officer, Eugene Sheehy, objected to the crown forces infringing legal privilege by seizing counsels' briefs at the offices of Mr Noyk. He was defence solicitor for IRA prisoners charged with murdering British officers.

May. General meeting of Irish Bar resolved to commission Oliver Sheppard as sculptor for war memorial.

July. Truce in the Anglo-Irish war, the Irish War of Independence, which had involved bitter fighting between the IRA and British forces, including actions of the controversial Auxiliaries and the Black and Tans. The legacy of those events included a prejudice against British forces and negative attitudes to remembering the Irish who served on the Allied side during the First World War.

November. Ulster Tower, Thiepval, Somme, France, is formally dedicated by Field Marshal Sir Henry Wilson, to commemorate the 36th (Ulster) Division.

1922

January. Dáil Eireann approves the Anglo-Irish Treaty by a narrow majority.

March. British army order no. 78, approved by King George V, led to disbandment of the main Irish regiments based south of the border, including those in which many lawyers had served : the Royal Dublin and Munster Fusiliers, the Connaught Rangers and the Royal Irish Regiment. Their flags were preserved at Windsor Castle.

June. Civil War. Four Courts, Dublin, held by anti-treaty republican forces, was bombarded by the artillery of the Free State army. The Four Courts building was destroyed and the superior courts were temporarily relocated to King's Inns and then to Dublin Castle.

1923
   May. Irish Civil War formally ends but violence continues.

1924
   May. Tim Healy, KC, first governor-general of the Irish Free State, attends ceremony in Dublin Castle, where Lord Chief Justice Molony unveils the memorial to the twenty-five barristers who died in the Great War. Oliver Sheppard also executed a war memorial to Irish solicitors, and the Cuchulainn sculpture, commemorating the Easter Rising in the GPO, Dublin.
   November. On the first Armistice Day after the Bar memorial was unveiled, there was an impressive remembrance service, in which judges, barristers and also the Bar of Northern Ireland and relatives of the deceased participated. Gerald Plunkett and Martin M.A. Lillis were specifically remembered.

1927
   July. The Menin Gate Memorial was unveiled by Field Marshal Plumer (who had been the commander at Messines, 1917), at 11 a.m. on 24 July in Ypres/Ieper, Flanders, Belgium.

1928
   November. A Hall of Honour is opened at Trinity College, Dublin, to commemorate graduates and others from Dublin University, including many barristers and solicitors who died in the war.

1931
   May. Bronze bust of Major Willie Redmond, MP, executed by the sculptor, Oliver Sheppard, is erected in public park, Wexford town.

1932
   July. The Prince of Wales, in the presence of the French president, unveils the Lutyens memorial at Thiepval, Somme, to remember the battle there in 1916 and the Allied soldiers without known graves.

1933
   A war memorial was placed at the new building of the Royal Courts of Justice, Belfast, to remember the Ulster lawyers who died in the Great War. At the formal ceremony, the duke of Abercorn, Northern Ireland governor, pleaded for peace. Meanwhile, the Bar memorial was moved from Dublin Castle to the restored Four Courts.

1937
   Bust of Tom Kettle, executed by the sculptor Albert Power and originally placed in 1921 at the Royal Hibernian Academy, Dublin, erected in St Stephen's Green, Dublin.

1939–1945 SECOND WORLD WAR

1945
May. VE Day marked the end of war in Europe.

1966
    50th anniversary of the Easter Rising. Taoiseach Sean Lemass, speaking at the King's Inns, Dublin, paid tribute to the Irish who 'motivated by the highest purposes fought and died in Flanders and Gallipoli, believing they were giving their lives in the cause of liberty everywhere, not excluding Ireland'.

1972
    January. Bloody Sunday. British soldiers of the Parachute Regiment shot dead 13 demonstrators following banned civil rights march in Derry. In reaction, polarised attitudes reinforced prejudices against remembrance of the Irish participation in British forces.

1987
    Remembrance Day. IRA bomb killed eleven people before service at war memorial in Enniskillen, Co. Fermanagh. In reaction to the outrage, Irish public opinion was influenced to honour remembrance occasions.

1990
    Election of Mary Robinson, SC, as president of Ireland, signalled a more inclusive attitude including presidential attendance at remembrance services in St Patrick's cathedral, Dublin.

1994
    After decades of neglect, the Irish National Memorial Gardens, Islandbridge, Dublin, were formally opened by Bertie Ahern, TD, then minister for finance and later taoiseach.

1998
    November. Mary McAleese, president of Ireland, in the presence of the British and Belgian monarchs, formally opened the Irish Peace Park at Messines/Mesen, Flanders, in an area where many Irish, including Willie Redmond, were killed during the Great War. Wreath placed at peace park in Mesen to honour Irish barristers who died in the First World War.

2001
    April. Taoiseach Bertie Ahern, TD, hosted a state reception at Dublin Castle for the Royal Dublin Fusiliers Association to honour the memory of the Irish who served in the First World War.
    August. Royal Dublin Fusiliers Association's ceremony at V beach in Gallipoli, in the presence of the local Turkish governor, to remember the Irish who served in

the Gallipoli campaign. A wreath was placed at Helles memorial in honour of the Irish lawyers killed in Gallipoli.

October. State funeral for 'the forgotten ten' IRA prisoners hanged by the British authorities in Mountjoy prison during the War of Independence, 1920–21. At the reburial of one of the ten, Patrick Maher, in Ballylanders, Co. Limerick, John O'Donoghue, TD, Minister for Justice, Equality and Law Reform, quoted Tom Kettle's poem about 'dying not for flag, nor King, nor Emperor' and paid tribute to the Irishmen who chose a different courageous path during the First World War by fighting for the rights of small nations.

2004

June. Remembrance service at Island of Ireland Peace Park, Mesen, Flanders. President McAleese recalls role of Irish from diverse traditions who were killed in the First World War.

Place-names

Many places have new names (sometimes a revised form of the original versions), mainly in Flemish and Turkish as appropriate. That may be confusing because the older names were used during the period of the First World War. Those older versions help to identify significant battles, for example Ypres, now locally called Ieper in the Flemish language. Modern names are vital when consulting current maps or visiting sites of battles and war fronts. Some colloquial names, which the soldiers used during the war, are shown in brackets after the old names. The lists below are not exhaustive.

WESTERN FRONT

Old name	Modern name	Old name	Modern name
Boesinghe	Boezinge	Passchendaele (Passiondale)	Passendale
Courtrai	Kortrijk	Ploegsteert (Plugstreet)	Ploegsteert
Dixmude	Dixmuide	Poperinghe	Poperinge
Fortuin	Fortuinhoek	St Jean	Sint-Jan
Frezenberg	Frezenberg	St Julien	Sint-Juliaan
Gravenstafel	Graventafel	St Eloi	Sint Elooi
Harelbeke	Harlebeke	Westhoek	Westhoek
Langemarck	Langemark	Wytschaete (Whitesheets)	Wijtschate
Locre	Loker	Ypres (Wipers)	Ieper
Messines	Mesen		

TURKEY INCLUDING GALLIPOLI AND THE WIDER OTTOMAN EMPIRE

Old name	Modern name	Old name	Modern name
Anzac Cove	Ari Burnu	Kiretch Tepe	Kirectepe
Achi Baba	Alcitepe	Krithia	Alcitepe
Chanak	Canakkale	Lala Baba	Lalababa Tepe
Chocolate Hill	Yilghin Burnu	Maidos	Eceabat
Chunuk Bair	Conkbayiri	Mesopotamia	Iraq (part)
Constantinople	Istanbul	(Mespot)	
Dardanelles	Canakkale Bogazi	Rodosto	Tekirdag
Gallipoli	Gelibolu	Salt Lake	Tuzla Golu
Helles	Gozcu Baba Tepe	Sedd-el-Bahr	Seddulbahir
(memorial site)		Suvla Plain	Anafarta Ova
Hill 10	Softatepe	Suvla Point	Buyukkemikli Burnu
Imbros	Gokceada or Imroz	Troy	Truva

IRELAND

Old name	Modern name
Kingstown, Co. Dublin	Dun Laoghaire
Londonderry (sometimes also used now)	Derry
Queenstown, Co. Cork	Cobh
Rutland Square, Dublin	Parnell Square
Sackville Street, Dublin	O'Connell Street

Glossary

Battalion. Tactical unit of the British army consisting of about 1,000 men, but 650–800 infantry men in 1917. Before the Great War, regiments consisted mainly of two regular battalions and an extra one for training. During the war, regular battalions were augmented by service battalions of inexperienced troops. Lt. Colonel in command.

Brass. Senior officers and general staff, so described by junior officers and troops.

Brigade. Group of regiments or battalions commanded by a brigadier-general.

Cheshires. Cheshire Regiment. Similar abbreviations refer to regiments based in, or associated with, specific areas, such as the Dublins, Munsters and Durhams.

Company. About 150 men in tactical sub-unit of four platoons, having a company headquarters, with a captain or major as officer commanding.

Connaughts. Connaught Rangers. An association to record and remember the history and members of the regiment was recently revived.

Commonwealth (formerly Imperial)
War Graves Commission.
The CWGC maintains the graves of members of the forces of the UK and other Commonwealth countries who were killed during the two world wars. It also maintains registers, records and memorials, including those at the Menin Gate and Thiepval, of those killed and those who have no known graves. The CWGC also maintains under contract the Irish Peace Park at Mesen.

Division. In Allied armies, tactical formation of three infantry brigades plus artillery, engineers and other supports, about 15,000–20,000 men with a major-general in command.

Dublin Metropolitan Police.
Established in 1835 for Dublin city area, amalgamated with Garda Síochána in 1925.

DU OTC,TCD.
Officers' Training Corps at Trinity College, Dublin University, established in 1910 to provide military training for students and opportunities for graduates to obtain commissions in the British Army.

Dublins.
Royal Dublin Fusiliers (RDF).

Fusilier.
Traditionally a soldier armed with a fusil, which was a light, flint-lock musket, but the term was inherited by certain regiments, such as the Dublins and the Munsters, and included in their titles.

Irish memorial records, 1914–1918.
Produced in 1923 under the auspices of the Irish National War Memorial, contains outlines of Irish people who died in the Great War. Copies are kept at the Memorial Gardens, Islandbridge, Dublin and in some libraries and by the Royal British Legion.

Inniskillings.
Royal Inniskilling Fusiliers (RIF).

inns of court.
Institutions for the training, admission and governance of barristers. Four inns of court in London–Lincoln's Inn, Gray's Inn, Inner Temple and Middle Temple–have authority to call qualified people to the Bar of England and Wales.

IRA.
Irish Republican Army, the name given to the Irish Volunteers after a resolution passed by Dail Eireann in 1919, and used during the War of Independence, and later for illegal organisations.

King's Inns.
The Honorable Society of the King's Inns. The educational and professional institution in Dublin for training barristers and admitting them to the degree of barrister-at-law before call to the Bar by the chief justice. It covered all Ireland, until the early 1920s when separate legal systems were established in the Irish Free State and Northern Ireland which now has a separate inn of court.

Military Cross.
Awarded to officers by British monarchs for bravery and gallantry. Details published in the *London Gazette*.

Munsters.
Royal Munster Fusiliers. An association records and remembers the history and members of this regiment.

RDFA.   Royal Dublin Fusiliers Association, formed during the 1990s to record, remember and honour those who served in that regiment.

RFC.   Royal Flying Corps, the air arm of the British army, created in 1912 from the Air Bn., Royal Engineers, merged into the Royal Air Force in 1918.

RND.   Royal Naval Division, used in the Gallipoli campaign, 1915 to provide ground troops on the initiative of Winston Churchill. Also served on Western Front.

RIC.   Royal Irish Constabulary, operated mainly outside the Dublin area, disbanded in 1922.

Royal Irish Regiment.
        This regiment was disbanded in 1921 with the other regiments based south of the Irish border, but the name was recently revived for the amalgamated British army units based in Northern Ireland.

Royal University of Ireland.
        Established in 1881, it organised examinations and awarded degrees, but it did not directly provide courses of lectures. The RUI was abolished when the National University of Ireland and Queen's University, Belfast were established in 1908.

Salient.   Bulge from front line protruding into enemy territory.

Territorials.   Territorial Force, British second-line reserve army, absorbing the Yeomanry and Volunteer regiments.

Trinity College, Dublin.
        TCD, the University of Dublin, provided some lectures for King's Inns students who were not necessarily registered for TCD degrees. Many students who aspired to become barristers obtained degrees in law or arts at TCD.

TCD Commencements.
        Formal sessions for conferring degrees at specified dates during the year as follows: Verna = Spring; Aestiva = Summer; Hiemalis = Winter.

University College, Dublin.
        It originated in Newman's Catholic University of Ireland and provided lectures for male students who aspired to degrees of the RUI. It became part of NUI in 1908 and granted autonomous status within the NUI framework in 1997.

Ulsters.   36th (Ulster) Division.

Volunteers.   Term generally used in Ireland to describe those who joined the
                nationalist paramilitary organisation formed in 1913. It later split
                into the National Volunteers, which favoured John Redmond's
                policy of enlisting in the British army, and the Irish Volunteers
                which adopted a more extreme nationalist approach leading to the
                Easter Rising 1916 and Irish independence. In its wider sense, the
                term 'volunteer' was applicable to most of the Irish who opted to
                enlist in the British army.

Ulster Volunteer Force.
                A paramilitary organisation formed to resist Home Rule. Many of
                its units and members enlisted in the British army, and especially in
                the 36th (Ulster) Division. During the recent terrorist violence in
                Northern Ireland, the term 'UVF' was revived and used by extreme
                loyalist paramilitary groups.

TCD WDL.   The list and hall of honour in Trinity College intended to include
                all members of College, including undergraduates, who died in the
                Great War. There are, however, some omissions. Names of some
                non-academic staff have been added in recent years. In the
                barristers' biographical outlines given in appendix 1, the numbers
                after WDL indicate relevant reference numbers.

Troubles.   The Anglo-Irish War of Independence, 1919–21, but the term is
                sometimes used in a wider context to include the subsequent Irish
                civil war and later the recent conflict in Northern Ireland.

Letters from the East by Herbert Tierney

Henry Tierney, Dublin, and his brother, the historian Fr Mark Tierney, OSB, Glenstal Abbey, Co. Limerick, kindly made available copies of letters and postcards written by their uncle, Herbert (Bertie) Tierney. Formerly a private in the Pals, D Company, 7th Dublins, he was commissioned as 2nd Lieutenant in the 8th Cheshires in November 1914. Further details of his career are given in appendix 1 and some aspects of it are placed in context elsewhere in this book.

Second Lt. Tierney's communications, signed 'Your fond son, Bertie', were sent to the family home, 14, Rostrevor Terrace, Rathgar, a middle-class suburb of Dublin and addressed to his 'Dear Mother'. She was Frances Tierney, née Healy from Co. Clare. This edited selection of extracts from the correspondence illustrates the human aspects of war and its effect on individuals and families.

HMT Ivernia, 3 July 1915

Here I am on a most lovely day sitting in a deal chair, got up in drill uniform, nice and cool, looking down into the loveliest sea that ever was. We are now a few hours from Malta where we hope to arrive about 4 or 5 this evening. The weather has been perfect … We have made a queer course from here to avoid submarines, and at night they take great precautions against any lights being shown … We heard there were some on the look out for us at the narrowest part between Sicily & Africa (Cape B). We have past that all right & now I think the coast is clear. I think the General is going to let us (officers) go ashore at Malta … This ship was out last voyage with the Naval Brigade and I find that Gerald Plunkett was aboard. It is a peculiar thing as the last time I saw him we were discussing which was the quickest way to the front. He got there first but had bad luck poor chap![1]

From the East, 11 July 1915

Now we have reached the stage when I can tell you practically nothing. Our letters are not really censored, but we may not say anything about our whereabouts, or the movements of other troops. We are still on board and have not been in action yet, nor have we yet any idea when we are going … This is a lovely climate, pretty hot in the daytime, but it does not get cold at night, so one need never be uncomfortable. I want you to send me something when you get this. You will get (it) at Crotty's or Elvery's or the Stores. It is a waterproof ground sheet, made of a kind

1. Gerald Plunkett, a barrister colleague of Bertie Tierney, had been killed in Gallipoli in June 1915, while serving with the Royal Naval Division. Both men from the Catholic middle class families of south Dublin had attended Belvedere College where they are now named on a memorial plaque.

of oil silk and it has a slit in the middle so that it may be used as a cape. The ones I have seen are a grey green colour & cost about 25/-. I have a ground sheet already but it is rather heavy … We still have a good time, everyone is full of buck & I think we all want to get into the scrap as soon as possible. I have seen quite a bit of the world in the last fortnight. It has been quite like a pleasure trip in the Mediterranean.

On land, 15 July 1915

I got a grand sheaf of letters on Sunday last … We have not got into the firing line yet but hope to do soon as this is a fairly rotten place. It is as hot as blazes. I took my knife out of my rucksack a few minutes ago and I could not hold the blessed thing it was so hot, but it's all in the game … Now I have some work for you. We have arranged that all Officers of each Company get a parcel of food sent out every week. We are all getting different things. It has fallen to my lot to have sauces and biscuits. Sauces mean chiefly Worcester and an occasional bottle of tomato sauce as a treat. Biscuits mean things like cream crackers or the crispy ones, I think you call them breakfast biscuits. The post is the only thing that reaches the trenches. There is no other way of getting extra supplies. If you feel like sending other things as well occasionally I will give you the complete list: Sauces, biscuits, potted meats, cakes, cocoa, soups, chutney, dried apples, condensed milk … I can't tell you where we are. We are in no danger but it is fairly rough. We are in bivouac which means we are under the skies, no tents or anything to give shade except what one can make by rigging up a blanket and a few sticks.

Gallipoli, 30 July 1915

Thanks awfully for a sheaf of letters I got this morning. The last was the 12th saying my valise had arrived and that you were sending me some chocolate. I also got one from Nance, she is a great sportsman. Well we have left the trenches and have been here on the beach since Wednesday night 29th. Tonight we are going some-where I believe Lemnos. Four hours sail, where we were before we came here. Then there is talk of a big start to finish the show here. I hope it does, we have had a rather dull time, always waiting and hoping for an attack that never came off. I have had rather bad luck, my pack has been lost. They were all handed into stores when we were going into the firing line, & when we came back mine was missing. All my shaving things were in it and my writing-pad (hence this paper), my Barberry (Burberry trench coat), cigs etc. It's rather a nuisance but I have got another pack now.

This beach is a complete rest. We do nothing all day but bathe and eat and we get a good sleep at night. They very rarely shell here, why I don't know, as they would get a great bang, the place is like a beehive. Yesterday, a little Greek ship came from God knows where, and landed a lot of cases and opened a sort of canteen. He (the dealer) sold milk (condensed), biscuits, cigs and Turkish delight and sardines. I think we all eat more Turkish delight than was good for us, but he did not come today so it was only a short orgy.

We were relieved in the trenches by the 2nd Munsters and the Captain of the Company that relieved us was a chap named Eager. They are Kerry people living at Greystones. I had known him in Tralee and in Dublin. We had quite a palaver until we went away.

Living in hope of letters & parcels. Don't forget cigs. Best love to all.

Lemnos, 3 August 1915

I like the way you grouse about the rain. I can't conceive anything more heavenly than a wet summer at home, everything green and fresh instead of the d-d sun and dust and drab colours of this place. We move tomorrow to the place where our big show is going to be. I am not sorry, resting here is not the sort of rest that one enjoys much. Give my love to Eleanor and of course to Paddy & Mrs Lynch when they come out again.[2] Nance will be on a hospital ship if she comes out here. There are dozens of them all lit up at night with green lights and a red cross, they look rippling. One feels that a slight wound would not be such a very unfortunate thing. All sorts of nice girls looking after one. One of our men was on one for a few days sick, he gave most glowing accounts. Now I must start censoring the men's letters.

Gallipoli, 13 August 1915

We are still acting as a sort of general support to anyone looking for help. We have been in a few tight spots but never had a chance to hit back. I have never seen a Turk yet except 'dead uns', and they were not very fresh. Of course, I have seen some prisoners. The big show is going on strong but just where we are there is an advance just now. I am in a wonderful dug-out now, perched upon the top of a hill, forming the side of a steep gully, with the enemy's trenches about 80 yds away – but they can't touch me. I can look out over the rest of the gully and away out to sea, and on the sea the navy is popping about. I keep extraordinary well, though this climate knocks some of the men about rather badly.[3] The main difficulty is to keep clean. Water is much too precious to wash with, and a change of clothes is an undreamed of luxury. When an army advances much it is hard enough to keep up supplies without bothering with mails. Now I must send my best love to you and Dad and all those people who have asked for me, I have not much chance of writing to them.

Gallipoli, 18 August 1915

The most important thing (to report) is the arrival of several boxes of food delicacies arranged before we left home. So now for a short while we live like fighting cocks. The only thing we haven't is bread. We are now in a position near a hill called 'Chenak'. Bere Ashmeade Bartlett was here yesterday; so most likely there will have been a long article by him in the papers, look back for it.[4] If you look at a map we are

2. Patrick Lynch, KC, of the Irish Parliamentary Party, a family friend from Mrs Tierney's native county of Clare, wrote to Bertie Tierney at the battlefront and kept him informed about legal topics. After the vacancy caused by the death of Willie Redmond, MP, in the battle of Messines, Lynch unsuccessfully contested the historic East Clare by-election in 1917 which was won by Eamon de Valera, Sinn Féin. During the 1930s, Lynch supported de Valera's Fianna Fáil government and became attorney general.
3. August 1915 was exceptionally hot and arid in Gallipoli and the Salt Lake near Suvla Bay, where Allied troops landed, dried-up. The climate and lack of drinking water aggravated the military problems.
4. Presumably this is a reference to Ellis Ashmeade Bartlett, an influential journalist who represented the London press. His pessimistic and critical reports of the Gallipoli operation irritated the army censors. When in London, he briefed Kitchener and Churchill and other cabinet ministers. Bartlett and also a young Australian journalist, Keith Arthur Murdoch,

a couple of miles inland at a point between Anzac and Suvla Bay. We are holding a new position and consolidating it. We have no time for any religious services here. Sunday is the same as any other (day).

Gallipoli, Thursday, 19 August 1915

For the first time it rained this morning since we left home, from 3.30 to 4.30. Now as my waterproof was lost when my pack disappeared I want you to send me the oilskin from home. I have the fleece of the Burbury (Burberry) it was not in the pack. The rainy season begins here in a month, so I want to be prepared, but with any luck the show will be over by then. Please address all letters etc. 8th Cheshires, 40th Inf. Bde. 13th Div. M.E.F. (Mediterranean Expeditionary Force).[5] Still no parcels – but we are doing ourselves proud now. I am looking forward to the cigs more than anything. The oil of lavender and the fly netting will be very useful though the flies are not nearly so bad here as in other places we sojourned in. Our rations today consisted of bread, bacon, eggs (one), rice, jam, tobacco, cigs, matches, rum, not so bad for a difficult position in the enemy's country. This of course is what the men get. We get the same.

Same place, Gallipoli, 22 August 1915

Thanks awfully for your parcel, the one containing cigarettes, Woodbines, this notepaper and chocolate. It was heaven sent. The parcel was a wreck and the chocolate all in putty, but like an old campaigner I kept it in my dugout all night in the cold and when it set I unwrapped it. There was a H-of a battle on our left about two miles away last evening. It is going on quietly now. I watched it for some time from our position, which is on a height about 600 ft. The Navy and our guns made a terrific bombardment, just like a picture in the illustrated papers. It was all Navy and sea and land out before us like a panorama, but you could not see the men moving it was too far. I hear they are getting on well. The attack was on a hill we call the W-hill. Its real name is 'Ismail Ogler Tepe'. At night I was detailed to take my platoon down to bathe. The sea is about two miles away. There was nearly a full moon & there is a lovely sandy beach, so we had the most delightful bathe I ever had. It was my first wash for a fortnight. The mail has just come in now. There was a parcel for me sent by Sir J and Miss Johnston of Listowel. The box was matchwood, the cake was powder but the cigs survived. A clean shirt (oh joy! oh rapture!). A piece of soap (heaven sent) some chocolates (yum). Good evening, I am going to supper.

Gallipoli, 23 September 1915

I have just re-read your letters of last week. There is very little to answer, you have not asked many questions. As for the Chaplain, he is still sick, but on Sunday last a Padre from another division came and said Mass for us of course, I went to

father of the media mogul, exposed military and political incompetence. That had caused the Dardanelles débâcle, terrible loss of life and Allied withdrawal from Gallipoli at the end of 1915. See M. Hickey, *Gallipoli* (London, 1995), pp. 83–84, 187, 311–12, 316–21.

5. For more information about the 8th Cheshires' role, see Hickey, *Gallipoli*, pp. ix, 257, 259, 293–97 and generally Crookenden, *The history of the Cheshire Regiment in the Great War*.

confession and communion. He is a little priest from Mallow. I always wear a scapular medal on my chain on my neck.

19th general hospital, Alexandria, 6 November 1915
… I did not expect to be here so long. I have never been really ill but it has taken a long time to get this thing quite shaken off. I was out all afternoon Monday last, but on Tuesday I had a temperature of 102, which came down to normal the next day. Nevertheless, they kept me in bed and starved me. I am longing to hear some news from you.

19th general hospital, Alexandria, 16 November 1915
I am feeling much better now, more like the man I was, more in *status quo ante bellum*. I was never very ill but just as I was getting well from jaundice, I suddenly got a temperature of 102–5. I am going to get some kit together here before I leave. Socks you might send me a pair now and again. I hope dear old Dad is keeping fit and Gerald. You said he was in great form due to golf. It is a great game for keeping you fit, almost as good as trying to strafe the Turks. I refused (to go to a convalescent home at a wonderful place called Luxor on the Nile) because I was afraid that I might not be able to do all the things I want to do before going back to the peninsula.

Mudros, 1 January 1916
Happy New Year! Here I am back at Mudros. This letter is being taken home by a Major Riddell who was commanding my regiment but is now sick … He sails tomorrow. My regiment was at Suvla to the end. They got away with the greatest success. They were here a week or so and went back to Helles in a hurry three days ago, I believe they will come back again. All this is strictly for your own consumption. I had a rippling Xmas Day in Alexandria at MacGrath's. I am glad the finger bowls arrived safely. I would very much like to give the P. Lynches some. We had a rippling time on the boat coming over. It is only a two days sail but they do some weird manoeuvring to dodge submarines. Eddie Healy was on board and he told me he was being attached to the Border Regt.

Lemnos, 11 January 1916
I am really awfully sorry for not writing for so long. I have been waiting Micaber like for something to turn up. I came here with a draft of officers and men for the regiment, which had just evacuated Suvla. We had expected to join up and go to Servia (Serbia). We were surprised to learn that they had gone to Helles only the day before we arrived. For some time past I have been on an engineering job building a road. Then it is rumoured we sail for Alexandria soon and for some time – short or long we won't be in action again. What will happen after we go to Egypt is very uncertain. There is a vague possibility that we may go home but don't be disappointed if we don't and don't tell anyone. I have great opportunities of seeing the passers by. During the past few days these have included two members of the Irish Bar – Joe Healy, Tim's son who is in the R.N.V.R. (Royal Naval Division) and Hugh Holmes, son of Judge Holmes, who is in the artillery, 10th (Irish) Div. I had a

long chat with both of them, and Holmes told me of another in the vicinity whom I looked up today. Henry Kennedy, he is in the A.S.C. (Army Service Corps). That was not all. When I found Kennedy he was in earnest conversation with D.G.T. Sherlock of the Munster Circuit. He is in the Irish Fusiliers and is now Adjutant on the Ordnance ship here in Lemnos. Isn't this a good record for the Irish Bar? Five members in a radius of a few miles.[6]

Port Said, Egypt, 6 February 1916

As you know I am only a 2nd Lieut. There are a number of 1st Lieuts. therefore my seniors, who have come out with drafts, many of them having never seen any active service. My company commander Capt. Boote did a very decent thing. He got the Co to put into the C company only those officers who were junior to me now that five of the original officers are gone home for a month's leave, I am left in command.

Basra or Bassora, Mesopotamia, 1 March 1916

What do you think of it? (Having voyaged on RMS *Briton*, Union Castle Line), here I am camped on the bank of the Euphrates, not far from the Garden of Eden, but oh! how it has changed. The place is about as Eastern as you can get. Basra is the military base and I hear its a pretty good town where one can buy most things necessary. It is now dark and now and then you can hear the jackals screeching and whining.

Final letter from the front, 7 April 1916.[7]

Dear Mother,

We started a deuce of a battle two days ago and we are still advancing, fighting heavily all the time. I have come through all safe & hope to say the same in a few days when the show is over. We are now in a position about 3 miles from where we started, but the first line is going forward well. You will read all about it all in the papers long since.

Best love,
Bertie

P.S. Have just had a parcel from you on the battlefield.
More welcome than anything could be. Cheerioh! Bertie

6. Joseph Healy, Munster Bar, was son of Tim Healy, KC, MP, a controversial nationalist politician who became first governor general of the Irish Free State in 1922. Lt. Hugh Oliver Holmes, North West Bar, was son of Hugh Holmes, lord justice of appeal, 1897–1913. Henry Kennedy also practised on North West circuit. David Sherlock, a barrister, had three sons serving in the war: David G. Sherlock, became a brigade-major; Capt. Edward was in the Royal Field Artillery (RFA); and Capt. Gerard Sherlock, 3rd (King's Own) Hussars, was killed in action in the German Cameroons, September, 1915.

7. Major-General Sir C.V.F. Townshend, *My campaign in Mesopotamia*, provides his perspective on the controversial siege of Kut-el-Amara. During attempts to relieve Kut, Herbert Tierney was lost and presumed dead.

POSTSCRIPT

Bertie Tierney survived the campaign in Gallipoli in 1915. During the attempt to relieve Major-General Townshend in the besieged Kut-el-Amara in Mesopotamia, Bertie Tierney was reported missing, believed dead, in April 1916. His family refused to believe that he was dead and wrote to the Red Cross and the military authorities to try and find their beloved son. Cpl. Kingsley, no. 282992, C Company, 8th Cheshires, in a letter to the British Red Cross enquiry department for wounded, missing and prisoners of war at 51, Dawson St., Dublin reported:

> Witness (Cpl. Kingsley) last saw Mr Tierney in charge on April 9th (1916). He was standing near the parapet of the first line of Turkish trenches, never taken that day, unwounded and firing his revolver. It was about 4.30 in the morning and still dark; but witness is quite positive that it was Mr. Tierney he saw, for as his officer he was easily able to recognise him. Three days later there was a truce, the ground was searched carefully, and no trace of Mr Tierney's body was found. It would seem therefore that two things might have happened: (1) that Mr Tierney might have been captured, wounded or unwounded, (2) that he might have been killed while fighting and fallen into the Turkish trench.

The War Office concluded that 2nd Lt. Herbert Tierney died on or since 9 April 1916, and a letter from Windsor Castle to his father Christopher Tierney, dated 18 September 1918, conveyed the king and queen's deep regrets for death in the country's service. Although Herbert Tierney had addressed his letters from the war zone to his mother, the official letter confirming his death was sent to his father.

Despite his assurances to his parents not to worry as he 'was not built to be done in by any bally Turk that infests Mesopotamia', he met his tragic end where he had heard the scavenging dog-like 'jackals screeching and whining'. Herbert Tierney is named in Iraq on the CWGC memorial at Basra (which featured in the recent Gulf and Iraq wars) near the place, which, in letters home, he mentioned as the Garden of Eden.

In memoriam

Herbert (Bertie) Tierney, Dublin Pals and Cheshire
Regiment, missing believed killed in action,
Mesopotamia (now Iraq), spring, 1916

At Basra, where jackals whined

Your name I read on stone –
At Basra's lonely scene,
A Dublin Pal, Bertie Tierney,
Missing, Spring nineteen sixteen.

Your mother read your censored notes –
From parched Gallipoli,
To fight in England's war
You crossed the Persian sea.

You survived the Dardanelles
But many fell at Suvla Bay,
And like Ledwidge of the Boyne
You lived to die another day.

Your fate was sadly sealed –
In the ancient vale of fears
Where Eden's garden grew,
With Eve the first mother's tears.

Relieve Kut el Amara –
The battle orders pealed,
While hungry jackals whined
On Ares the war god's fated field.

You'll walk no more in Dublin –
Nor sail its pleasant Bay,
But sleep in Basra's peace
Where jackals no longer prey.

Anthony P. Quinn

This elegy was awarded a highly commended certificate in a competition organised by the
Inchicore Ledwidge Society, Dublin, December 2002.

Bibliography

MANUSCRIPT SOURCES

Dublin
Dublin City Archives
    UDC/1/min 1/7a/pp. 500 and 501, minutes of Rathmines Urban Council, 2 and 18 June 1915 re G. Plunkett.
Honorable Society of King's Inns
    Clancy J. (ed.), Index to Barristers' memorials, 1998.
    Memorials for admission of students and call to the Bar.
Law Library, Four Courts
    Bar Council minutes, especially 21 October 1931.
National Archives
    Dept. of the Taoiseach papers DTS 3743, 31 March 1924, letter from Chief Justice Kennedy to President Cosgrave.
    OPW file. NA 2007, memorandum 14 July 1936.
National Library
    W.G. Fallon papers MS 22, 589.
    Sheehy-Skeffington papers.
Trinity College, Dublin, Library, manuscripts department
    Bernard papers, 2328/95, 163.
    O'Sullivan MS 4633/634.
    Samuels collection, papers 2/58.
University College, Dublin, archives
    LA 34, 413–423, re T.M. Kettle.

London
Honorable Society of the Middle Temple
    Archives, MT 3ROH/1 re J.H. Edgar.
National Archives (TNA), formerly PRO, Kew, London
War Office papers (WO)
    339/21334, letter of 13 October 1914 from Brig.-Gen. T.E. Hickman, MP, to Adjutant General, 36th (Ulster) Division.
    339/5485, letter of 21 December 1914 from Dr Mahaffy, provost of TCD, recommending H. O'Connor for commission in Hampshire Regiment.
    339/14609, Burgess, R.B.
    339/21334, Crozier, W.M.
    339/18517, Cullinan, R.H.
    95/2840, War diary of 9th Durhams re J.H. Edgar.
    339/58010, Farran, E.C.L.
    339/12366, Hickman, P.H.

339/20466, Julian, E.L.
339/38456, Kenny, C.S.
339/13445, Kettle, T.M.
95/3496, War diary of 6th Munsters re J.B. Lee.
374/41658, Leland, J.H.F., extract from marriage certificate.
339/23219, F.H. Lewin.
374/41658, Lillis, M.M.A.
339/53232, MacCarthy, C.A.
3741/48507, Moore, A.R.
339/5483, O'Connor, H.M.
339/21332, Proctor, J.C.B.
95/1970, War diary of 6th Royal Irish Regiment re W.H.K. Redmond.
339/19182, Redmond, W.H.K.
339/13357, Samuels A.P.I.
339/28638, Shaw, J.R.
339/11541, Smyth, G.B.J.

BOOKS AND ARTICLES

Andrews, C.S., *Dublin made me: an autobiography*, Dublin and Cork, 1979 and 2001.
Andrews, D., 'Andrews on Saturday', *Irish Times*, 4 August 2001.
Axelrod, A., *The complete idiots' guide to World War I*. Indianapolis, 2000.
Barnier, A., 'Ireland, sport and empire' in Keith Jeffery (ed.), *An Irish empire? Aspects of Ireland and the British empire*, Manchester, 1996.
Banks, A., *A military atlas of the First World War*, Barnsley, 2003.
Barnes, B.S., *This righteous war*, Huddersfield, 1990.
Barry, T., *Guerilla days in Ireland*, Dublin 1949, Cork 1955, Dublin, 1989, 1991.
Bartlett, T. and Jeffery, K. (eds) *A military history of Ireland*, Cambridge, 1996.
Belloc, H., *The cruise of the Nona*, 1925 and Penguin, Harmondsworth, 1958.
Betjeman, J., 'Ireland with Emily' from *Collected poems*, quoted in Frank O'Connor (ed.), *A book of Ireland*, London and Glasgow, 1959.
Bennett, R., *The Black and Tans*, Staplehurst, Kent, 1959 and 2001.
Bentley, J., *Some corner of a foreign field: poetry of the Great War*, London, Boston, Toronto, 1992.
Bew, P., *John Redmond*, Dublin, 1996.
Bhreathnach-Lynch, S., 'Commemorating the hero in newly independent Ireland' in L.W. McBride (ed.), *Images, icons and the Irish nationalist imagination*, Dublin, 1999.
Biggs-Davison, J. and Chowdharay-Best, G., *The Cross of Saint Patrick: the Catholic unionist tradition in Ireland*, Abbotsbrook, Bucks., 1984.
Binyon, L., 'For the fallen', *The Times*, 21 September 1914.
Bishop, A. and Bostridge, M. (eds), *Letters from a lost generation*, London, 1999.
Blake, R., *In black and white: the history of rowing at Trinity College, Dublin*, Dublin, 1991.
Bowman J. and O'Donoghue R. (eds), *Portraits: Belvedere College, 1832–1982*, Dublin, 1982.
Bowman, T., 'Carson's army or Kitchener's men: the Ulster Volunteer Force and the formation of the 36th (Ulster Division)', lecture to Royal Dublin Fusiliers Association, 13 October 2001.

Bowman, T., 'The Ulster Volunteers 1913–1914: force or farce', *History Ireland*, vol. 10, no. 1, spring 2002, pp. 43–47.

Boylan, H., *A dictionary of Irish biography*, 3rd ed., Dublin, 1998.

Brearton, F., *The Great War in Irish poetry: W.B. Yeats to Michael Longley*, Oxford, 2000, 2003.

Brittain, V., *Testament of youth: an autobiographical study of the years 1900–1925*, London, 1933 and 1979.

Budd, D. and Hinds, R., *The Hist and Edmund Burke's club*, Dublin, 1997.

Burke's *Landed gentry of Ireland*, London, 1958.

Burke, T., 'The story of Lt. Robert Stanton, 6th battalion, Royal Dublin Fusiliers', *The Blue Cap*, journal of the Royal Dublin Fusiliers Association, vol. 4, March 1997, pp. 1–2.

——— , 'In memory of Tom Kettle', *The Blue Cap*, vol. 9, 2002.

Callanan, F., *T.M. Healy*, Cork, 1996.

Campbell, G.L., *Royal Flying Corps, casualties and honours during the war of 1914–1917*, London, 1917.

Carey, T., *Hanged for Ireland: the forgotten ten, executed 1920–1921: a documentary history*, Dublin, 2001.

Carnegie, A., *Autobiography*, London, 1920.

Carrothers, D.S. (compiler), *Memoirs of a young lieutenant, 1898–1917*, Enniskillen, 1992.

Carty, M.R., *History of Killeen Castle, County Meath*, Dunsany, Co. Meath, 1991.

Casey, P.J., 'Irish casualties in the first world war', *Irish Sword*, vol. xx, no. 81, summer, 1997.

Christian Brothers Community, *Christians: a celebration of one hundred years of CBC, Cork*, Cork, 1988.

Christie, N., *For king and empire*, 1: *the Canadians at Ypres, 22–26 April 1915*, Ottawa, 1999.

Clarke, A., *The donkeys*, London, 1961; Pimlico, London, 1991.

Clery, A., Obituary and memoir of Tom Kettle, *The Clongownian, 1918*, pp. 148–50.

Collins, S., 'Ireland's prodigal sons', *Sunday Tribune*, Dublin, 17 February 2002.

Cogan, M.J., 'The Great War', in Christian Brothers Community, *Christians: a celebration of one hundred years of CBC, Cork*, Cork, 1988.

Commonwealth (formerly Imperial) War Graves Commission, *Introduction to the register of the Thiepval memorial, France*, London, 1930.

Coogan, T.P., *Michael Collins*, London, 1991.

Cooper, B., *The Tenth (Irish) Division in Gallipoli*, London, 1918, revised edition with foreword by Dr J. Bowman, Dublin, 1993 and 2003.

Costello, C. (ed.), *The Four Courts: two hundred years*, Dublin, 1996.

Creeslough-Dunfanaghy guide book, Donegal, 1987.

Cronin, A., 'Till the boys come home', *Irish Times*, 9 July 1976.

Cronin, P., *South County Dublin and East Wicklow during the 1914–1918 war*, Foxrock Local History Club, lecture publication no. 23, Dublin, 1986.

Cross, T., *The lost voices of World War: an international anthology*, London, 1998.

Crookenden, A., *The history of the Cheshire Regiment in the Great War, 1914–1918*, Chester, 1939.

Crozier, F.P., *A brass hat in no man's land*, London, 1930 and Gliddon Books, Norfolk, Great War Classics, 1989.

Curtayne, A., *The complete poems of Francis Ledwidge*, London, 1974 and 1986.

Dancocks, D.G., *Welcome to Flanders Fields: the first Canadian battle of the Great War: Ypres, 1915*, Toronto, 1988.

De Bréadún, D., Feature on state papers, *Irish Times*, 3 January 2002.

Delany, V.T.H., *Christopher Palles, lord chief baron of her majesty's court of exchequer in Ireland 1874–1914, his life and times*, Dublin, 1960.

Denman, T., *Ireland's unknown soldiers: the 16th (Irish) Division in the Great War*, Dublin, 1992.

——, *A lonely grave: the life and death of William Redmond*, Dublin, 1995.

——, 'A voice from the lonely grave: the death in action of Major William Redmond, MP, 7 June, 1917', *Irish Sword*, journal of the Military History Society of Ireland, vol. xviii, no. 73, summer 1992, pp. 286–297.

Doherty, R., *Irish volunteers in the Second World War*, Dublin, 2001.

——, and Truesdale, D., *Irish winners of the Victoria Cross*, Dublin, 2000.

Donegal Book of Honour, the Great War, 1914–1918, Donegal, 2002.

Dooley, T., *The decline of the big house in Ireland*, Dublin, 2001.

Dooley, T.P., *Irishmen or English soldiers? The times and world of a southern Catholic Irish man (1876–1916) enlisting in the British army during the First World War*, Liverpool, 1995.

Dooney, L. 'Trinity College and the war', in Fitzpatrick, D. (ed.), *Ireland and the First World War*. Dublin, 1986 and 1988.

Doyle, M., 'The combined Irish regiments OCA annual commemorative parade', *The Gallipolian*, journal of the Gallipoli Association, no. 96, autumn, 2001, pp. 20 and 56.

Dublin Book of Honour, the Great War 1914–1918, Dublin, 2003.

Dudley Edwards, R., *The faithful tribe: an intimate portrait of the loyal institutions*, London, 2000.

——, *Patrick Pearse: the triumph of failure*, 1990; London, 1997.

Duffy, S. (ed.), *An atlas of Irish history*, Dublin, 1997.

Dungan, M., *Irish voices from the Great War*, Dublin, 1995.

——, *They shall grow not old: Irish soldiers and the Great War*, Dublin, 1997.

Dyer, G., *The missing of the Somme*, London, 1994 and 1995.

Eckhert, R.P., *Edward Thomas*, London, 1937.

Ellis, J.S., 'The degenerate and the martyr: nationalist propaganda and the contestation of Irishness, 1914–1918', in *Eire-Ireland*, xxxv, 3–4, fall/winter, 2000/1, pp. 7–33, Morristown, N.J., with references to the Samuels Collection, Trinity College Library, Dublin.

Errington, F.H.L., *Inns of Court OTC during the Great War*, 1922, reprinted Uckfield, East Sussex, 2003.

Fallon, O., 'Irishman's diary' re siege of Kut-el-Amara, 1915, *Irish Times*, 22 March 2003.

Falls, C., *The history of the 36th (Ulster) Division*, Belfast and London, 1922, London, 1996, 1998.

Farran, E.C.L., *The law relating to purchase of land*, with R.A Walker, Dublin, 1903–04 and supplement, 1906.

Feilding, R., *War letters to a wife: France and Flanders 1915–1918*, London, 1930, Norfolk, 1989.

Ferguson, N., *The pity of war*, London, 1998, Penguin edition, 1999.

Findlater, A., *Findlaters: the story of an Irish merchant family, 1771–2001*, Dublin, 2001.

Fingall, Elizabeth, Countess of, *Seventy years young: memoir*, London, 1937, Dublin, 1991.

Fitzpatrick, D., 'Militarism in Ireland, 1900–1922', in Bartlett, T. and Jeffery, K. (eds) *A military history of Ireland*, Cambridge, 1966.

—— , 'The logic of collective sacrifice: Ireland and the British Army, 1914–1918', *Historical Journal*, 38, (1995), pp. 1017–30.

—— (ed.), *Ireland and the First World War*, Dublin, 1986.

Fitzpatrick, G., *St Andrew's College, 1894–1994: Ardens sed virens*, Dublin, 1994.

Foster, R., *The Irish story: telling tales and making it up in Ireland*, London, 2001.

Foy, M. and Barton, B., *The Easter Rising*, Stroud, Glos., 1999.

Fraser, T.G. and Jeffery, K., *Men, women and war*, Dublin, 1993.

Fussell, P., *The Great War and modern memory*, Oxford, 1975.

Geary, S., *The Collingwood battalion, Royal Naval Division*, Hastings, 1919.

Geoghegan, P.M., *1798 and the Irish Bar*, Dublin, 1998.

Giddings, R., *The war poets: lives and writings of the 1914–1918 war poets*, London, 1988.

Gilbert, M., *First World War*, London, 1994, 1995.

Goodenough, S., *The greatest good fortune: Andrew Carnegie's gift for today*, Edinburgh, 1985.

Grand Lodge of Free and Accepted Masons in Ireland, *Roll of Honour, Great War, 1914–1919*.

Greer, D.S. and Dawson, N.M. (eds) *Mysteries and solutions in Irish legal history*, Dublin, 2001.

Gray, T., *The lost years: the Emergency in Ireland, 1939–1945*, London, 1998.

Gregory, A. and Paseta, S. (eds) *Ireland and the Great War: a war to unite us all?*, Manchester, 2002.

Gwynn, D., 'Thomas M. Kettle (1880–1916)', *Studies*, lv, no. 220, winter, 1966.

—— , *The Irish Free State 1922–1927*, London, 1928.

Hall, E., book review of M.Healy, *The old Munster circuit*, *Law Society Gazette*, vol. 95, no. 6, July 2001, p. 27.

—— and Hogan, D. (eds), *The Law Society of Ireland, 1852–2002: portrait of a profession*, Dublin, 2002.

Hanley, B., *A guide to Irish military heritage*, Dublin, 2004.

Hanna, H., *The pals at Suvla Bay, being the record of the 'D' company of the 7th Royal Dublin Fusiliers*, with a foreword by Lt.–Gen. Sir Bryan Mahon, Dublin, 1917, reprinted Uckfield, Sussex, 2002.

Harding, B., *Keeping faith: the history of the Royal British Legion*, London, 2001.

Harris, H., *The Irish regiments in the First World War*, Cork, 1968.

Hart, A.R., *A history of the king's serjeants at law in Ireland: honour rather than advantage?*, Dublin, 2000.

Haughey, J., *The First World War in Irish poetry*, London and Cranbury, NJ, 2002.

Healy, M., *The old Munster circuit*, London and Dublin, 1939; new ed. with biographical note by C. Lysaght, London, 2001.

Hickey, M., *Gallipoli*, London, 1995.

Herbert, B., 'Tom Kettle, 1880–1916', *Capuchin Annual*, 1967, pp. 420–27.

Hobson, C., *Airmen died in the Great War, 1914–1918*, Polstead, Suffolk, 1995.

Hogan, D., *The legal profession in Ireland, 1789–1922*, Dublin, 1986.

—— , 'Irish lawyers and the great war', *Law Society Gazette*, xcii, no. 10, December, 1999.

—— , 'R.R. Cherry, lord chief justice of Ireland', in Greer, D.S. and Dawson, N.M. (eds) *Mysteries and solutions in Irish legal history*, Dublin, 2001.

Hogan, G., 'Return to the Four Courts', in Costello, C. (ed.), *The Four Courts: two hundred years*, Dublin, 1996.

Hogan, M.J.R., 'The Great War', in Christian Brothers Community, *Christians: a celebration of one hundred years of CBC, Cork*, Cork, 1988, pp. 168–179.

Hogarty, P., *The old toughs: history of the 2nd Bn., Royal Dublin Fusiliers*, Dublin, 2001.

Holt, T. and V., *Major and Mrs Holt's battlefield guide to Gallipoli*, Barnsley, 2001.

—— , *Poets of the Great War*, Barnsley, 2000.

Horne, J. and Kramer, A., *German atrocities 1914: a history of denial*, New Haven, Conn., 2001.

Hughes, T., *Tom Brown's schooldays*, London, 1857 and reprints.

Hull, M.M., *Irish secrets: German espionage in wartime Ireland, 1939–1945*, Dublin and Portland, OR, 2003.

Hume, D. 'Empire Day in Ireland 1896–1962' in Jeffery, K. (ed.), *An Irish empire? Aspects of Ireland and the British empire*, Manchester, 1966.

Inner Templars who volunteered and died in the Great War. London, n.d.

Ireland's memorial records, 1914–1918, 8 vols., Dublin, 1923.

Irish Catholic directory, Dublin, 1896.

James, Rhodes R., *Gallipoli*, London, 1965, 1999.

Jeffery, K., *Ireland and the Great War*, Cambridge, 2000.

—— 'The Great War in modern Irish memory' in Fraser, T.G. and Jeffery K. (eds), *Men, women and war*, Dublin, 1993.

—— 'The Irish military tradition and the British Empire' in *An Irish empire? Aspects of Ireland and the British empire*, Manchester, 1996.

—— in Department of Foreign Affairs, *Cuimhneachán*, Dublin, 1966, p. 47.

—— (ed.), *An Irish empire? Aspects of Ireland and the British empire*, Manchester, 1996.

Jerrold, D., *The Royal Naval Division*, London, 1923, reprinted Uckfield, Sussex, 2002.

Johnston, Col., *Queen's University of Belfast OTC: history of the corps, 1908–1998*, Belfast, 1999.

Johnstone, T., *Orange, green and khaki: the story of the Irish regiments in the Great War 1914–1918*, Dublin, 1992, 2001.

Keane, R., 'A mass of crumbling ruins, the destruction of the Four Courts in June, 1922', in Costello, C. (ed.), *The Four Courts: two hundred years*, Dublin, 1996.

Keegan, J., *The First World War*, London, 1999.

Kehoe, E., review of television documentary 'An seamróg agus an swastika', *Sunday Business Post*, Agenda, 3 February 2002.

Kennedy, D., *Local heroes of the 1914–1918 war*, Foxrock Local History Club lecture publication no. 41, Dublin, 1999.

Kenny, C., *Tristram Kennedy and the revival of Irish legal training, 1835–1885*, Dublin, 1996.

Kettle, A.J. and Kettle, L.J. (eds) *Material for victory*, Dublin, 1958.

Kettle, T., *The day's burden and other essays*, with memoir by his wife, Mary Sheehy Kettle and introduction by James Meenan, Dublin, 1968.

—— , *Poems and parodies*, with a preface by William Dawson, Dublin, 1916.

Kiberd, D., 'Belvedere boy who did not like royalty', Agenda, *Sunday Business Post*, 30 September, 2001.

—— , *Inventing Ireland: the literature of modern Ireland*, London, 1995.

Knox, R., *Patrick Shaw-Stewart*, London, 1920.

Kostick, C. and Collins, L., *Easter Rising: guide to Dublin in 1916*, Dublin, 2000.

Laffan, M., *Count Plunkett and his times*, Foxrock Local History Club lecture publication no. 29, 1992.

—— and Ui Chléirigh, M., 'The story of Muckross Park' in *Dominican College, Muckross Park, a centenary of memories*, 1900–2000, Dublin, 2000.

Laffin, J., *Panorama of the Western Front*, London, 1994.

Ledwidge, F., 'The Irish in Gallipoli', versions of poem in Cooper, 1993, Curtayne, 1974 and 1986 and O'Meara, 1997.

Lee, J., *A soldier's life, General Sir Ian Hamilton, 1853–1947*, London, 2000.

—— , 'A modest proposal for commemorating the dead', *Sunday Tribune*, Dublin, 11 November 2001.

—— , 'The canon of Irish history – a challenge reconsidered', in Toner Quinn (ed.), *Desmond Fennell, his life and work*, Dublin, 2001.

Lee, J.B., *Shops Acts, 1912 and Irish regulations, notices and forms*, Dublin, 1912.

—— with Moloney, H.J., *The law relating to compensation for criminal injuries to person and property*, Dublin, 1912.

Leonard, J. 'Lest we forget', in Fitzpatrick, D. (ed.), *Ireland and the First World War*, Dublin, 1986.

Levenson, L., *With wooden sword: a portrait of Francis Sheehy Skeffington, militant pacifist*, Dublin, 1983.

Luce, J.V., *Trinity College, Dublin, the first 400 years*, Dublin, 1992.

Lyons, J.B., *The enigma of Tom Kettle, Irish patriot, essayist, poet, British soldier, 1880–1916*, Dublin, 1983.

MacArdle, D., *The Irish republic*, London, 1937; 4th ed., Dublin, 1951.

MacFhionnghaile, N., *Donegal, Ireland and the First World War*, Letterkenny, 1987; 2nd ed., 2005.

McBride, L.W., *The greening of Dublin Castle: the transformation of bureaucratic and judicial personnel in Ireland, 1892–1922*, Washington DC, 1991.

McBride, L.W. (ed.), *Images, icons and the Irish nationalist imagination*, Dublin, 1999.

McCague, E., *Arthur Cox, 1891–1965*, Dublin, 1994.

McCandless, P., *Smyths of the Bann*, Newcastle, Co. Down, 2002.

McCoole, S., *Guns and chiffon: women revolutionaries and Kilmainham Gaol, 1916–1923*, Dublin, 1997.

McDaniel, D., *Enniskillen, the Remembrance Sunday bombing*, Dublin, 1997.

MacDonagh, M., *The Irish at the front*, London, New York and Toronto, 1916.

Macdonald, L., *Somme*, London, 1985; Penguin ed. 1993.

—— , *They called it Passchendaele: The story of the third battle of Ypres and the men who fought in it*, London, 1978, 1990.

McManus, R., *Dublin 1910–1940: shaping the city and suburbs*, Dublin, 2002.

McMaster, N., *Flanders fields*, 75th Anniversary tape of the battle of the Somme, Somme Association, Belfast, 1991.

Manning, M., *James Dillon, a biography*, Dublin, 1999 and 2000.

Martin, F.X., 'Did Belvedere change, 1916–1922' in Bowman, J. and O'Donoghue, R. (eds), *Portraits: Belvedere College, 1832–1982*, Dublin, 1982.

Maye, B., 'Irishman's diary', *Irish Times*, 7 January 2002.

Molohan, C., *Germany and Ireland, 1945–1955: two nations' friendship*. Dublin and Portland, Oregon, 1999.

Moloney, E., *A secret history of the IRA*, London, 2002.

Moloney, H.J. and Lee, J.B., *The law relating to compensation for criminal injuries to person and property*, Dublin, 1912.

Molony, J.N., *A soul came into Ireland, Thomas Davis, 1814–1845: a biography*, Dublin, 1985.

Morgan, G., 'The legacy of Tom Kettle', letter, *Irish Times*, 11 December 2001.

Morrissey, T.J., *William J. Walsh, archbishop of Dublin, 1841–1921*, Dublin, 2000.

Mortimer, G., *Fields of glory: the extraordinary lives of sixteen warrior sportsmen*, London, 2001.

Moses, H., *The Gateshead Gurkas: a history of the 9th battalion, Durham Light Infantry, 1959–1967*, Durham, 2001.

Murphy, J.H. and Collins M. (eds) *Nos autem: Castleknock College and its contribution*, Dublin, 1996.

Murphy, O., with foreword by K. Myers, *The cruel clouds of war, Belvederians killed in 20th century conflict*, Dublin, 2003.

Murray, P., 'Why venerating our killers is wrong', *Sunday Tribune*, 23 September 2001.

Myers, K., 'Irishman's diary', *Irish Times*, 14 March, 3 October and 13 November 2001.

—— , 'First to last, Irishmen led the 1914–1918 sacrifice', *Irish Times*, 15 November 1982.

Ní Dhuibhne, E., 'Sources – Family values: the Sheehy Skeffington papers in the National Library of Ireland', *History Ireland*, vol. 10, no. 1, spring 2002.

Novick, B., *Conceiving revolution: Irish nationalist propaganda during the First World War*, Dublin, 2001.

Noyk, M., 'Thomas Whelan', *An tÓglach*, Dublin, winter 1967.

O'Brien, C.C., *Memoir: my life and themes*, Dublin, 1999.

Ó Cathaoir, B., *John Blake Dillon, Young Irelander*, Dublin, 1999.

O'Connor, F. (ed.), *A book of Ireland*, London and Glasgow, 1959.

O'Connor, U., *The Ulick O'Connor diaries, 1970–1981: a cavalier Irishman*, London, 2001.

——— , 'Pearse's high place in the story of our country', book review, *Sunday Independent*, 22 May 1977.

Ó Dubhghaill, M., *Insurrection fires at Eastertide*, Cork, 1966.

Ó Maitiu, S., *Dublin's suburban towns, 1834–1930*, Dublin, 2003.

O'Meara, L. *Francis Ledwidge, the poems complete*, Newbridge, Co. Kildare, 1997.

Ó Muiri, P., 'Before I joined the army, I lived in Donegal', exhibition described in 'Tuarascáil', *Irish Times*, 3 October 2001.

O'Neill, M., *Grace Gifford Plunkett and Irish freedom: tragic bride of 1916*, Dublin and Portland, Oregon, 2000.

O'Rahilly, A., *Father William Doyle, S.J.*, London, 1920.

Ó Tuathail, S., *Gaeilge agus bunreacht*, Baile Atha Cliath, 2002.

Orr, P., *The road to the Somme: men of the Ulster division tell their story*, Belfast, 1987.

Osborough, W.N., 'The title of the last lord chief justice of Ireland', *Ir. Jur.*, ix (1974), 87–98.

Page, C., 'The Royal Naval Division memorial to return to Horseguards', *The Gallipolian*, no. 97, winter 2001–02.

Paseta, S., *Before the revolution: nationalism, social change and Ireland's Catholic elite*, Cork, 1999.

Passingham, I., *Pillars of fire: the battle of Messines ridge, June, 1917*, Stroud, Glos., 1998.

Pope, S. and Wheal, E., *A dictionary of the First World War*, Barnsley, 2003.

Powell, A., *A deep cry: First World War soldier-poets killed in France and Flanders*, Stroud, Glos., 1998.

Plunkett Dillon, G., 'The North Roscommon election', *Capuchin Annual*, 1967, pp. 338–40.

Power O'Donoghue, Mrs, 'Castlegrove House', originally published in *Lady's Pictorial*, 1894, reprinted in John A. Claffey (ed.), *Glimpses of Tuam since the famine*, Old Tuam Society, Tuam, 1997.

Quinn, A.P., '"But for a dream", a quest for Tom Kettle', *The Cross*, Dublin, 1976.

———, 'Flanders fields and Irish recollections', *Capuchin Annual*, Dublin, 1977.

———, *The golden triangle, the Æ commemorative lectures*, Society for Co-operative Studies in Ireland, Dublin, 1989.

———, 'A brief encounter with the last serjeant', *Irish Law Times* (n.s.), vol. 12, no. 11, December 1994, p. 293.

———, 'A wreath for Willie Redmond', broadcast on *Sunday Miscellany*, RTE 1, 1994.

———, 'A briefed encounter with Chief Baron Palles', *Irish Law Times* (n.s.), vol. 13, no. 12, 1995, p. 294.

———, 'The chaplain in the war trenches, *in memoriam* Fr Willie Doyle', in *Dun Laoghaire Journal*, Dun Laoghaire Borough Historical Society, no. 4, 1995.

———, 'Harmony between diverse traditions may be found in the ideals of Davis', *Sunday Tribune*, Dublin, 24 September 1995.

——, 'Happy wanderers' in *Walking World Ireland Annual*, Dublin, 1997.

——, letters to *Irish Times*, 3 and 23 February 1999, 25 September 2000, 24 March and 14 November 2001, and *The Examiner*, 19 February, 1999.

——, 'Wigs and guns', *Irish Law Times*, vol. 18, no. 6, April, 2000, pp. 90–92.

——, 'The Irish in Flanders', and 'The Irish in Gallipoli', broadcast on *Sunday Miscellany*, Remembrance Sunday, 2000 and 28 November 2004 respectively.

——, 'Remembering the Irish in World War One is relevant to reconciliation and peace', *The Blue Cap*, journal of the Royal Dublin Fusiliers Association, vol. 8, June, 2001.

——, 'Gallipoli, where 4,000 Irish were slaughtered', *Sunday Business Post*, Dublin, 11 November 2001.

——, book review of *Irish volunteers in the Second World War* by Richard Doherty. *Sunday Business Post*, 25 November, 2001.

——, outlining local connections, articles in the *Dun Laoghaire Journal*, Dun Laoghaire Borough Historical Society: 'Wigs and guns', no. 9, 2000, pp. 43–49, 'Irish recollections in France and Flanders, no. 10, 2001, pp. 55–56, 'Irish recollections in Gallipoli', no. 11, 2002, pp. 41–44.

——, '1916 deaths of brothers in law, Kettle and Sheehy Skeffington, makes case for war and peace', *Sunday Business Post*, 23 March, 2003.

——, 'Gallipoli names amongst those remembered in Dublin' in *The Gallipolian*, 103, winter 2003–4.

——, 'Rededication of Royal Naval Division memorial', *Ireland's Own: St Patrick's Day Annual*, Wexford, 2004.

Quinn, Toner (ed.), *Desmond Fennell, his life and work*, Dublin, 2001.

Redmond, W., *Trench pictures from France*, London, 1917; reprinted Uckfield, Sussex, 2004.

Remarque, E.M., *All quiet on the Western Front* (original: *Im Westen nichts Neues*, Berlin, 1929), translated by Brian Murdoch, London, 1994.

Rivlin, R., *A social history of Jews in modern Ireland*, Dublin, 2003.

Russell, G. (Æ), letter to *Irish Times*, 17 December, 1917.

Samuels, A.P.I. and D.G.S., *With the Ulster Division in France, a story of the 11th battalion, Royal Irish Rifles (South Antrim Rifles) from Borden to Thiepval, including war diaries of Arthur Samuels*. Belfast, n.d., *c.*1920; reprinted Uckfield, Sussex, 2003.

Samuels, A.P.I., *Early life, correspondence and writings of the Rt. Hon. Edmund Burke, LL.D.*, with a transcript of the minute book of the debating 'club' founded by him in Trinity College, Dublin, with extra material by A.W. Samuels, Cambridge, 1923.

—— (ed.), with foreword by his father, A.W. Samuels, *The early life, correspondence and writings of Rt. Hon. Edmund Burke*, Cambridge, 1923, reviewed in the *Dublin Magazine*, February, 1925.

Savage-Armstrong, G.F., *Poems: national and international*, Dublin, 1917.

Scannell, J., 'German World War Two espionage in County Dublin', lecture to Foxrock Local History Club, 13 November 2001.

Sewell, E.D.H., *The Rugby internationals' roll of honour*, London and Edinburgh, 1919, pp. 1–2, 118–19.

Shaw, F., 'The canon of Irish history – a challenge', *Studies*, lxi, no. 242, summer, 1972.

Sheehy, E., *May it please the court*, Dublin, 1951.

Sheffield, G., *Forgotten victory: the First World War, myths and realities*, London, 2001.

Silkin, J. (ed.), *The Penguin book of First World War poetry*, 2nd ed., London, 1996.

Simkins, P., *Kitchener's army: the raising of the new armies, 1914–1916*, Manchester and New York, 1988.

Simon Commission, *Report of Royal Commission of Inquiry, 1916*.

Sinn Féin (1916) Rebellion handbook, Dublin, *Irish Times*, 1916 and revised edition with introduction by Declan Kiberd, 1998.

Sisson, E., *Pearse's patriots: St Enda's and the cult of boyhood*, Dublin, 2004.

Smith, C.F., *Newtownpark Avenue, its people and their houses*, Dublin, 2001.

Snoddy, O., 'Three by-elections of 1917', *Capuchin Annual*, Dublin, 1967, pp. 341–47.

Solomons, B., *One doctor and his time*, London, 1956.

Spagnoly, T. and Smith, T., *Salient points: cameos of the Western Front; Ypres, 1914–1918*, London, 1993.

Spiers, E.M. 'Army organization and society', in Bartlett, T. and Jeffery, K. (eds) *A military history of Ireland*, Cambridge, 1996.

Stallworthy, J., *Anthem for doomed youth*, London, 2002.

Sullivan, A.M., *The last serjeant*, London, 1952.

Summerfield, H., *That myriad minded man: Æ*, Gerards Cross, Bucks., 1975.

Swinnerton, I., *The location of British army records, 1914–1918*, revd. 4th ed., Federation of Family History Societies, Bury, Lancs., 1999.

Taaffe, M., *Those days are gone away*, London, 1959.

Taylor, J.W., *The First Royal Irish Rifles in the Great War*, Dublin, 2002.

Temple Church, Pitkin Guides, Andover, Hants., 1997.

Thorpe, B., *Private memorials of the Great War on the Western Front*, Western Front Association, Reading, Berks., 1999.

Tomkin, N., letter in *The Clongownian*, 1918, p. 141.

Townshend, C.V.F., *My campaign in Mesopotamia*, London, 1920.

Turpin, J., *Oliver Sheppard, symbolist sculptor of the Irish cultural revival*, Dublin, 2000.

——, 'Oliver Sheppard and Albert Power, State sculptural commissions', *Dublin Historical Record*, journal of the Old Dublin Society, vol. lv, no. 1, spring 2002.

Tynan Hinkson, K., 'Joining the colours', in Bentley, J. (ed.), *Some corner of a foreign field, poetry of the Great War*, London, Toronto, Boston, 1992 and 1993.

University of Dublin TCD War Dead List, Hodges Figgis, Dublin, 1922.

Vinen, R., *A history in fragments, Europe in the twentieth century*, London, 2000.

Von Falkenhayn, E., *Memoirs: German headquarters, 1914–1918 and its critical decisions*, English translation, HMSO, London, 1919.

Warner, R. (ed.), *Icons of identity*, Belfast, 2000.

Walker, R.W., *To what end did they die? Officers died at Gallipoli*, Worcester, 1985.

West, T., *Dublin University Football Club, 1854–2004: 150 years of Trinity rugby*, Dublin, 2004.

Willoughby, R., *A military history of the University of Dublin and its Officers Training Corps, 1910–1922*, Limerick, 1989.

Wise T. and S., *A guide to military museums and other places of military interest*, 10th revised ed., Knighton, Powys, 2001.

Wyse Jackson, P. and Falkiner, N., *A portrait of St Columba's College*, Dublin, 1993.

PERIODICALS

Banbridge Chronicle, 10 May 1924

Bar Review, journal of the Bar of Ireland, vol. 7, issue 1, October/November 2001

Capuchin Annual

Court Service News

Dublin Historical Record, journal of the Old Dublin Society

Dublin Magazine

Dublin University Calendar, annual

Dun Laoghaire Journal

Edward Thomas Fellowship Newsletter, in particular no. 48, January 2003

Gazette of Law Society of Ireland

History Ireland

Ireland's Own

Irish Law Times and Solicitors' Journal (ILT&SJ)
    xlvii (1913); xlviii (1914), 247, 281, 316, 323; xlix (1915), 72; l (1916), 54, 80; l War supplement, 1916; li (1917), 168, 216–17, 308; liii (1919), 132–33; liv (1920), 76; lv (1921), 83, 186, 187, 303; lviii (1924), 125, 137–39, 283, 303; lxii (1928), 276–77; lxvii (1933), 161; (new series), vol. 12, no. 11 (1994); vol. 13, no. 12 (1995); vol. 18, no. 6 (2000).

Irish Life supplement: *Our heroes, Mons to the Somme*, Dublin, 1916; reprinted Uckfield, East Sussex, 2002.

Irish Reports [1906] 2 IR: *McGovern v. McBride*.

Irish Sword, journal of the Military History Society of Ireland

London Gazette, 3rd supplement, 17 September 1915.

Stand To, journal of the Western Front Association, no. 70, April 2004.

The Blue Cap, journal of the Royal Dublin Fusiliers Association, vol. 8, June 2001 and vol. 9, 2002.

The Gallipolian, journal of the Gallipoli Association: spring and autumn, 2000, spring and winter, 2001, autumn 2002, winter 2003–04.

The New Ranger, journal of the Connaught Rangers Association, vol 1, issue 1, July 2003.

Walking World Ireland, Annual, 1997 and nos. 17 and 51.

NEWSPAPERS

Freeman's Journal
Irish Times
Sunday Business Post
Sunday Independent
Sunday Tribune

COLLEGE ANNUALS

St Andrew's College Magazine, Easter, 1919.
The Cheltonian, various years, especially 1916 (Roll of Honour).
The Collegian, 1917, school annual, material republished in Christian Brothers
    Community, *Christians: a celebration of one hundred years of C.B.C., Cork*, Cork,
    1989.
The Reptonian, 1916.
The Clongownian, 1915, 1916, 1918.
The Castleknock College Chronicle, 1914–18.
The Belvederian, 1916, 1917.

SITE VISITS

Ireland, England and Europe: Western Front (Belgium and France) and Turkey
    (Gallipoli)

WEBSITES

Commonwealth War Graves Commission	www.cwgc.org.
Edward Thomas Fellowship	www.edward-thomas-fellowship.org.uk
Eneclann, Irish Memorial Records 1914–18 on CD-ROM	www.eneclann.ie
Gallipoli Association	www.gallipoli-association.org
Imperial War Museum	www.iwm.org.uk
Journey of Reconciliation Trust	www.iol.ie/jrtrust
Royal Dublin Fusiliers Association	www.greatwar.ie
Western Front Association	www.westernfront.co.uk

Index

Compiled by Julitta Clancy, Registered Indexer

Note: Entries are filed word-by-word. **Boldface** entries are given for the 25 barristers recorded in this book. Locators followed by (*illus.*) indicate *illustration* numbers; those followed by *n* indicate footnote page references. Authors and titles mentioned in footnotes are included.

Ballymena, Co. Antrim, 63
Ballyshannon, Co. Donegal, 103, 104
Ballytrent House, Co. Wexford, 112
Banbridge, Co. Down, 116, 117
Banbridge Chronicle, 117
Bandon, Co. Cork, 9, 104, 105
Bar Council, 55, 58n, 61, 61n
Bar Memorial, Belfast: *see* Royal Courts of
    Justice
Bar Memorial, Four Courts, Dublin, 2, 9,
    19 (*illus.*), 21, 48, 56–9, 60, 61, 62, 70
  commissioning of, 57, 126
  description, 58–9
  initiation of project, 55–7, 126
  list of barristers, 8
    biographies, 88–119
  remembrance ceremonies, 8, 61–2, 81–2
  sculptor, 57, 59
  unveiling ceremony (1924), 57–8, 127
Bar of Ireland, 5, 126
  Noyk motion (1921), 21, 60
  remembrance ceremonies, 8–9, 61–2
  war memorial: *see* Bar Memorial
Bar Review, 67n
Barbarians, the, 88
Barnes, B.S., 53n
barristers, 8–9; *see also* Bar Memorial (Four
    Courts); Bar of Ireland; King's Inns
  biographical notes, 87–119
  British army, in, 1–2
  training, 133
Barristers' Corps of Volunteers, 51
Barron, Louis, 120
Barry, Kevin, 35, 85
Barry, Tom, 17, 118, 119
Bartlett, Ellis Ashmeade, 138n–139n
Bartlett, Thomas, 25n
Barton, Brian, 39n
Barton, Dunbar Plunket, judge of the High
    Court, 51
Basra, Mesopotamia (Iraq), 141, 143
  war memorial, 68, 105, 119, 142
Battersby, F.J.G., 67
Battersby, T.S. Frank, KC, 67
Battlefield guide to Gallipoli (Holt), 19n, 22n
Bayeux Tapestry, 10
Bayna House, Co. Meath, 110
Before the revolution (Paseta), 29n, 36n, 37n,
    46n
Belfast, 62, 63, 81, 90, 116
Belfast Agreement (1998), 83

Belfast News-letter, 17n
Belgian Bar, 62
Belgium, 23, 49, 50, 62, 64, 84, 91, 92, 96;
    see also Flanders; Messines (Mesen);
    Ypres (Ieper)
  German atrocities, 23, 84
  German invasion, 50, 121
  place names, 130
  war graves, 10n, 15, 91, 108, 113, 114,
    117, 130
  war memorials, 12–15 (*illus.*), 64–5, 68;
    see also Island of Ireland Peace
    Park (Mesen/Messines); Menin
    Gate Memorial (Ypres/Ieper)
Bellewaarde, Ypres/Ieper, Belgium, 92, 122
Belloc, Hilaire, 5
Belvedere College, Dublin, 7, 20, 25, 32,
    33–5, 45, 136n
  barristers' biographies, 109, 110, 118
  Great War, impact of, 35
  war memorial plaque, 71
Belvederian, The, 33n, 35n, 44n, 110, 119
Bennett, F.E., 90
Bennett, Richard, 21n
Bennett, R.L., 28n, 70n
Bentley, James, 6n, 54n
Bernard, Revd John, 80
Bernert, Fritz Otto, 102, 124
Betjeman, John, 11
Beveridge, James O'Shaughnessy, 119
Beveridge, John, 119
Bew, Paul, 31n
Bhreathnach-Lynch, Sighle, 75n
Big Push (1917), 124
Biggs-Davison, John, 45
Bin Laden, Osama, 21
Binyon, Laurence, 82, 122
Birr, Co. Offaly, 94
Bishop, Alan, 27n, 82n
Black and Tans, 7, 101, 126
Black and Tans, The (Bennett), 21n
Black Watch (Royal Highlanders), 10
Blackall, Sir Henry, 118
Blackhall Place, Dublin, 59
Blackrock, Co. Dublin, 53, 98, 99, 100
Blair, Tony, MP, 104
Blake, R., 94
Blandford, Dorset, England, 73
Blomfield, Sir Reginald, 64
Bloody Sunday, 1920 (Dublin), 126
Bloody Sunday, 1972 (Derry), 128

Laffan, Moira, 33n, 73n

Laffin, John, 3

Lagnicourt, France, 102

Lala Baba/Lalababa Tepe, Turkey, 131

Lancashire Hussars, 48

Land League, 31, 96, 97

landed gentry of Ireland, The (Burke), 11

Langemarck/Langemark, Belgium, 15, 30, 65, 108, 124, 130

last years, The (Dixon), 6n

Law Journal, 1

Law Library, Four Courts, Dublin, 44, 56, 57, 61

Law Society Gazette, 32n, 61n

Law Society of Ireland, 48, 57, 106
  war memorial, Four Courts, 59, 60–1, 120

Law Society of Ireland, The (Hall and Hogan, eds), 4, 59n

law students, 49–50

Law Students' Debating Society, King's Inns, Dublin, 93, 98

Lawyers' Corps of Yeomanry, 2

Leader, 36

Ledwidge, Francis, 4, 6n, 16n, 19, 20, 22n, 27, 110
  death, 124
  'The Irish in Gallipoli', 19n, 28n

Ledwidge, Francis, *Complete poems* (Curtayne, ed.), 19n

Ledwidge, Francis, *Poems complete* (O'Meara, ed.), 19n

Ledwidge commemoration (Inchicore Ledwidge Society), 16n, 30n

Lee, Alfred T., 98

Lee, Edward, JP, 98

Lee, Joe (historian), 22, 47n

Lee, John, 66n

Lee, Joseph Bagnall (1888–1915), 42
  army career, 98
  biographical notes, 98–9
  death, 98
  education, 98
  legal career, 98
  memorials, 8, 20, 62, 63, 67, 98–9, 122
  writings, 98

Lee, Michael, 98

Lee, Capt. Robert Ernest, 98–9

Lees (drapery store), Dublin, 98

legal profession: *see also* Bar Memorial; Bar of Ireland; Inner Temple; King's Inns; Middle Temple; solicitors
  war effort, support for, 48–53

legal profession in Ireland, 1789–1922, The (Hogan), 4

Legion of Honour/Légion d'Honneur, France, 74, 113

Leighton, Christine, 26n

Leinster Bar, 106, 108

Leinster Regiment, 46, 66, 112, 115

Leland, Florence Mary, 53, 100

Leland, Henry, 99

Leland, John Henry Frederick (1884–1915)
  army career, 43–4, 99
  biographical notes, 99–100
  death, 63, 99
  legal career, 99
  marriage, 52–3
  memorials, 8, 20, 62–3, 67, 80, 99, 122

Leland, Laura, 99

Lemass, Sean, TD, viii, 80n, 128

Lemnos, 138, 140, 141

Leofwin (Lewin), Earl, 10

Leonard, Jane, 4, 55n, 64n

Letitia (ship), 116

Letterkenny, Co. Donegal
  war exhibition (county museum, 2001), 13n

Letters from a lost generation (Bishop and Bostridge, eds), 27, 82n

Levenson, Leah, 15n

Lewin, Brig.-Gen. Arthur Corrie, 101

Lewin, Frederick Henry (1877–1915), 2 (*illus.*), *3* (*illus.*), 10–12, 26
  army career, 100
  biographical notes, 100–2
  death, 100–1, 123
  education, 11–12, 100
  family, 10–11, 12
  grave, *4* (illus.), 11, 101
  legal career, 100
  memorials, 8, 64, 69, 70, 101

Lewin, Frederick Thomas, DL, JP, 11, 100

Lewin, Patrick T.C., 12n, 26n, 70n, 102

Lewin family (Galway/Mayo), 11–12, 26, 64, 101–2

Lillis, Frank, 61

The Irish Legal History Society

Established in 1988 to encourage the study and advance the knowledge of the history of Irish law, especially by the publication of original documents and of works relating to the history of Irish law, including its institutions, doctrines and personalities, and the reprinting or editing of works of sufficient rarity or importance.

PATRONS

The Hon. Mr Justice Murray
Chief Justice of Ireland

Rt. Hon. Sir Brian Kerr
Lord Chief Justice of Northern Ireland

COUNCIL 2004/05

President

His Honour Judge Martin QC

Vice-Presidents

James I. McGuire, esq.

Professor Norma Dawson

Honorary Secretaries

Kevin Costello, esq.

Ms Sheena Grattan

Honorary Treasurers

John G. Gordon, esq.

R.D. Marshall, esq.

Council Members

Dr Jack Anderson
Ms Rosemary Carson
The Hon. Mr Justice Geoghegan
Professor D. Greer QC (hon.)
The Hon. Mr Justice Hart
Daire Hogan, esq.

Dr Sean Donlan
Professor Colum Kenny
Eanna Mulloy SC
Professor J.O. Ohlmeyer
Professor W.N. Osborough
  (ex officio)

Website address: www.irishlegalhistorysociety.com